Stakeholder Involvement in Social Marketing

This book is the first to provide evidence-based experience to showcase how stakeholder management can be applied within social marketing programs, as well providing contemporary discussions of social marketing research. The book aims to bring practitioners and academics together to address the calls made by scholars to address inherent challenges involved in identifying, involving and prioritising different stakeholders in social marketing interventions.

Through sharing real-world experience, the text aims to extend and synthesise current knowledge in the field and contribute to establishing stronger and long-lasting alliances with stakeholders involved in social marketing interventions with an aim of ensuring sustainable behavioural change. This book features a diverse series of case studies from different countries (including but not limited to Australia, Finland, Ireland, Slovenia, the United Kingdom) conducted in various behaviour change contexts (including alcohol consumption, nutrition intake, and breast feeding). Leading international social marketing and social science scholars provide case studies on stakeholder involvement in an intervention or multiple interventions and elucidate relevant lessons to inform theoretical as well as practical implications for multi-stakeholder social marketing interventions.

This volume will be of interest to researchers, advanced students, practitioners, and policymakers in social marketing and health policy.

Kathy Knox, Ph.D. is a research psychologist with expertise in human development, health education, social marketing, and applied health behaviour change across a range of settings.

Krzysztof Kubacki is Professor of Marketing and Society at Auckland University of Technology, New Zealand. Most of his recent work focuses on the identification, trial, evaluation and critique of behaviour change programs, but Krzysztof is also interested in the intersecting roles of ethics, power and vulnerability in behaviour change and social marketing systems.

Sharyn Rundle-Thiele is director of Social Marketing, Griffith Business School and editor-in-chief of *Journal of Social Marketing*. Drawing on her commercial marketing background Sharyn's research focuses on applying marketing tools and techniques to change behaviour for the better.

Routledge Studies in Marketing

This series welcomes proposals for original research projects that are either single or multi-authored or an edited collection from both established and emerging scholars working on any aspect of marketing theory and practice and provides an outlet for studies dealing with elements of marketing theory, thought, pedagogy and practice.

It aims to reflect the evolving role of marketing and bring together the most innovative work across all aspects of the marketing "mix" – from product development, consumer behaviour, marketing analysis, branding, and customer relationships to sustainability, ethics, and the new opportunities and challenges presented by digital and online marketing.

12 Understanding the Higher Education Market in Africa
Edited by Emmanuel Mogaji, Felix Maringe and Robert Ebo Hinson

13 Internal Marketing
Theories, Perspectives and Stakeholders
David M. Brown

14 Stakeholder Involvement in Social Marketing
Challenges and Approaches to Engagement
Edited by Kathy Knox, Krzysztof Kubacki and Sharyn Rundle-Thiele

15 Decoding Coca-Cola
A Biography of a Global Brand
Edited by Robert Crawford, Linda Brennan and Susie Khamis

16 Luxury and Fashion Marketing
The Global Perspective
Satyendra Singh

For more information about this series, please visit: www.routledge.com/ Routledge-Studies-in-Marketing/book-series/RMKT

Stakeholder Involvement in Social Marketing

Challenges and Approaches to Engagement

Edited by Kathy Knox,
Krzysztof Kubacki, and
Sharyn Rundle-Thiele

LONDON AND NEW YORK

First published 2021
by Routledge
2 Park Square, Milton Park, Abingdon, Oxon OX14 4RN

and by Routledge
52 Vanderbilt Avenue, New York, NY 10017

Routledge is an imprint of the Taylor & Francis Group, an informa business

© 2021 selection and editorial matter, Kathy Knox, Krzysztof Kubacki
and Sharyn Rundle-Thiele; individual chapters, the contributors

The right of Kathy Knox, Krzysztof Kubacki and Sharyn Rundle-Thiele
to be identified as the authors of the editorial material, and of the authors
for their individual chapters, has been asserted in accordance with sections
77 and 78 of the Copyright, Designs and Patents Act 1988.

All rights reserved. No part of this book may be reprinted or reproduced or utilised
in any form or by any electronic, mechanical, or other means, now known or
hereafter invented, including photocopying and recording, or in any information
storage or retrieval system, without permission in writing from the publishers.

Trademark notice: Product or corporate names may be trademarks or registered trademarks,
and are used only for identification and explanation without intent to infringe.

British Library Cataloguing-in-Publication Data
A catalogue record for this book is available from the British Library

Library of Congress Cataloging-in-Publication Data
Names: Knox, Kathy, editor. | Kubacki, Krzysztof, editor. |
Rundle-Thiele, Sharyn, editor.
Title: Stakeholder involvement in social marketing : challenges and
approaches to engagement / edited by Kathy Knox,
Krzysztof Kubacki and Sharyn Rundle-Thiele.
Description: Abingdon, Oxon; New York, NY: Routledge, 2021. |
Series: Routledge studies in marketing; volume 14 |
Includes bibliographical references and index.
Identifiers: LCCN 2020028812 (print) | LCCN 2020028813 (ebook) |
ISBN 9780367172695 (hbk) | ISBN 9780429055898 (ebk)
Subjects: LCSH: Social marketing. | Stakeholder management. | Social change.
Classification: LCC HF5414 .S73 2021 (print) |
LCC HF5414 (ebook) | DDC 658.8–dc23
LC record available at https://lccn.loc.gov/2020028812
LC ebook record available at https://lccn.loc.gov/2020028813

ISBN: 978-0-367-17269-5 (hbk)
ISBN: 978-0-429-05589-8 (ebk)

Typeset in Bembo
by Newgen Publishing UK

Contents

List of figures	ix
List of tables	x
List of contributors	xi
Acknowledgements	xiii

1 Introduction   1

KRZYSZTOF KUBACKI, KATHY KNOX, AND SHARYN RUNDLE-THIELE

The growing importance of stakeholder involvement in social marketing 1
Structure of the book 3
Future directions and considerations in stakeholder engagement 6
Identity and role of stakeholders 6
Challenges and assumptions 7
Respect for indigenous ways of knowing and being 8
Researcher reflexivity and the role of researchers as stakeholders in social
 marketing programmes 9

2 Ending tyrannic man's dominion: In search of new
partners and new stories   12

GERARD HASTINGS

Introduction: Time to change the narrative 12
Power 13
Inertia 16
Dogmatism 18
New stories and new partners 19
The chances of success 22

3 Ethical tension in working with stakeholders   25

KRZYSZTOF KUBACKI, NATALIA SZABLEWSKA, AND DARIUSZ SIEMIENIAKO

Introduction 25
What is a stakeholder? 27

vi *Contents*

Power asymmetry as a cause of ethical tension and conflict 29
Addressing ethical tension and conflict between stakeholders 32
Conclusion 35

4 Stakeholder involvement in social marketing anti-smoking
   interventions   39
   V. DAO TRUONG, QUYNH PHAM, AND STEPHEN SAUNDERS

   Introduction 39
   Marketing stakeholder theory 41
   Methods 42
   Results 43
   Stakeholder groups 43
   Conclusion 50

5 MOSA: Addressing alcohol issues in Slovenia through an
   upstream multiple stakeholder approach   55
   TANJA KAMIN AND MAJA ROŠKAR

   Introduction 55
   MOSA: A social marketing approach to addressing
     alcohol-related problems 56
   Stakeholder approach to tackling alcohol issues on a national level 57
   Stakeholder analysis 58
   Stakeholder identification and categorisation 60
   MOSA stakeholder network for enhancing empowerment
     processes and capacity building 64
   Changes introduced by MOSA stakeholder approach 66
   Conclusion 68

6 Challenges in conducting social marketing-based alcohol
   prevention trials in schools   72
   CHRISTIANE STOCK, TIMO DIETRICH, LOTTE VALLENTIN-HOLBECH,
   AND SHARYN RUNDLE-THIELE

   Introduction 72
   Case description of the two programs and three cluster RCTs 76
   Challenges and implications of stakeholder involvement 78
   Conclusions and recommendations 84

7 Engaging dissensus: Innovating social change   89
   MARIE-LOUISE FRY, LINDA BRENNAN, AND JOSEPHINE PREVITE

   Introduction 89
   Dissensus in alcohol social change 90

Contents vii

Engaging dissensus: Harnessing collective intelligence 92
DrinkWise How to drink properly: *Challenging the alcohol
social change space 93*
Moving forward 103

8 Stakeholder analysis in a systems setting: An Active Travel
case study in Ireland 108
CHRISTINE DOMEGAN, PATRICIA MCHUGH, DMITRY BRYCHKOV,
AND FIONA DONOVAN

Introduction 108
The importance of stakeholders in a systems setting 109
An Active Travel case study in Ireland 112
Step 1 – Conduct a focal system boundary analysis 113
Step 2 – Classify the focal system stakeholders 115
*Step 3 – Identify stakeholders' interests and benefits/barriers
to participation 121*
Step 4 – Map the stakeholder dynamics of the focal system 124
Conclusion 128

9 Co-production of social experiments to promote health
and well-being among disadvantaged groups together with
key stakeholders 132
TOMI MÄKI-OPAS, JANET CARTER ANAND, CSILLA VESZTEG,
AND MARJA VAARAMA

*Social inequalities in health and well-being are a well-acknowledged
societal challenge – Why do we still fail to tackle it? 132*
Four social experiments with disadvantaged groups 135
Discussion 143

10 Plural rationality approach to stakeholder engagement 150
KATHY KNOX AND JOY PARKINSON

Introduction 150
Stakeholder engagement in environmental issues 151
Plural rationality approach 155
Case study – Reducing domestic dog and koala interactions 157
Discussion 170

11 From care to prevention in the NHS 176
TONY CONWAY AND MARGARET HYDE

Stakeholder analysis: The social marketing and healthcare context 176
A role for relationship marketing 178

viii *Contents*

The changing structure of health and social care in the United Kingdom 181
Our case: The Greater Manchester Health and Social Care Partnership 183
The Greater Manchester Health and Social Care Partnership model 184
Conclusion 187

12 Towards universal helmet use: Advocating for change
    in Vietnam   191
    LUKAS PARKER, MIRJAM SIDIK, AND TRUONG THI NGUYET TRANG

Background 191
Engaging and mobilising stakeholders to promote sustainable change 192
AIP Foundation and its stakeholders 194
Building better stakeholder engagement and coordination 199
Conclusion 201

Index   204

Figures

5.1	MOSA Interest-Power Matrix	63
5.2	Two pillars of the MOSA network	65
5.3	MOSA network sustainability	66
5.4	MOSA interactive webpage with number of visits	67
6.1	Evolution of alcohol and drug education	73
7.1	DrinkWise target audience matrix	96
7.2	How to drink properly character and tag line	101
7.3	Drinks coaster	102
8.1	A system of stakeholders	110
8.2	Map of Galway city	113
8.3	Stakeholder power/influence grid of Active Travel in Galway city	124
8.4	Tourists stakeholder value-based exchange map of the focal system	125
8.5	Festival stakeholder value-based exchange map of the complementary system	125
8.6	Stakeholders dynamic focal system mapping	126
9.1	Social marketing as a triangle of social relations in PROMEQ	134
10.1	Koala conservation in the Redland City Council is a heated topic	153
10.2	Examples for the fuzzy compromise solution program design	171
11.1	Example of a potential network of stakeholders in public health	178
11.2	Relationship marketing and stakeholder approach to "local" UK Health Care	180
11.3	Greater Manchester structure	185
11.4	Stakeholders in the Greater Manchester Health and Social Care Partnership	187
11.5	Map comparing GMHSP current priorities with future desired priorities	188
12.1	Tripartite model of behavioural compliance	194
12.2	Relationships between the stakeholders	196

Tables

4.1	Stakeholder involvement in social marketing anti-smoking interventions (2009–2018)	44
5.1	Steps of stakeholder analysis	59
7.1	Multiple stakeholders informed the design of the HTDP campaign	97
7.2	HTDP print creative examples	102
8.1	Active Travel stakeholders boundary analysis	116
8.2	Freeman's categorisation of stakeholders in Active Travel	118
8.3	Layton's stakeholder classification mechanism	119
8.4	Stakeholders power and interest	122
9.1	PROMEQ approach to social marketing of tailored experiments: Co-design and co-creation together with PPP partnership	136
9.2	The needs and resource profiles of the disadvantaged groups	138
9.3	Experimental designs and mixed methods approach applied to evaluate the effectiveness of the tailored social marketing experiments	144
10.1	Characteristics of stakeholders classified by rationality typologies	160
10.2	Archetypal rationalities, thematic categories, and exemplar quotes	161
10.3	Stakeholder framework and number of interviews	167
10.4	Campaign concepts to reduce dog and koala interactions	168
11.1	Examples of classifications of stakeholders	177
11.2	Six-market stakeholder model	179
12.1	Fostering child helmet compliance	198

Contributors

Janet Carter Anand, University of Eastern Finland, Department of Social Sciences, Kuopio, Finland.

Linda Brennan, School of Media and Communication, RMIT University, Australia.

Dmitry Brychkov, National University of Ireland, Galway, Ireland.

Tony Conway, Department of Marketing, Retail and Tourism, Business School, Manchester Metropolitan University, Manchester, United Kingdom.

Timo Dietrich, Social Marketing @ Griffith, Department of Marketing, Griffith University, Nathan, Australia & Centre for Youth Substance Abuse, Faculty of Health and Behavioural Sciences, University of Queensland, Brisbane, Australia.

Christine Domegan, National University of Ireland, Galway, Ireland.

Fiona Donovan, Healthy Ireland, Ireland.

Marie-Louise Fry, Griffith Business School, Griffith University, Australia.

Gerard Hastings, Professor Emeritus, Stirling University, Scotland.

Margaret Hyde, Department of Marketing, Retail and Tourism, Business School, Manchester Metropolitan U.

Tanja Kamin, Faculty of Social Sciences, University of Ljubljana, Ljubljana, Slovenia.

Kathy Knox, Social Marketing @ Griffith, Department of Marketing, Griffith University, Nathan, Australia.

Krzysztof Kubacki, Marketing Department, Faculty of Business, Economics and Law, Auckland University of Technology, Auckland, New Zealand.

Tomi Mäki-Opas, University of Eastern Finland, Department of Social Sciences, Kuopio, Finland.

Patricia McHugh, National University of Ireland, Galway, Ireland.

xii   *List of contributors*

Lukas Parker, School of Media and Communication, RMIT University, Australia.

Joy Parkinson, Social Marketing @ Griffith, Department of Marketing, Griffith University, Nathan, Australia.

Quynh Pham, Department of Economics, National Economics University, Hanoi, Vietnam.

Josephine Previte, UQ Business School, University of Queensland, Australia.

Maja Roškar, National Institute of Public Health, Slovenia.

Sharyn Rundle-Thiele, Social Marketing @ Griffith, Department of Marketing, Griffith University, Nathan, Australia.

Stephen Saunders, Department of Marketing, Monash University, Frankston, Australia.

Mirjam Sidik, AIP Foundation, Vietnam.

Dariusz Siemieniako, Department of Marketing and Tourism, Faculty of Engineering Management, Białystok University of Technology, Poland.

Christiane Stock, Charité Universitätsmedizin Berlin, Institute for Health and Nursing Science, Berlin, Germany.

Natalia Szablewska, Law School, Faculty of Business, Economics and Law, Auckland University of Technology, New Zealand.

Truong Thi Nguyet Trang, AIP Foundation, Vietnamniversity, Manchester, United Kingdom.

V. Dao Truong, Department of Tourism and Hotel Management, National Economics University, Hanoi, Vietnam.

Marja Vaarama, University of Eastern Finland, Department of Social Sciences, Kuopio, Finland.

Lotte Vallentin-Holbech, Institute of Psychology, Centre for Drug Research, Aarhus University, Denmark.

Csilla Veszteg, University of Eastern Finland, Department of Social Sciences, Kuopio, Finland.

Acknowledgements

This book was inspired by the many conversations we had with Dr. Nuray Buyucek during her doctoral research at Social Marketing @ Griffith. Nuray, following the completion of her PhD, embarked on a career in government, and her work commitments did not allow her to continue working with us to bring her concept for this book to reality. We would like to acknowledge Nuray's contribution in the process of converting our conversations into a book proposal. Further, we would like to thank staff at Routledge for creating the opportunity for us to deliver this book. Your enthusiasm for our idea and support from the first conversation over a year ago made our work much easier. We also want to acknowledge the work of the reviewers who each patiently provided their constructive feedback on every chapter – it is possible to deliver books like this one only because of our supportive colleagues who are always willing to give us a few hours of their time so that we and all contributing authors can benefit from your expertise and experience. Finally, this book would not be possible without hard work and dedication of all contributing authors, who willingly shared their knowledge of stakeholder involvement in social marketing programmes.

1 Introduction

*Krzysztof Kubacki, Kathy Knox,
and Sharyn Rundle-Thiele*

The growing importance of stakeholder involvement in social marketing

For a large part of the twentieth century, since Kotler and Zaltman (1971) coined the term *social marketing* to describe the use of marketing to achieve social goals, our discipline was focused on promoting social ideas to individuals. In fact, in their social marketing periodisation study, Duane and Domegan (2019) observed that social marketing practice was predominantly driven by a micro-marketing management model, concentrating on downstream approaches involving a small number of stakeholders. While cooperation between stakeholders, often referred to as *intermediaries* (Duane & Domegan, 2019), was evident, for example using existing distribution channels to deliver social products such as condoms to individuals considered to be in need, initiatives were in most cases ad hoc and short term.

However, a growing awareness of the limitations of downstream and individual-focused social marketing programmes has begun to emerge. Identifying practical solutions to address increasingly complex and multi-faceted social issues requires sophisticated programmes, conducted over the longer term that engage an increasing number of stakeholders at all levels, from individual organisations to broader government, inter-organisational, and cross-national frames. As a result of the growing awareness of the complexity and inter-relatedness of the health, environmental, and social challenges, social marketing literature often includes references to partnerships, recognising the necessity for formation and effective management of stakeholders, given that multiple stakeholders are needed for social transformation to occur benefitting people and the planet (Duane & Domegan, 2019). A shift from micro-level behavioural interventions to social marketing systems has begun (e.g. see Venturini, 2016).

A stakeholder approach has been applied in strategic management for many decades, and a considerable base of evidence exists indicating that effectiveness is increased when multiple stakeholders are involved (Bryson, 2004). When stakeholders are managed effectively in business settings, outcomes tend to be beneficial to companies and to all stakeholders (Lafreniere, Deshpande,

2 *Krzysztof Kubacki et al.*

Bjornlund, & Hunter, 2013). With social marketing maturing as an academic discipline and practice, in the first two decades of the twenty-first century we have witnessed social marketers engaging in conversations about macro-social marketing (Kennedy, 2020), wicked problems (Brennan, Previte, & Fry, 2016), systems thinking (Domegan et al., 2016), and stakeholder involvement in delivery of behavioural change (Domegan, McHugh, Flaherty, & Duane, 2019). Yet one common denominator runs across all those different approaches to social marketing – social marketing programmes take place in complex settings, often involving multiple stakeholders in social marketing processes (Buyucek, Kubacki, Rundle-Thiele, & Pang, 2016). A holistic approach across the down-, mid-, and upstream continuum has been proposed as one means to increase the likelihood of success of social marketing programmes over the longer term (Hoek & Jones, 2011), which requires the involvement of multiple parties and management of their relationships. Multi-stakeholder partnerships involving a broad array of stakeholders including government bodies, organisations and individuals, are needed to create a supportive context facilitating behaviour change and social transformation efforts (Lefebvre, 2006; McHugh & Domegan, 2017).

Although partnerships are essential for social marketing to deliver effective change, there is only a handful of scholarly resources that discuss stakeholder involvement and share experiences on how multiple parties with different agendas (Domegan, Collins, Stead, McHugh, & Hughes, 2013), conflicting interests (Andreasen, 2006), and expectations (Temple et al., 2008) are managed together to deliver lasting change. The current book is, therefore, the first to integrate the latest theoretical developments and evidence-based experience to guide stakeholder involvement and management in social marketing programmes. This book was born from our desire to put together a scholarly resource, outlining current practices and experiences as well as encouraging discussion in the social marketing field, addressing challenges and experiences arising within the management of different parties' involvement in social marketing programmes. Given related literature was scattered across numerous academic journals, conference proceedings, and government and industry reports, often inaccessible to those who work in multi-stakeholder social marketing systems; we hope that this book will become a valuable reference for social marketing researchers and practitioners.

The aim of this book is to integrate and extend the current literature concerning stakeholder involvement in the social marketing field. Therefore, it provides a broad array of case studies and theoretical chapters discussing stakeholder involvement in social marketing programme development, delivery, and evaluation, broadening the current discussions on relational thinking in the field and their implications for the practice of social marketing. Experienced international scholars and social marketing practitioners were invited to share their experiences of stakeholder involvement in social marketing. Contributing chapters explore contemporary frameworks, issues, and practices relevant to establishing partnerships; overcoming difficulties and barriers in managing

Introduction 3

programmes with multiple stakeholders; and criteria and best practice principles for establishing alliances, stakeholder identification and management.

This book is unique in the discussion on stakeholder involvement in social marketing as it brings practitioners and academics together to address the calls made by scholars to take up inherent challenges involved in identifying, involving, and prioritising different stakeholders in social marketing interventions (Hastings, 2003). Through sharing real-world experiences, the text synthesises and extends current knowledge in the field and contributes to establishing stronger and long-lasting alliances with stakeholders involved in social marketing programmes with the aim of further supporting and facilitating sustainable change.

Structure of the book

This book consists of two parts. The first part includes three chapters exploring different issues affecting stakeholder involvement in social marketing. In Chapter 2, Gerard Hastings sets the tone for the book by advocating a new way to think about partnerships. In his view, traditional approaches to partnerships involving stakeholders such as multinational corporations (MNCs) stifle true change. Unconstrained power corrupts MNCs and shapes all stakeholder relationships in their favour; from power comes inertia, or as Hastings argues, the unwillingness of the elites to embrace truly radical change that may undermine the current status quo which benefits them the most. In his call for changing our partnership approach, Hastings reminds us that the dogmatism that limits innovation in partnerships is often used by MNCs to hijack any new ideas and incorporate them into the existing, dominant market discourse through partnerships with, among others, unsuspecting social marketers. Hastings' words of warning lead to a call for new stories through a partnership with nature rather than MNCs.

Continuing with the topic of power, in Chapter 3, Krzysztof Kubacki, Natalia Szablewska, and Dariusz Siemieniako focus on the issue of ethical tension and conflict between various groups of stakeholders in social marketing systems. Like Hastings, they consider power as an inseparable part of the environment of every social marketing system, yet Kubacki and colleagues approach the issue of power through the lens of power asymmetry and a human rights framework. In their proposed human rights-based approach, including three sets of human rights principles – transparency and accountability, equality and non-discrimination, and participation and inclusion – they show how social marketers can facilitate the process of addressing the conflicting interests of various stakeholders and the power asymmetry in a social marketing system.

Dao Truong, Quynh Pham, and Stephen Saunders discuss in Chapter 4 the level of involvement of various stakeholders in social marketing interventions aiming to encourage individuals to quit smoking. Their systematic literature review of studies published between 2009 and 2018 synthesises key insights from 12 interventions, adding to the growing evidence (see, e.g. Buyucek,

4   *Krzysztof Kubacki et al.*

Kubacki, Rundle-Thiele, & Pang, 2016) that stakeholder involvement tends to be concentrated in the early stages of social marketing, such as formative research and intervention design, while the number of stakeholders involved in programme delivery tends to decrease as interventions progress, beyond formative research, to implementation and evaluation. Further, the impact of stakeholder involvement on outcomes is rarely reported, adding to the concern that different stakeholders do not play a sufficient role throughout an intervention's life, limiting their potential contribution to the success of the intervention and any programme longevity.

The second part of this book includes eight chapters describing case studies that report stakeholder involvement in different social marketing programmes, providing brief reflections and overviews of the most relevant lessons learned to inform theoretical as well as practical implications for multi-stakeholder social marketing, which in turn can inform future social marketing programme development and delivery. This part features a diverse series of case studies from different countries (including Australia, Finland, Ireland, Slovenia, the United Kingdom, and Vietnam) conducted in various behaviour change contexts (including alcohol harm minimisation, Active Travel, road safety, health-care systems, and reducing health and well-being inequalities). Case studies explore theoretical issues with practical implications such as stakeholder selection processes; formative research processes; issues emerging during programme delivery, such as conflicts between different stakeholders and how those conflicts were dealt with; approaches taken to solve problems; management techniques; and benefits versus downsides of stakeholder involvement.

In Chapter 5 readers can find a fascinating overview of efforts to minimise the impact of harmful alcohol consumption in Slovenia. Through establishing MOSA – mobilising community for responsibility towards alcohol – Tanja Kamin and Maja Roškar reflect on the programme's approach to systematically identifying the most relevant stakeholders and synchronising their scattered alcohol harm minimisation efforts. Over the last ten years, the MOSA network has become an example of an important and successful multi-stakeholder government-funded platform facilitating the process of sharing up-to-date data on alcohol research between all involved stakeholders and knowledge about strategic development, implementation, and evaluation of interventions, providing open access and regularly updated databases.

Chapter 6 explores the challenges of adhering to the highest possible research standards, such as randomised control trials, when delivering alcohol education programmes for local communities and schools in Australia and Denmark. Christiane Stock, Timo Dietrich, Lotte Vallentin-Holbech, and Sharyn Rundle-Thiele reflect on their experiences of delivering programmes involving multiple stakeholders in school settings. School administrators are the initial gatekeepers, providing or restricting access to students depending on their perceived need for alcohol education programmes; next, teachers can have a significant impact on the programme implementation process, and they can impact programme fidelity; finally, the engagement of all support

Introduction 5

staff and students is important to deliver reliable programme evaluations. Stock and colleagues provide detailed recommendations for successful delivery of programmes in school settings.

In Chapter 7, Marie-Louise Fry, Linda Brennan, and Josephine Previte explore the development of Australia's DrinkWise initiative *How to drink properly*. Their case study provides an alternative approach to stakeholder analysis, employing Willis et al.'s (2016) collective intelligence framework to identify multisectoral partnerships consisting of six phases of prioritising needs, evidence mapping, using relevant methods and tools, analysing and synthesising data, providing feedback to multisectoral partners, and taking action. The case study provides insights into the highly contested role of industry in the development of alcohol change interventions and presents counterarguments to Hastings' view of the alcohol industry's involvement in social change as "dancing with the devil."

Christine Domegan, Patricia McHugh, Dmitry Brychkov, and Fiona Donovan in Chapter 8 take us on a journey through stakeholder analysis informed by systems thinking, using an example drawn from an Irish Active Travel programme that has been implemented within the urban community of Galway city. Incorporating macromarketing and systems thinking together with the more traditional stakeholder theory approach proposed in the earlier chapter, Domegan and colleagues propose a systemic and holistic multi-stakeholder assessment involving system boundary analysis, classification of stakeholders, identification of their interests, benefits and barriers to participation, and mapping stakeholder dynamics. Their systematic and systemic approach to stakeholder analysis provides a robust foundation for co-designing and co-creating social marketing change interventions that can be implemented with the support of a range of stakeholders identified within complex systems.

In Chapter 9, Tomi Mäki-Opas, Janet Anand, Cilla Veszteg, and Marja Vaarama undertake an analysis of why past and current health and welfare promotion strategies in Finland have failed to reduce health and well-being inequalities. Focusing on the PROMEQ programme (*Inclusive Promotion of Health and Well-Being*), which sought to establish partnerships between researchers, public services, private enterprises, and third sector organisations over a three-year period, the authors reflect on the effectiveness of interventions targeting four distinct groups: youth not in education, employment, or training (NEETS), long-term unemployed, refugees in early stage of resettlement, and older people with multiple care needs and living alone at home.

In Chapter 10, Kathy Knox and Joy Parkinson introduce the plural rationality approach to integrating stakeholder perspectives in environmental planning, a context fraught with values and conflicting motives. In the example a community behaviour change initiative is described to address the declining koala population in South East Queensland, Australia: an area characterised by discrepancies between community attitudes and actions. Applying the plural rationality framework, the authors demonstrate how stakeholders' socially

6   *Krzysztof Kubacki et al.*

constructed ways of interpreting the issue were worked into designing a fuzzy compromise solution that addressed barriers to behaviour change.

Tony Conway and Margaret Hyde in Chapter 11 take us to Greater Manchester, England, to explore issues associated with stakeholders and stakeholder analysis within one of the largest and most important health organisations in the world – the United Kingdom's National Health Service (NHS). The authors suggest that stakeholder theory working with relationship marketing as a philosophy and as a strategic tool can enhance the management of the Greater Manchester Health and Social Care Partnership comprising of health and social care agencies such as NHS and local authorities, as well as the community, voluntary, and social enterprise sector, and a host of other agencies.

In Chapter 12, Lukas Parker, Mirjam Sidik, and Truong Thi Nguyet Trang discuss AIP Foundation's efforts to increase child helmet use when travelling on motorbikes in Vietnam. The foundation employs multisectoral collaborations across its programmes to engage public, private, and government road safety stakeholders. The authors reflect on some of the key challenges and benefits of bringing a very diverse group of stakeholders together, and the evolving role of the foundation, from creating and owning road safety campaigns to building capacity and coordinating government-led road safety efforts across multiple stakeholders.

Future directions and considerations in stakeholder engagement

A contemporary conceptualisation of stakeholders has evolved from Freeman's definition towards a holistic orientation in which stakeholders are networks within systems – connected in structures and engaged in processes. This collection of critical reviews and overviews (Part 1) and contemporary social marketing case studies (Part 2) is intended to provide practitioners and academics with useful source material to help guide a modern approach to developing stakeholder involvement in programmes. Considering the worked case examples as a whole, some observations can be made drawing together common threads across theoretical perspectives, settings, and contexts.

Identity and role of stakeholders

In social marketing contexts such as social welfare, health care, or alcohol and drug education, the primary motive for stakeholder involvement is not commercial profit. Therefore, our interpretation of the identity and role of stakeholders differs from the traditional commercial setting. Chapters in this edited volume demonstrate the diversity of identities of stakeholders and diversity among their roles. Authors agree that it is important to identify stakeholders, and we can slice and dice them in various ways, for example according to power relations or rationalities. Multiple approaches and detailed frameworks describing steps and stages in the process of identification and classification of stakeholders are presented throughout the case studies contained herein. However, the reader should note a few important caveats: not all stakeholders (i.e. all those who affect or are affected by the phenomena) are self-evident (see Chapter 5); not all stakeholders have a voice (i.e. forests, koalas), and as noted in the systematic literature review presented in Chapter 4, social marketing practitioners may have a role in formative research and evaluation, but direct involvement during program implementation of social marketers as a stakeholder group is less evident (Chapter 4). Various sources of difference among stakeholder identities, such as the form of power (see Chapters 3 and 9), varying and at time ill-aligned goal outcomes, morality, religion, culture, and professional practice, often translate into tensions (see Chapters 2 and 7). Contributing authors have exposed their approaches, spelling out how modern social marketing applications have navigated divergent identities and roles of stakeholders to ensure health, environmental, and social gains are delivered as intended.

Challenges and assumptions

As shown in case studies in this edited volume, it is hard to generalise about a stakeholder groups' expectations and assumptions. It is equally difficult to predict in advance which methods for engaging stakeholders in social marketing efforts might be met with success. Indeed, significant challenges exist in navigating unique stakeholder needs and wants, ethics and values, power relations, and the scale and complexity of the social and behavioural ecosystems (such as schools – see Chapter 6, health services – see Chapters 9 and 11, and road safety systems – see Chapters 8 and 12) in which social phenomena exist and thus, the settings for our work.

Social marketers are faced with resource constraints, and there is no algorithm for assigning priority as well as establishing and maintaining trust among interested parties. Stakeholder involvement in social marketing takes time and effort, and project timeframes and funding reduce the potential to realise gains in the longer term. Contemporary approaches to stakeholder involvement recognise these challenges and remain agile and committed to questioning assumptions. Practical tactics for managing the challenges and for conceptualising and integrating stakeholder input described in this edited volume include (but are not limited to):

- a human rights framework (Chapter 3)
- relationship marketing approach (Chapter 11)
- Christopher's et al. (1991) six-markets model (Chapter 11)
- Willis's et al. (2016) collective intelligence framework (Chapter 7)
- a plural rationality approach (Chapter 10).

Examples herein serve to integrate a macro perspective, shifting the focus upstream to institutional and organisational change, and show how international social marketing applications have been able to intentionally integrate

8 *Krzysztof Kubacki et al.*

stakeholders at levels of government and society. Together with judicious use of formative research (Kubacki & Rundle-Thiele, 2016) and programme evaluation (Weinreich, 2010), practical tactics and frameworks offered in the examples provided herein combine to enable the scholar, researcher, and social marketing practitioner community to adapt their approach to the unique challenges presented by stakeholder engagement and management. We hope that by examining examples the reader takes away the importance of genuine engagement with stakeholders in multiple phases of the social marketing process (see Chapter 4), not just asking them to adopt a behaviour.

We would like to draw the readers' attention to two ideas touched on briefly in the preceding pages which will no doubt remain important in future directions and considerations for stakeholder engagement in social marketing as well as other social change agendas. The ideas are respect for indigenous ways of knowing and being (see Chapter 2 for examples from Sierra Nevada's Kogi people and the Amazon's Kayapo people), researcher reflexivity, and role as stakeholders in social marketing.

Respect for indigenous ways of knowing and being

Currently in Australia it is a commonplace to commence meetings and public addresses with an appropriate Acknowledgement of Traditional Owners. On the path to reconciliation in Australia, this is an important step and a positive cultural change. However, to listen to indigenous stakeholder voices, wherever in the world, requires meaningful engagement and partnership with communities to shape programmes and policies. In her 2019 Boyer Lecture series, *The End of Silence*, Rachel Perkins describes examples for how such listening can be done well, and how it has been done poorly:

> [21:35] Ways of hearing indigenous voices already exist throughout Australia, and one structure that I'm familiar with is the Central Land Council back home in the Northern Territory. My father was its first chair and we recently celebrated its 40th anniversary. It's an example of the kind of bottom up approach, a grass roots structure that is effective in giving the voice to the people on the ground. For this reason, the Central Land Council is relied upon by governments to give advice on matters relating to land in central Australia which in turn has contributed to much better policy outcomes.
>
> A different structure exists in Cape York. In Cape York we find leading examples of community policies that have been developed through consultation and this has led to greater buy-in by the local communities and as a result, more effective policy outcomes such as the Family Responsibilities Commission where the community decides who will be the recipient of welfare management. This is to be contrasted with the outcomes in the NT during what's known as "the intervention." Policies were imposed upon the local communities by the federal government without

Introduction   9

consultation, rather than emanating out of those communities. **However well-intentioned the intervention may have been, history shows that policies imposed on people without adequate consultation and not done in partnership are rarely successful in the long term and can be, as they are in the Northern Territory, widely resented** [23.11][emphasis added]

(Perkins, 2019).

Seeking consultation and partnership with those who are affected by and affect outcomes and programmes entails openly acknowledging indigenous voices. Contemporary social marketing practice and future directions in this field will need to engage with systems and networks of stakeholders at all levels, including first nations people. What can social marketers contribute to engaging with and listening to indigenous voices?

Researcher reflexivity and the role of researchers as stakeholders in social marketing programmes

Practitioners, researchers, and scholars hold stake in the programmes and campaigns we develop and evaluate. Our reputations, career trajectories, higher degree progress, and our next client contract (and maybe our pride) depend on the success or at least the absence of negative consequences of our work. In this regard, we have an interest in shaping the way a programme is built; how it is delivered, received, assessed, evaluated, communicated, and recognised. Indeed, we participate in and exist within the societal groups that we target with social marketing interventions: We are members of the communities we seek to change, and we are party to the behaviours that we study. At the extreme, our practice is an intervention and our very being in any setting that we are charged to change means we necessarily have a stake in the outcomes achieved. As a result of our status as stakeholders in our work, social marketers need to practice reflexivity: Thinking in a metacognitive way and critically reflecting on experiences, expectations, and assumptions. Researchers and practitioners must be able to state and actively examine our assumptions – about how a programme might drive change, how collateral might be received, about who should or will do what, etc. – and we must be open to having our assumptions challenged by other stakeholders and the communities we serve, including indigenous peoples. As Hastings poetically put it in Chapter 2: "The submerged hazard here is … inherent rigidity" when stakeholders or partners cling dogmatically to their assumptions. Uncovering and understanding our assumptions are important because the criteria for success is delivery of shared value. That is, each stakeholder must recognise value from changing away from business as usual (what we currently know and do) if change is to occur. Reflexivity is practised in the process of evaluating programmes, where our assumptions and position as stakeholders become apparent. The word 'evaluation' has at its core, both literally and metaphorically, the concept of 'value.' The value we place on

10 *Krzysztof Kubacki et al.*

a particular action and its outcome defines its importance, how we interpret information, and, in many cases, how we assess success or failure. These values are contestable, as we have seen in this edited volume.

Policymakers, academic researchers, frontline staff, and the wider community may all have different views on what represents 'value' from public investment in social change initiatives. The values held by one group of stakeholders differ substantially from those of another: *A policymaker, a frontline employee, a scientist, and a community member walk into a bar.* Each of these groups holds a stake in social change initiatives, but the point is their values, assumptions, and criteria for success differ widely. While the policymaker might value financial return on investment, time frames for realising this value may be short term and linked to the capacity to generate headlines and positive press for incumbent governments. As such the long-term sustainability of social or environmental change may not be a priority. Frontline employees, on the other hand, are on the ground dealing with real-life situations such as those covered in our case studies of health-care service (Chapter 11) and school settings (Chapter 12). Stakeholders at the frontline are the health-care professionals, the educators, and third sector partners in our social marketing programmes. The frontline values practicality of programmes (e.g. ease of implementation and program outcomes), long-term sustainability of solutions, and as such, evidence for success may be measured in terms of changes observed as captured in case reports. Scientists (social scientists included) measure success of social change programmes against prevailing standards, defined by rigour and integrity. The scientific community values the quality of measures employed, and so the concepts of validity and reliability shape our understanding and evaluation of outcomes. In terms of what the community members value from social change initiatives, the focus shifts to methodology and implementation. As we have seen in examples given in Chapter 2 and quote from the Boyer Lecture, stakeholder communities value observable changes (e.g. improved quality of life, health or productivity gains) and opportunities for engagement, consultation, and voice. What is important to members of communities is to be understood, and this can only be gained through shared decision-making and opportunities to be heard, given that the value each stakeholder obtains from change is different.

"Nothing about me without me."

References

Andreasen, A.R. (2006). *Social Marketing the 21st Century*. Sage.

Brennan, L., Previte, J., & Fry, M.L. (2016). Social marketing's consumer myopia: Applying a behavioural ecological model to address wicked problems. *Journal of Social Marketing*, 6(3), 219–239.

Bryson, J.M. (2004). What to do when stakeholders matter. *Public Management Review*, 6(1), 21–53.

Buyucek, N., Kubacki, K., Rundle-Thiele, S., & Pang, B. (2016). A systematic review of stakeholder involvement in social marketing interventions. *Australasian Marketing Journal*, 24(1), 8–19.

Christopher, M., Payne, A., & Ballantyne, D. (1991). *Relationship Marketing: Bringing Quality, Customer Service and Marketing Together*. Butterworth Heinemann.

Domegan, C., Collins, K., Stead, M., McHugh, P., & Hughes, T. (2013). Value co-creation in social marketing: Functional or fanciful? *Journal of Social Marketing*, 3(3), 239–256.

Domegan, C., McHugh, P., Devaney, M., Duane, S., Hogan, M., Broome, B.J., Layton, R.A., Joyce, J., Mazzonetto, M., & Piwowarczyk, J. (2016). Systems-thinking social marketing: Conceptual extensions and empirical investigations. *Journal of Marketing Management*, 32(11–12), 1123–1144.

Domegan, C., McHugh, P., Flaherty, T., & Duane, S. (2019). A dynamic stakeholders' framework in a marketing systems setting. *Journal of Macromarketing*, 39(2), 136–150.

Duane, S., & Domegan, C. (2019). Social marketing partnerships: Evolution, scope and substance. *Marketing Theory*, 19(2), 169–193.

Hastings, G. (2003). Relational paradigms in social marketing. *Journal of Macromarketing*, 23(1), 6–15.

Hoek, J., & Jones, S.C. (2011). Regulation, public health and social marketing: A behaviour change trinity. *Journal of Social Marketing*, 1(1), 32–44.

Kennedy, A.M. (2020). *Macro-social Marketing Insights. Systems Thinking for Wicked Problems*. Routledge.

Kotler, P., & Zaltman, G. (1971). Social marketing: An approach to planned social change, *Journal of Marketing*, 35(3), 3–12.

Kubacki, K., & Rundle-Thiele, S. (2016). *Formative Research in Social Marketing: Innovative Methods to Gain Consumer Insights*. Springer.

Lafreniere, K.C., Deshpande, S., Bjornlund, H., & Hunter, M.G. (2013). Extending stakeholder theory to promote resource management initiatives to key stakeholders: A case study of water transfers in Alberta, Canada. *Journal of Environmental Management*, 129, 81–91.

Lefebvre, C. (2006). Partnerships for social marketing programs: An example from the National Bone Health Campaign. *Social Marketing Quarterly*, 12(1), 41–54.

McHugh, P., & Domegan, C. (2017). Evaluate development! Develop evaluation! Answering the call for a reflexive turn in social marketing. *Journal of Social Marketing*, 7(2), 135–155.

Perkins, Rachel. The End of Silence (part 2, *With the consent of the natives*), Boyer Lectures, ABC Radio National, 23 November 2019; https://podcasts.google.com/?feed=aHR0cHM6Ly93d3cuYWJjLm5ldC5hdS9yYWRpb25hdGlvbmFsL2ZlZWQvMjg4NTc3Ni9wb2RjYXN0LnhtbA%3D%3D&hl=en-AU.

Temple, S., Long, T., Wayman, J., Taubenheim, A.M., & Patterson, J. (2008). Alliance building: Mobilizing partners to share The Heart Truth with American women. *Social Marketing Quarterly*, 14(3), 68–79.

Venturini, R. (2016). Social marketing and big social change: Personal social marketing insights from a complex system obesity prevention intervention. *Journal of Marketing Management*, 32(11–12), 1190–1199.

Weinreich, N.K. (2010). *Hands-on Social Marketing: A Step-by-Step Guide to Designing Change for Good*. Sage.

Willis, C.D., Greene, J.K., Abramowicz, A., & Riley, B.L. (2016). Strengthening the evidence and action on multi-sectoral partnerships in public health: An action research initiative. *Health Promotion and Chronic Disease Prevention in Canada*, 36(6), 101–111.

2 Ending tyrannic man's dominion

In search of new partners and new stories

Gerard Hastings

Introduction: Time to change the narrative

Social marketers are tasked with wicked problems which require partnered approaches to deliver change.

Partnership working has a reasonable and inclusive ring to it: two can achieve more than one; mutual respect can be nurtured; we are all, ultimately, on the same side – the side of good. And in times of crisis, such as we now face with climate breakdown, we surely need every hand to the pump, a team response to a collective calamity.

However much depends on the choice of partner. I well remember as a child partnering with an older and bigger friend on an apple-scrumping[1] project; all went well until the gardener spotted us, then my pal's longer legs left me facing the music. A partnership of equals will work, but if there is a power imbalance, the stronger is likely to prevail when things get tricky, and collaboration can quickly dissolve into division.

When the aim is to deliver change, a partner who is overly attached to the status quo is also likely to be troublesome. Marriages predicated on 'curing' one partner's addiction to alcohol or gambling so often fail because the dependent one – the alcoholic or the gambler – does not want to, or cannot, change. Again, this drawback is hidden, or at least downplayed, at the outset; only when real life intervenes do the flaws in the deal begin to assert themselves.

Partnership working has a third, more profound and even better camouflaged pitfall. If one partner is committed to a particular worldview, has a fixed idea of how problems are defined and solved, is convinced they have the answer – or the means of divining the answer – to every question, then collaboration becomes unworkable. A group of committed Christians can comfortably agree (indeed, assume) that God and prayer will provide a resolution to world poverty; an atheist joining the group will struggle with this. The submerged hazard here is that this inherent rigidity, this (often unacknowledged) dogmatism, prevents the emergence of alternative narratives, of novel ways of thinking about the problem, about life. At this point in human history, as we contend with the unsustainability, the impasse of our current way of life, we have never been in greater need of new stories.

Ending tyrannic man's dominion   13

These three problems of power, inertia, and dogmatism are writ large when the partner is a multinational corporation (MNC). This chapter will examine the disorienting power, the built-in intransigence and the deafness to new ways of thinking that result when the architects and principal beneficiaries of the current failing system decide to try and fix its faults; when the fox elects to renovate the hen house. It will then explore what might be possible if we were to start afresh; to embrace the undoubted benefits of partnership working but to choose different partners and, instead of patching up the old threadbare narrative of a world "made up of dead stuff plus active minds and acquisitive wills" (Williams, 2019), to start telling a new story.

Power

Power is a dangerous commodity. It is innately and achingly attractive; like sex and money, with which it shapeshifts ineluctably, we can never get enough of it. Those who have it always want more and will do all they can to prevent any weakening of their position. Paradoxically, then, the powerful are also vulnerable and insecure. The most potent dictators in history left nothing to chance, building what Thomas Piketty calls a "repressive apparatus of control" to see off any threats; the Stasi, KGB[2], and Gestapo are names that live on in infamy.

Most of us, however, do not have much power, so the temptation is to gravitate to those who have and to hope we can gain some by association. Politicians, who depend more than any of us on power, are drawn to it like moths to a candle. And who can blame them? Power is their life's blood; without it they flounder and fade away. We are all of us susceptible to this magnetism of power. The powerful can get things done; they do hold the reins. So, our inclination is to get close, holding our noses if necessary, and try and make a difference. It may be a little malodorous, but at least there is the hope of progress. This has always been a hazardous thing to do; the powerful can be crotchety – we only have to recall the brutality of Peterloo, Solzhenitsyn, or Tiananmen Square. In the modern era we may not need to worry about the gulag and the militia, but other more insidious traps await us.

Power can distort our moral judgement, much as a block of metal confuses a compass. Someone with wealth and power is obviously a winner – society has judged them a success. Any reservations we may harbour about how they attained power, or what they might be doing with it, are eased by this social acceptance, this acquired status. Just look how quickly Trump and Johnson moved from being judged as totally unsuitable for high office to heroes of their respective caucuses as they acquired power.

In our consumer society, business – and its apotheosis the multinational corporation – has acquired immense power. MNCs have not only become staggeringly rich, they are getting richer all the time because they have something even governments can only dream of – a continuing and growing income stream. A recent analysis by Oxfam showed that the combined revenue of the ten biggest corporations now exceeds that of 180 countries put together

14   *Gerard Hastings*

(Oxfam, 2017). This affords them immense status, which executive jets and conspicuous consumption reinforce. We even refer to them reverentially as wealth creators, despite creation – making something from nothing – being the preserve of the divine.

This modern elite has many of the qualities of its historical antecedents. The same hunger for more power and anxiety about losing it; the same pull for the wannabe powerful; the same ability to suspend disbelief; the same control of the reins. It also has a crucial additional strength: charm. The discipline of corporate marketing has grown up as a means of making the overweening power of big business not just palatable but positively appealing. As Bakan explains, branding emerged when General Electric wanted to give its monolithic reality a human face. The company went about this quite literally, using the faces of its workforce to put across a down-home, couthy image of what had become an early example of the corporate behemoth.

Marketing, without the corporate appellation, is something different: a genuine attempt to meet consumer need, if only because not doing so will give other businesses a competitive advantage. It has its origins in the mists of human history, where collaboration was the prerequisite of survival, and marketing, with the idea of the mutually beneficial deal at its core, provides a protocol for facilitating this cooperation (Gerard Hastings, 2013).

All this changes with the acquisition of power. In the hands of an MNC marketing, axioms like 'consumer sovereignty' and the 'customer always comes first' are eviscerated by the fiduciary imperative and the precedence of the shareholder. Customer service becomes an Orwellian construct when the commercial determinants of ill-health are so well recognised; when so many products – tobacco, processed food, alcohol, pharmaceuticals, petrochemicals, leaded paint, guns – are known to have caused such harm, even when used as intended, that a new descriptor, the 'industrial epidemic' (Jahiel & Babor, 2007), has had to be coined. If we extend the definition of harm beyond the individual to the collective and then the planetary, the list of products multiplies. Arguably it becomes endless; the problem is consumption and a system honed to command it is of very questionable value. In these circumstances, marketing is a tool for manipulation not cooperation. Teenagers are beguiled with tobacco; gamblers are captivated by fixed-odds betting terminals; and everyone is being enthralled by their devices; "in an attention economy, addiction is not so much a scourge as a means of production" (Seymour, 2019).

Corporate marketers do not stop at we consumers; their stakeholder marketing is equally focussed. Powerful lobbying and corporate affairs functions are used to engage policymakers, politicians, and other decision makers, including academics and teachers. This partnership working is an immensely effective marketing tactic; with it soda (soft-drink) manufacturers can influence the Centres for Disease Control and Prevention (the CDC) (Maani Hessari, Ruskin, McKee, & Stuckler, 2019); oil companies undermine climate science (Supran & Oreskes, 2017); and the paint industry exonerates lead (Kessler, 2014).

The CDC case illustrates how subtle and slippery this process becomes. Coca-Cola staff deliberately set about building relationships with civil servants at CDC in order to influence them and reframe the debate about a potential threat to the company's profits, the imposition of taxes on sugar-sweetened beverages (SSBs):

> One particular email exchange sheds light on the seriousness with which the industry takes the threat of taxing SSBs and the possibility that ongoing relationships between the CDC and SSB companies could alleviate this threat. Alex Malaspina (from Coca-Cola) described Margaret Chan's support of a sugar tax as a "global threat to our business." This statement, while striking, is consistent with Coca-Cola's communications to shareholders in its annual reports, which make clear that "possible new or increased taxes on sugar-sweetened beverages to reduce consumption or to raise revenue ... could adversely affect our profitability." Malaspina then asked for and received advice from a senior CDC contact on how to arrange a meeting with Margaret Chan in order to influence her.

Furthermore, the case is neither dated (the events took place in 2015) nor atypical – the soda industry spent nearly US$70 million between 2009 and 2016 undermining public health interventions to reduce sugary drink consumption (Centre for Science in the Public Interest, 2016). This track record has led to the conclusion that self-regulation will never work, and statutory measures are needed (Ronit & Jensen, 2014); it also calls into serious question any attempt at partnership working (Freedhoff, 2014).

The energy-dense food industry is not exceptional; the same pattern emerges in other well-studied sectors such as tobacco and alcohol. The problem is not one of bad apples or wicked people, it is systemic. A corporation simply cannot serve two masters simultaneously: either it goes after profits or better public health; it cannot do both. Those who would partner with the corporate sector face exactly the same dilemma.

It is clear then that when a corporation works with social marketers and other good causes it does so to enhance its core business. It might do good as well, but this will be secondary to shareholder returns and, when it comes to a choice between the two, profits will always win out. If you are in any doubt about this seemingly cynical conclusion, consult the horse's mouth: business textbooks explicitly state that partnership working is a function of hard-headed business decisions. Causes are selected and partners chosen according to the benefits they can bring to the bottom line, not the needs of society. It is as far away from philanthropy as the sex industry is from everlasting love. The benefits are numerous but typically fall into three groups:

> **Reputation management.** Being associated with good causes brings kudos and respectability. Coke's support of the Olympics is buying a small slice of the organisation's high regard; Philip Morris's funding of

16   *Gerard Hastings*

women's refuges makes its tobacco-predations just a little less obvious; and the Diageo Foundation grants are "building partnerships with community groups and NGOs" (fundsforNGOs, n.d). In a world where the brand is so important and emotional associations a vital plank of consumer and stakeholder marketing, the ready-made prestige of a beneficent organisation or good cause is a valuable commodity. The companies also acquire allies and potential champions; my athletics career, job in a refuge or foundation grant will make me − contractually and genuinely − grateful to the sponsor. As the CDC example shows, it can even turn into friendships. The indirect, covert nature of this messaging and relationship building only makes it more powerful; where a billboard claiming Coke to be Olympian would be absurd, a link-up with the International Olympic Committee (IOC) bypasses our critical radar and soon becomes normal.

Avoiding regulation. Partnership working, in the form of Corporate Social Responsibility (CSR), first came to prominence in the early 1990s when Shell got into serious trouble in the Niger Delta. The company was being heavily criticised for despoiling the homeland of the Ogoni people and became implicated in the execution of Ken Saro-Wiwa by the then-military junta. It responded, like Coke, with a charm offensive but little concrete action. The story has continued since, with local communities having to sue the corporation for proper compensation (which was increased from a mere US$4000 to £55m) and until this day "the Niger Delta is one of the most polluted places on earth" (Amnesty International, n.d). The court case points up the gulf between voluntary and compulsory measures, and staving off the latter is a key purpose of stakeholder marketing.

Distraction. The 'look over there' has become a feature of populist politics; Donald Trump's success in deflecting criticism with diversionary 'noises off' has become infamous. Personable partnerships and charismatic causes can perform the same purpose for the corporation. Women's refuges do provide a vital service, do bring immense help to a vulnerable group − and take our attention away from lung cancer. The related concern here is that good causes will be chosen for their ability to distract, their popular allure: donkey sanctuaries stand a much better chance of being funded than ex-offender services. This begs the question: who should decide what good causes to address; the marketing director of Philip Morris International (PMI) or the UN Rapporteur on refugees? Such decisions are fraught enough without the disorienting effects of the profit motive.

Inertia

These strategic questions are thrown into relief when we start to consider radical change. The compelling example is climate. The prognosis is now

Ending tyrannic man's dominion 17

so disturbing that we can no longer avoid debating the need for systemic transformation; the kind of thinking which is being curated by the Great Transition Initiative (GTI, 2019), "an online forum of ideas and an international network for the critical exploration of concepts, strategies, and visions for a transition to a future of enriched lives, human solidarity, and a resilient biosphere." As Patel and Moore point out: "great transitions occur when business as usual no longer works" but "the powerful have a way of sticking to time-honoured strategies even when the reality is radically changing" (Patel & Moore, 2017).

Humankind has undergone previous transformations: from hunter gatherer to settled agriculture, to industrialisation to digital; from tribe to city state, to nation state to the global community; from speaking to writing, to printing, to posting. Change, then, is inevitable, it is part of the human condition; the only question is whether it will be managed and informed or chaotic. In this debate the current elite is an obstacle, not a bridge, to progress. Any solution it favours will be

> inadequate for the task, as it treats the symptoms of unsustainability instead of the underlying disease … it will be unable to overcome powerful countervailing forces: the growth imperative of conventional development, the resistance of vested interests, and a spreading consumerist culture.
>
> (GTI, 2019)

When viewed exclusively through the half-blocked keyhole of profit and loss, transformation is simply not on the agenda; a social marketing project funded by an oil company will not even broach such radical ideas.

So, as with war, truth is the first casualty of corporate partnership. The Civil Rights Movement famously argued that progressive change starts by "speaking truth to power"; this is impossible when power joins in on both sides of the conversation. The possibility that the most sustainable outcome would be to put your oil company partner out of business will not even get a mention. Anyway, it would be so rude, would it not, when you are just about to have lunch together?

More broadly, if climate breakdown requires us to cut back radically on our consumption – to stop flying altogether, to give up eating meat, to reject our cars (even the electric ones) – how can a corporation which depends for its very existence on our current shopping behaviour even acknowledge this, let alone address it? They will innovate, you might say, and come up with carbon neutral versions of all these products. But would they do so willingly? Or would they obstruct and delay? Take the argument a stage further: suppose it becomes clear that it is the exploitation of nature that is the problem, that materialism does not bring contentment, that profit and loss are alien and damaging constructs that humankind has invented to aid and abet its despoliation of the planet. Will any corporation even entertain such a conversation? So, if social marketers link arms with them, they are at risk of consolidating the

18 *Gerard Hastings*

system which the Civil Rights Movement set out to challenge, where power speaks to power untroubled by truth.

Dogmatism

Life exacerbates this obfuscation and encourages our collaboration in it. The protagonist rarely knows the story: the narrator relates it, the other characters may observe and divine it, but the protagonist is too busy living the reality to do so. She is preoccupied with overcoming obstacles, fighting corners, enjoying successes, and so has little time to think about the big picture. She is struggling to keep on top of emails, anxious about her *h*-score on Google Scholar and hungry for promotion; she cannot afford the luxury of worrying about the conflict minerals in her multiple electronic devices.

Anyway, if we do start picking at the loose threads of our system, the whole fabric begins to unravel. Conflict minerals speak of exploitation and extraction; sweat shops hove into view; strip mining and arctic oil conjure up uncomfortable pictures of despoliation; the fate of the Ogoni people in the Niger Delta disturbs our sleep. Reading about it only makes matters worse. When Raj Patel (Patel & Moore, 2017) reminds us that the conflict minerals are just the latest in the long history of the Rich North taking advantage of the Global South, that capitalism followed the path trodden down by colonialism, we get an uncomfortable sense of connection with an era of exploitation we thought had vanished. When we are reminded that the world's most successful economy was built on genocide, and that the oppression continues to this day, the temptation to turn a blind eye is great. When we learn that the climate is in meltdown and more than half the carbon our lifestyles have injected into the Earth's atmosphere has been put there *since* the first Intergovernmental Panel on Climate Change (IPCC) report in 1988 (Wallace-Wells, 2019) the cognitive dissonance becomes unbearable. We just want nurse to make the pain stop.

And nurse, in the form of the corporate marketer, will do just that. One of the principal purposes of the barrage of consumer and stakeholder marketing that engulfs us every moment of our lives is to keep us onside with the great project: perpetual economic growth driven by spiralling consumption; to help us forget, or at least downplay: the negative side effects of inequalities, exploitation, sweatshops, and climate chaos. A shocking dimension of humankind's current predicament is that we are not only collaborating in all the self-harm and planetary degradation, but that we are OK about doing so; complicity is surpassed only by self-justification. In this light, slogans like 'I'm loving it' and 'because you're worth it' acquire an ominous tinge, and partnership working – Coke blessed by the IOC, vulnerable women harboured by PMI, social marketing funded by Big Oil – become distinctly sinister.

Piketty argues that this "apparatus of justification" outguns even the "repressive apparatus" as a means of social control (Piketty, 2014); in a consumer society, gulags and secret police are bested by the mall and the smartphone.

Ending tyrannic man's dominion 19

The speed with which the latter has taken control of our lives is daunting: in twenty years we have moved from dalliance to dependency and our phones from intriguing accessories to life support machines. We now spend more time on devices than we do sleeping; our every move, decision, and sentiment are monitored, recorded, and analysed – then bought and sold. Algorithms, big data, and precision targeting mean our grip on reality is being badly distorted, and, as Cambridge Analytica demonstrates, democracy itself is now under siege. The Stasi could only dream of such intricate surveillance, such as social, psychological, and political control.

Furthermore, it is all so pleasing that we collaborate willingly; we do not just volunteer our data, we pay for the privilege of handing it over. Meanwhile we cravenly accede to conflict minerals, sweatshops, and reflex Siri questions. These last require multiple energy-sapping servers to jump into action at our whim, but we think nothing of the carbon footprint – we just get petulant when the answer does not come back quickly enough. Postman (1985) argues that Huxley rather than Orwell got it right about human oppression: volunteer consumers who willingly embrace their servitude are much easier to control than coerced citizens. Social marketers partnering with the corporate sector become part of this apparatus of justification.

But still this is not the worst. Harari (2014) is the latest of many to point out that humankind progresses through stories. We need to be able to think, plan, and aspire beyond our immediate social and geographical boundaries if we are to move forward. Corporate marketing stifles the emergence of new stories. It dominates the media, both analogue and digital, links the current system with all that is good in life, and sells us contentment and self-satisfaction. Stakeholders, who should be challenging this smothering dream, offering alternative stories, are instead diverted into curating it with partnership working.

New stories and new partners

What could the new story be?

Given the devastation we have caused and are still causing, it seems appropriate to begin with an apology; a recognition that we have gone wrong, that our current story is untenable. Our apparent inability to do this, to grasp the enormity and imminence of climate breakdown, and turn this into alternative stories is what Amitav Ghosh calls our 'Great Derangement' (Ghosh, 2017). He contrasts the tepid language of the 2015 Paris Agreement on Climate with the Vatican encyclical Laudate Si which appeared at the same time:

> while words like catastrophe and disaster occur several times in the Encyclical, the Agreement talks only of the adverse impacts or effects of climate change. The word catastrophe is never used and even disaster occurs only once and that too because it figures in the title of a previous conference.
>
> (Ghosh, 2017, p. 154)

20   *Gerard Hastings*

He puts this down to the involvement of "various billionaires, corporations and climate entrepreneurs" in the negotiations. He argues that the text itself betrays this bias:

> as is often the case with texts, the Agreement's rhetoric serves to clarify much that it leaves unsaid: namely that its intention, and the essence of what it has achieved, is to create yet another neo-liberal frontier where corporations, entrepreneurs and public officials will be able to join forces in enriching each other.
>
> (Ghosh, 2017, p. 156)

Perhaps there is a need to update Shelley's Ozymandias, with the King of Kings surviving to experience the despair, decay, and colossal wreck which his works have produced. For the new story to "warn, as so many of the old stories do, against taking too much, against reaching too far, against leaving too little for others" (Bringhurst & Zwicky, 2018, p. 22).

Partnership working with corporations pulls stakeholders into this same disreputable space, perpetually retelling a discredited story instead of devising a new one. The Encyclical offers us social marketers this stark warning:

> many professionals, opinion makers, communications media and centres of power, being located in affluent urban areas, are far removed from the poor, with little direct contact with their problems. They live and reason from the comfortable position of a high level of development and a quality of life well beyond the reach of the majority of the world's population ... this attitude exists side by side with a green rhetoric.

This suggests that, when it comes to partnership working, we should be thinking of partnerships with the poor, with the victims of the current system, not its architects and beneficiaries. The economic establishment may be incapable of contrition and reinvention, but other sectors of society, those not dominated by the market and money − or excluded from them − are capable of questioning and rethinking the narrative. Furthermore, our story is unlikely to progress without clear links to social justice:

> we have to realize that a true ecological approach always becomes a social approach; it must integrate questions of justice in debates on the environment, so as to hear both the cry of the earth and the cry of the poor.

There is a particular need to apologise to and connect with indigenous peoples. It is sobering to think that as our way of life has been pushed across the world it has caused the deaths not just of countless people but countless peoples. Alternative social systems, ways of contemplating the human condition, unique insights, and intuitions, have been swept away from every continent of the world (bar Antarctica where there were none in the first place).

Ending tyrannic man's dominion   21

And to the apology could be added a dose of humility. Regret is sometimes expressed about the loss of scientific knowledge that comes with the reduction in biodiversity, the new drugs and cures that might be disappearing before even being found, as the Amazon burns. But what about the learning from different social systems? From the people "who still know the secrets of sustainable living" who "are not relics of the past, but the guides to our future" (Gupta, 2011). Here partnership working makes abundant sense.

Interestingly, moves towards such a partnership have been made, but not by the economic establishment or multinational corporations, despite their state-of-the-art communications. Rather it has come from the Kogi people of the Sierra Nevada, whose way of life dates back to pre-Colombian times, who have used their connections with a BBC journalist to make a film called Aluna (2018). In it they explain that they see themselves as stewards of the planet and feel a compelling need to warn us, their "younger brothers," of the harms our economic system is causing. They express deep unease about the devastation that mining, power generation, and modern living in general are reeking on the world; they call on us to change course. Despite a lack of modern scientific method, they explain basic ecology, the connectedness of nature, and the harm being done to the climate.

A similar plea came recently from the Amazon's Kayapó people: "We call on you to stop what you are doing, to stop the destruction … If the land dies – if our Earth dies – then none of us will be able to live. We will all die" (Metuktire, 2019). Their chief, Raoni Metuktire, explains that we share the same fears about the future, we are in the same perilous predicament.

They can also give us a new perspective on things we take for granted. They refer to money, for example, as *piu caprim*, which means sad leaves, because it causes so much division:

> When your money comes into our communities it often drives our people apart. And we can see that it does the same thing in your cities, where what you call rich people live isolated from everyone else, afraid that others will come to take their piu caprim away from them. Meanwhile other people live in misery because they don't have enough money for food.

Partnering with the Kogis and the Kayapós makes a lot of sense. It can open our minds to new ways of thinking, new ways of being that have stood the test of time. Note it is not a matter of accepting wholesale everything they say, adopting all their customs and every aspect of their culture; in a partnership of equals there is room for compromise and negotiation – both partners are free to learn. By contrast, partnering with a multinational corporation does require us to accept their view of the world – from a foundation myth extolling growth and consumption to shamanistic branding practices.

A recurring theme in indigenous cultures, including that of the Kogis and the Kayapós, is our relationship with nature. While our current narrative sees it as something to be exploited, "a portfolio of resources for us or our species to buy and sell or manage or squander as we please" (Bringhurst & Zwicky, 2018, p. 12), indigenous culture recognises our dependence on it, our symbiotic relationship with it. So, our story might continue with us "trying to think like an ecosystem instead of like a disconnected visitor" (Bringhurst & Zwicky, 2018, p. 8), by recognising that we are part of nature not the master of it; that the world is a living, breathing network of mutually dependent life forms. Once we embrace this "Gaia Principle" of mutual dependence, then extraction becomes much more difficult and brute exploitation impossible. When we accept that rivers connect mountain and sea and benefit both, hydro-electric schemes need much more careful thought. If we see trees as sentient creatures that can comprise ecosystems in their own right, logging becomes a much more questionable activity. The Kogis see nature herself as a living, sentient being; Aluna is the mother of everything, and they say in their film "if you knew she could feel you would stop." The reverse is also true: as long as we do not know that nature can feel, we will never stop; we urgently need a story of the world that will bring this lesson home to us.

This does not mean we can never harvest anything from nature; humankind, as do other animals, need to do this to survive, let alone flourish. It is a question of how we do it; a question of restraint; a question of respect. The native American Indians were horrified by the logging operations of the European settlers and their unsustainable hunting practices. It was not that they never cut down trees or hunted wildlife, but that they did so with respect. They would apologise to the trees and animals, thanking them for the life they gave up and the life they sustained. To quote Raoni Metuktire again: "to live you must respect the world, the trees, the plants, the animals, the rivers and even the very earth itself." Partnership working is essential, but we need a partnership with nature not the MNC.

The chances of success

What are the chances of a new story emerging and prevailing? The augers are pretty grim. The IPCC gave us 12 years to save the planet in 2018, and it is a notoriously careful and politically constrained organisation whose pronouncements are therefore innately conservative. So, as Wallace-Wells says in the opening words of *The Uninhabitable Planet*: "it is worse, much worse, than you think" (Wallace-Wells, 2019, p. 1). The speed of degradation is also daunting. *Homo sapiens* has been around for 20,000 years, but more than half the harm we have done to the planet has been perpetrated in the last three decades. There is much to be pessimistic about.

Nonetheless, as the former Archbishop of Canterbury says in his recent essay, it might just work. Despite the inertia, the vested interests, the obtuseness of the "collectively wealthy of the world" and what Walt Whitman calls our "mania for owning things," he argues that "some serious adjustments might be made." If we can stop partnering with the status quo and instead partner with the poor, the indigenous, and the natural world, things could change. If we can embrace humility and hope, the clouds may begin to lift.

But just as importantly, perhaps more so for our own peace of mind, as we embrace these alternative perspectives, we will escape the discomfort of living in denial and complicity. In his classic book on the French Resistance, Joseph Kessel explains how the emergence of a putative opposition, weak and ineffective though it seemed in 1940, immediately made people feel better. Despite the Nazi dominance, the ruthlessness of the Gestapo and the complicity of many French people, most significantly Marshal Petain, just doing something – an old woman tripping up an enemy soldier with her walking stick, an official turning a blind eye – and knowing the others were also doing something – gave a sense of agency and hope. As a résistant in the book explains: "Je suis bien content de connaitre la résistance. Je ne vais plus être tellement malheureux. Je comprends la vie et je l'aime. J'ai la foi." ("I am so happy to know about the resistance. I am no longer despondent; I understand life and love it. Now I have hope.")

Our individual decisions to avoid flying or dispense with our SUV might have a trifling effect on the planet and on their own will never avert climate breakdown, but they will, in Rowan Williams words, help us "escape the toxicity of the mindset that brought us here." These small steps also have the power to connect us with others of like mind and generate hope. If this can develop into a growing sense of resistance, this hope might even, as for Kessel's résistant, grow into success.

When this happens, our new story will write itself.

Notes

1 This is an act of stealing from an apple orchard.
2 Komitet Gosudarstvennoy Bezopasnosti: the former Soviet Union's secret police.

References

Aluna (2018). Retrieved from www.youtube.com/watch?v=ftFbCwJfs1I&t=4117s.
Amnesty International (n.d.). Niger delta negligence. Retrieved from www.amnesty. org/en/latest/news/2018/03/Niger-Delta-Oil-Spills-Decoders/.
Bringhurst, R., & Zwicky, J. (2018). *Learning to Die: Wisdom in the Age of Climate Crisis.* Saskatchewan, Canada: University of Regina Press.
Centre for Science in the Public Interest (2016). Big soda vs. public health (2016 Edition). A Report. 21 September 2016. Retrieved from https://cspinet.org/ resource/big-soda-vs-public-health-1.
Freedhoff, Y. (2014). The food industry is neither friend, nor foe, nor partner. *Obesity Reviews, 15*(1), 6–8.
fundsforNGOs (n.d.). The Diageo Foundation grants: Call for applications. Retrieved from www.fundsforngos.org/environment-2/the-diageo-foundation-grants-call-for-applications/.

Ghosh, A. (2017). *The Great Derangement: Climate Change and the Unthinkable*. Chicago: University of Chicago Press.

Gupta, A. (2011). Arundhati Roy: The people who created the crisis will not be the ones that come up with a solution. *The Guardian*. Retrieved from www.theguardian. com/world/2011/nov/30/arundhati-roy-interview.

GTI (2019). Great Transition Initiative. Retrieved from https://greattransition.org/about/aims-and-background.

Harari, Y.N. (2014). *Sapiens: A Brief History of Humankind*. London: Harper.

Hastings, G. (2013). *The Marketing Matrix: How the Corporation Gets Its Power – and How We Can Reclaim It*. London: Routledge.

Jahiel, R.I., & Babor, T.F. (2007). Industrial epidemics, public health advocacy and the alcohol industry: Lessons from other fields. *Addiction, 102*(9), 1335–1339.

Kessler, R. (2014). Lead-based decorative paints: Where are they still sold – and why? *National Institute of Environmental Health Sciences*.

Maani Hessari, N., Ruskin, G., McKee, M., & Stuckler, D. (2019). Public peets private: Conversations between Coca-Cola and the CDC. *The Milbank Quarterly, 97*(1), 74–90.

Metuktire, R. (2019). We, the peoples of the Amazon, are full of fear. Soon you will be too. *The Guardian*. Retrieved from www.theguardian.com/commentisfree/2019/sep/02/amazon-destruction-earth-brazilian-kayapo-people.

Oxfam (2017). Retrieved from www.oxfam.org/sites/www.oxfam.org/files/file_attachments/bp-economy-for-99-percent-160117-en.pdf.

Patel, R., & Moore, J.W. (2017). *A History of the World in Seven Cheap Things: A Guide to Capitalism, Nature, and the Future of the Planet*. California: University of California Press.

Piketty, T. (2014). *Capital in the Twenty-First Century* (A. Goldhammer, Trans.). Cambridge: Harvard University Press.

Postman, N. (1985). *Amusing Ourselves to Death: Public Discourse in the Age of Show Business*. London: Penguin Books.

Ronit, K., & Jensen, J.D. (2014). Obesity and industry self-regulation of food and beverage marketing: A literature review. *European Journal of Clinical Nutrition, 68*(7), 753.

Seymour, R. (2019). *The Twittering Machine*. Canada: Indigo Press.

Supran, G., & Oreskes, N. (2017). Assessing ExxonMobil's climate change communications (1977–2014). *Environmental Research Letters, 12*(8), 084019.

Wallace-Wells, D. (2019). *The Uninhabitable Earth. A Story of the Future*. New York: Penguin Random House.

Williams, R. (2019). Afterword to *This Is Not A Drill. An Extinction Rebellion Handbook*. London: Penguin.

3 Ethical tension in working with stakeholders

Krzysztof Kubacki, Natalia Szablewska, and Dariusz Siemieniako

Introduction

The purpose of this chapter is to engage in a debate about the ethical tension and conflict that can arise from working with multiple and diverse stakeholders in the context of social marketing. The practice of social marketing has always involved some degree of collaboration between social marketers and a range of different stakeholders. Stakeholder interactions include building relationships with funding agencies to gather the resources needed to support social marketing programmes, working with advertising and other related agencies to develop marketing communications strategies and materials, and engaging with target audiences to understand their needs and implement citizen-centric behaviour change strategies. Yet, in the last 30 years, we have observed a shift in typical stakeholder engagement. According to Duane and Domegan's (2018) periodisation study, initial social marketing practices (1969–1990) often involved only limited cooperation between a small number of stakeholders and focused on the promotion of social ideas to individuals in an attempt to change their behaviour. Although this kind of downstream approach might have been effective (at least in the short term) and remains popular in practice, it has attracted significant criticism for overlooking the wider social, cultural, economic, and political contexts of social issues (see, for example, Kennedy, 2016; Luca, Hibbert, & McDonald, 2016). Addressing the limitations of downstream, often individual-focused, social marketing, social marketers have more recently begun to integrate a macro-perspective into their work, recognising that most social issues and their causes and potential solutions require more sophisticated and systemic programmes with greater engagement of a large number of stakeholders at all levels, from the individual to the government and society.

However, generating any change in a social marketing system that consists of multiple stakeholders unavoidably leads to ethical tension and conflict between the stakeholders in that system. In this chapter, we follow McHugh, Domegan, and Duane's (2018) understanding of a social marketing system as "a multiplicity of people and stakeholder groups interacting to create patterns of behaviours, choices, and values over time in a dynamic macro–micro context" (p. 165). Most social marketing systems include target audiences and any other individuals or groups that may be affected by the operations of the system (e.g. families, friends, peers, and communities), commercial organisations, industry bodies, the media, the government, non-governmental organisations (NGOs), not-for-profits, research organisations, and community groups, among others. Social marketers operate in a system where these diverse stakeholders may have very different understandings of a social issue that needs to be addressed, its causes, and its importance, and, hence, what the potential solutions are and which of them should be prioritised over other potential solutions.

The sources of modern ethics can be rich and diverse, including morality, religion, culture, professional practice, and law. In relationships between stakeholders, these sources translate into differences in "standards of conduct and moral judgement applied to marketing practice" (Gaski, 1999, p. 316) that often lie at the centre of ethical tension and conflict. Consider a social issue such as excessive alcohol consumption and its social marketing system and key stakeholders. The World Health Organization's *Global Status Report on Alcohol and Health* (WHO, 2018) showed that each year, three million people die due to the harmful use of alcohol, which contributes to over 200 different disease and injury conditions. Hence, there is no doubt that alcohol is a dangerous drug, and the medical profession's view of alcohol will be shaped by scientific research and medical practitioners' exposure to the wide range of diseases and injuries caused by alcohol consumption. Another relevant stakeholder group, law enforcement, will focus on the harms caused by drink driving, violence, and other anti-social behaviours. Social workers will prioritise the social costs and consequences for families affected by excessive alcohol consumption and alcoholism. However, for many people, alcohol is a source of pleasure, and their drinking may not result in any immediately visible negative consequences. In the absence of any direct adverse alcohol drinking experience, many drinkers will view alcohol drinking as a matter of exercising personal choice. At the same time, alcohol manufacturers and distributors will emphasise the good time that people have when consuming alcohol, and the industry bodies will focus on the positive economic contributions that alcohol manufacturing and consumption make to society, including jobs. The media will recognise the social issue but cannot ignore the revenue from alcohol advertising. The government will be torn between the economic benefits and tax revenue generated by the alcohol industry and all the negative consequences of alcohol consumption.

We can see that even when considering only some of the key stakeholders in the alcohol consumption system, there are inherent differences emerging between various stakeholders' roles in the system and their views on the issue. Yet, achieving social marketing objectives requires at least some degree of collaboration between stakeholders in a social marketing system, despite and beyond any differences between them. While ethical dimensions of social marketing and commonly used ethical frameworks such as deontology and teleology have been examined more broadly elsewhere (see, for example, Eagle, Dahl, & Low, 2020), the specific focus of this chapter is on how the differences in perspectives can lead to ethical tension and conflict between stakeholders, which in turn may jeopardise social marketing efforts. In what follows, we first attempt to define what we mean by a stakeholder in this chapter, and we identify the different groups of stakeholders between which we can observe ethical tension and conflict. Next, we examine power asymmetry as a cause of ethical tension and conflict. Finally, we consider how human rights principles can help us to address the ethical tension and conflict arising from the power asymmetry between the different groups of stakeholders in social marketing systems.

What is a stakeholder?

Before we consider the sources of conflict and ethical tension between the stakeholders involved in social marketing programmes, we need to clarify what we understand by the term 'stakeholder.' As we highlighted in the introduction, social marketing research has shifted towards understanding social issues as integrated systems, and social marketing practice involves working with other participants in the system, often referred to as 'partnerships,' 'coalitions,' 'collaborations,' 'cooperation,' 'agencies,' 'alliances,' 'initiatives,' and 'stakeholders' (Duane & Domegan, 2018). Yet, despite the richness of the terminology used to describe the relationships between participant stakeholder groups, the social marketing literature provides very limited understanding of the differences between these terms and their distinct characteristics. We recognise that they are used to describe relationships of different natures; however, as it is often difficult to distinguish between them, in this chapter, we use 'stakeholders' as an umbrella term encompassing all the different types of participants in a social marketing system.

Edward Freeman, who proposed stakeholder theory in 1983, described a stakeholder as "any group or individual who can affect or is affected by the achievement of the organization's objectives" (Freeman, 1984, p. 46). Although stakeholder theory was originally developed as an approach to managing corporations, Niblett (2005) believes that, as social marketing focuses on complex social issues where economic, political, and social interests often conflict, considering stakeholders in social marketing systems seems even more important than it is in a commercial environment. Hence, we define social marketing stakeholders as all the participants in a social marketing system who can affect, or are affected by, the achievement of social marketing objectives.

Working with a wide range of stakeholders may encourage strong commitments to behaviour change (Domegan, Collins, Stead, McHugh, & Hughes, 2013) and remains paramount to the creation of environments supportive of behaviour change (Lefebvre, 2006). However, where different stakeholders control the resources essential to achieving social marketing objectives, they can facilitate the desired change, but, in certain circumstances, they may work against social marketing objectives (Kennedy, 2016; McHugh et al., 2018). At the same time, while a small group of stakeholders may lack the resources required to address complex social issues, there is evidence indicating that increasing the number and type of stakeholders in social marketing

28 *Krzysztof Kubacki et al.*

programmes may increase chances of success (Gregson et al., 2001). It is therefore important for social marketers to identify all relevant stakeholders in the social marketing system and understand their roles and objectives.

Although different classifications of stakeholders have been offered in the management literature (see, for example, Clulow, 2005; Freeman, 1984; Kennedy, Kapitan, Bajaj, Bakonji, & Sands, 2017; Smith & Fischbacher, 2005), a persuasive classification has been provided in the social marketing literature by Hastings and Domegan (2017), who divided stakeholders into *incumbents*, *challengers*, and *regulating agencies*. The Hastings and Domegan (2017) classification focuses on the distribution and nature of power and influence among the stakeholders in a social marketing system. While unequally distributed power gives some stakeholders more ability to resolve conflict and ethical tension in their self-interests, power that is spread out more equally among many stakeholders may lead to compromise.

The first group of stakeholders are the most powerful stakeholders in a social marketing system: they aim to maintain the status quo and may impede any attempts to introduce change into the system. *Incumbents* are highly influential and benefit from the current situation; their privileged position and resources allow them to shape the system in their favour. For instance, in the alcohol consumption example provided earlier, some of the world's largest alcoholic beverage companies may be described as incumbents. *Challengers*, on the other hand, are stakeholders who have less power and influence than incumbents, yet they will use innovation and an entrepreneurial spirit to disrupt the status quo and change the balance of power in the system. They will use any opportunity to introduce change and rewrite the rules governing the system. For instance, social marketers aiming to minimise the harm from alcohol consumption will engage with other stakeholders to reduce alcohol consumption, acting against the commercial self-interests of large alcoholic beverage companies. Further, local micro-brewers may also act as challengers, albeit their objectives are different to social marketing objectives, as they attempt to change consumption patterns in the industry by shifting consumption away from large brands towards locally produced alcoholic beverages. *Regulating agencies* are stakeholders who oversee the system by enforcing the existing rules and laws. Some of these stakeholders, such as industry groups, may be formed to represent the interests of incumbents and protect them from the intervention of government agencies and other organisations representing the interests of the state and other stakeholders (e.g. consumer groups and medical associations). In the alcohol consumption example, it is the role of the state to introduce and enforce licensing laws.

However, one of the main limitations of stakeholder theory is that it does not provide much guidance to social marketers on how to identify and manage the inevitable conflict and ethical tension between the stakeholders who have different perspectives, objectives (both commercial and social), and ideas regarding how the system should work as a whole. Therefore, other approaches and principles beyond stakeholder theory are needed to assist social marketers in managing stakeholders towards a social objective, considering the needs, interests, claims, rights, and duties of all in the social marketing system.

Power asymmetry as a cause of ethical tension and conflict

In an ideal scenario, social marketing programmes would be developed by stakeholders who share similar values and agree to pursue shared objectives via the same methods. However, as we have seen in the example of the alcohol industry, stakeholders often have very different understandings of the social issue that lies at the centre of the social marketing system; they have varying perspectives on the causes of the issue and hence the best way to address the issue. They may also have different commercial interests that enable their survival. Therefore, different stakeholders often work together to enhance their individual positions in the system and protect their interests. As a result, conflict and ethical tension between self-interests and the interests of other stakeholders in the social marketing system will arise, emanating from one important stakeholder attribute: power (Jones, Felps, & Bigley, 2007).

Power, in this context, is defined as "the potential to affect another's behaviour, manifest when a firm demands something incompatible with another firm's desire, and the firm receiving the demand shows resistance" (Cowan, Paswan, & Van Steenburg, 2015, p. 142). In other words, when one stakeholder in a social marketing system requests another stakeholder to change their behaviour, they can either conform to the demands (avoiding conflict) or confront the demands (creating conflict), yet in both cases the demands may lead to some ethical tension and potentially conflict due to opposed interests. Power is an inseparable part of the environment of every social marketing system, and different levels of power in a system lead to power asymmetry, where some stakeholders may be more influential (e.g. incumbents) than other stakeholders (e.g. challengers). In social marketing systems, social marketers most commonly act as challengers trying to disrupt the status quo and to empower those whose interests and needs are not being served. Therefore, in their attempts to disrupt the system, social marketers need to consider the various sources of power and power asymmetry that will shape their ability to succeed.

Power asymmetry in business relationships has been studied extensively, first of all in buyer–supplier dyads (see, for example, Lacoste & Johnsen, 2015, Siemieniako & Mitręga, 2018) and in business networks (see, for example, Olsen, Prenkert, Hoholm, & Harrison, 2014; Zolkiewski, 2011), yet it has not attracted any attention in the social marketing literature. However, stakeholders in social marketing systems will have different levels of power and influence in the system, and their ability to introduce, facilitate, or impede change will vary accordingly. If we consider social marketers as challengers who attempt to redress the balance in the system, we need to acknowledge the various sources of power asymmetry. The sources have been frequently discussed in the management and marketing literature with reference to the seminal work

30 *Krzysztof Kubacki et al.*

of French and Raven (1959), who distinguished between five key sources of power possession:

1. *Reward* power is the ability to reward other stakeholders in the social marketing system. All funding bodies who participate in the system either as regulating agencies (e.g. government-sponsored social marketing programmes) or as challengers (e.g. social marketing campaigns supported by NGOs or charities) use reward power to influence the system. Funding bodies use financial rewards to motivate other stakeholders to participate in and/or initiate programmes that will allow them to achieve their strategic social marketing objectives. Stakeholders who are willing to comply and are able to deliver satisfactory results are rewarded with funding that can increase their ability to influence the system and achieve their own commercial and/or social objectives. Further, commercial sponsors can also support social marketing programmes to achieve their commercial objectives (e.g. relating to reputation and brand image) through associating themselves with social marketing objectives. Other commercial stakeholders in social marketing systems who often act as competitors to social marketing programmes also employ reward power to achieve their strictly commercial objectives (e.g. increasing sales and market share). For example, while large alcoholic beverage companies will try to increase their sales, their efforts may run counter to social marketers trying to reduce the harm from alcohol consumption. They use traditional marketing exchanges to encourage alcohol consumption and reward loyal consumers through, for example, loyalty programmes and sales promotions. The stakeholders with the largest financial resources (e.g. incumbents such as large commercial organisations and large funding bodies) will have a greater ability to shape the exchanges within a social marketing system to increase their own benefits.

2. *Coercive* power gives one stakeholder the ability to influence another stakeholder through punishment (Siemieniako & Mitręga, 2018). Coercive power may be a source of conflict and ethical tension when partnerships are formed between commercial and social marketing stakeholders. For example, a commercial sponsor of a social marketing programme may attempt to withdraw their support if they believe that the achievement of some social marketing objectives will jeopardise their commercial interests. In heavily regulated markets, such as alcohol and tobacco, coercive power may also be used by regulating agencies to exercise control over other stakeholders and ensure that they follow the established rules, regulations, and policies, as well as to protect the most vulnerable in the social marketing system. Tension may therefore occur between incumbents, who would like to maintain the status quo, challengers, who would like to challenge the status quo, and regulatory agencies, who are tasked with monitoring the system to create a safe and just environment for all stakeholders. Consequently, regulatory agencies may be granted coercive power to provide a counterbalance to incumbents' reward power.

Ethical tension in working with stakeholders   31

3. *Legitimate* power is the most complex source of power, involving social norms, social structures, cultural values, and normative ethics. All the stakeholders within a social marketing system should accept and follow the advice provided by regulating agencies such as government departments and other monitoring organisations, including self-regulatory industry bodies. Consequently, regulatory agencies possess the legitimate power to intervene in a social marketing system when they believe that the rules governing the system are not being adhered to by a stakeholder or a group of stakeholders without invoking their coercive power. Their role is to use their legitimate power to enforce compliance with all the norms and values accepted in the system, monitoring and identifying right and wrong actions (Weiss, 2014). Incumbents and challengers (including the media) may also use their legitimate power to enforce non-legally binding rules such as social norms and ethics to put pressure on stakeholders when their actions or the consequences of those actions may harm another stakeholder within a social marketing system.

4. *Expert* power consists of the expertise and knowledge possessed by stakeholders in a social marketing system. Incumbents may use their market, marketing or product knowledge to create competitive barriers for new challengers; at the same time, challengers may develop expertise in niche markets or products that becomes a threat to incumbents, challenging their position over time. A specific category of expert power is scientific research, which is often used by challengers such as social marketers to compete against incumbents who may have significant reward and/or coercive power. Ethical tension will also occur between scientists who may have differing views, stemming, for example, from the fact that their research is funded by commercial organisations, leading to a potential conflict of interest. Therefore, the generation and acceptance of useful facts and knowledge within a social marketing system depend on each stakeholder's expert power. Social marketers often act as challengers and use expert power (e.g. academic and government research) to introduce change into the system and influence how other key stakeholders, such as consumers and regulating agencies, perceive the social issue at the centre of the social marketing system.

5. *Referent* power refers to the reputation of a stakeholder that makes them an attractive partner for other stakeholders. Incumbents and challengers may decide to work together because they admire some aspects of each other's business models and they want to learn from each other or create synergy. Commercial organisations may also engage in corporate social marketing with reputable social marketing partners to increase the credibility of their actions, and social marketers may choose to partner with commercial organisations because they believe that they can help each other to achieve both commercial and social marketing objectives. Prominent university scientists and research institutes may use their referent power to develop balanced partnerships with reputable challengers such as NGOs, charities,

32 *Krzysztof Kubacki et al.*

and government organisations to influence a social marketing system for the social good. Regulatory agencies also rely on stakeholders with significant referent and expert power to develop their understanding of a social marketing system and any changes that may be required to make sure that the system is fair and just for all.

Power asymmetry is inevitable in all social marketing systems and remains an interplay of some or all the five power sources: reward, coercive, expert, referent, and legitimate (Cowan, Paswan, & Van Steenburg, 2015; Handley & Benton, 2012; Siemieniako & Mitręga, 2018). However, although categorising stakeholders into incumbents, challengers, and regulating agencies and identifying the main sources of power asymmetry in a social marketing system are likely to help us to better understand the mechanics of the system, the trade-offs between self-interests and other stakeholders' interests require other frameworks beyond stakeholder theory that will help to guide all of the stakeholders in the social marketing system towards the social good.

Addressing ethical tension and conflict between stakeholders

One approach developed to support the analysis of power relations and to recognise and address the vulnerabilities of certain stakeholder groups and individuals is a human rights framework. In practice, the framework can be achieved by applying a human rights perspective or following a human-rights-based approach (see Szablewska & Kubacki, 2019). Therefore, the process of addressing the ethical tension and conflict stemming from the power asymmetry in a social marketing system can be guided by human rights principles.

Human rights principles have been developed to facilitate the implementation of and adherence to human rights as legal entitlements of individuals, and in certain circumstances groups, against the state or state-like entities to protect and guarantee the fundamental rights, freedoms, and dignity of all (Universal Declaration of Human Rights, 1948, Preamble). However, these principles have applications beyond the strictly legal context (in relation to legal rights and corresponding obligations) and can facilitate the fair and just distribution of power, protect the interests of the weakest groups, and unveil existing biases and underlying motives for (in)action. In other words, they have been used and followed in different contexts to aid decision-making processes by ensuring that these processes are *transparent*, that decision-makers remain *accountable*, and that those affected by the decisions are treated *equitably* and in a *non-discriminatory* manner, which is achieved by enabling the meaningful *participation* and *inclusion* of all those affected by decision-making. These human rights principles – of transparency, accountability, equality, non-discrimination, participation, and inclusion – are known as 'process principles' (United Nations Development Group, 2011) and have been utilised widely in the fields of policy development and (government and public authority) service delivery (see, for example, Audit Commission, 2003; Ministry of Justice, 2008), in relation to socially responsible corporate practices (see, for example, United Nations Global Compact, 2015) or in relation to humanitarian aid and international development (see, for example, Broberg & Sano, 2018).

Participation and inclusion

The principles of participation and inclusion focus on the mechanisms for involving all stakeholders within the social marketing system in decision-making processes. Social marketing programmes must facilitate opportunities for participation for all stakeholders and allow them to develop their capacity for inclusion in the development, delivery, and assessment of the programmes by identifying and removing any perceived and real barriers to participation and inclusion. The Victorian Equal Opportunity & Human Rights Commission (VEOHRC) (2008) called for stakeholder participation that is active, free, and meaningful: "participants must be able to shape and determine the decision-making process, as well as contribute significantly to the realisation and monitoring of the program itself" (p. 14). In practice, creating the capacity for participation and addressing the power asymmetry between stakeholders stemming from their different and often-conflicting roles in the social marketing system, such as incumbents and challengers, may require social marketers to identify and provide resources and to reach out to those who otherwise might end up being excluded (e.g. vulnerable populations). Broberg and Sano (2018) argued that participation and inclusion in practice should increase stakeholders' capacity for autonomous action.

Shand and Arnberg (1996) distinguished between five types of participation approaches that can be employed by social marketers to address the power asymmetry between stakeholders and its potential negative consequences (i.e. ethical tension and conflict):

1. Information: Gaining access to information, for example, about social marketing programmes, offered services, current policies, and sources of available funding; supporting challengers with information and know-how (e.g. expert knowledge) increases their capacity to directly compete against incumbents.
2. Consultation: Creating two-way communication channels between stakeholders beyond just formative research enables them to be continuously involved in decision-making processes, addressing the risk of those with the most resources (e.g. reward power) or influence (e.g. referent power) having the loudest voices.
3. Partnership: According to Duane and Domegan (2018), partners are stakeholders who are actively engaged in the social marketing programme; partnerships extend beyond information exchange and consultation to form long-term relationships in a social marketing system, aiming to create change in the system. Different stakeholders come together to address power asymmetry through the effect of synergy.

34   *Krzysztof Kubacki et al.*

4. Delegation: Active participation and inclusion can be achieved through regulating agencies allowing stakeholders to be involved in, or even become responsible for, policy development in a social marketing system. Although the overall control over the regulatory framework must be maintained by the regulating agency (e.g. a government department), some elements of policies governing a social marketing system may be developed, monitored, and enforced by the stakeholders themselves (e.g. self-regulation).
5. Control: When the well-being of some stakeholders is at risk, regulating agencies may attempt to take control over a social marketing system through policy and law. The most influential stakeholders (usually incumbents) will be required to behave in a prescribed way to minimise the harmful effects of their actions on other stakeholders and the entire system. For example, industries such as alcohol, tobacco, and gambling are heavily regulated in most countries to reduce power asymmetry through legitimate power. Upstream social marketing may be used by challengers to advocate an increased level of control in a system with high power asymmetry.

Equality and non-discrimination

Discrimination, inequality, and marginalisation lie at the heart of most social issues (Broberg & Sano, 2018). The principles of equality and non-discrimination determine that all people have an equal right to protection and respect, and attention must be paid to vulnerable stakeholders (both individuals and groups) with limited economic, social, and political resources (i.e. power). Social marketers must develop mechanisms within social marketing systems to identify those who might be vulnerable and at risk of discrimination and provide them with direct opportunities for engagement in social marketing programmes, creating a level playing field. The mechanisms must include three key steps: (1) identifying vulnerable stakeholders, (2) assessing the impact of the social marketing programmes on them, and (3) assessing whether actual or potential discrimination has been addressed (VEOHRC, 2008). Therefore, evaluations of social marketing programmes should include whole-of-system impact evaluations in addition to process and outcome evaluations to ensure that the voices of all relevant stakeholders are heard and considered, in particular those with less power and those who are often marginalised in decision-making processes.

Transparency and accountability

The principles of transparency and accountability address the need for transparent processes for the determination of the social issues at the centre of social marketing systems and for all stakeholders to be accountable for decision-making. It is the responsibility of regulating bodies (e.g. the government and its agencies) to set clear accountabilities in a social marketing system. Responsibilities and objectives for all stakeholders need to be identified, and processes need to be established to enforce appropriate accountabilities by regulating agencies. Voluntary reporting channels may be adopted by individual stakeholders so that they can become champions for good causes (and enjoy at the same time reputational benefits increasing their expert and referent powers). In social marketing systems with significant harm risks (e.g. alcohol, tobacco, and gambling), compulsory monitoring and reporting mechanisms may be enforced by regulating bodies to reduce the ethical tension and conflict between social marketing and commercial stakeholders and to deliver on the social good.

Conclusion

This chapter offers a critical discussion on the potential sources of conflict and ethical tension arising from working with multiple and diverse stakeholders in the context of social marketing. We argue that human rights principles may provide us with a compelling approach to address the tension. Human rights principles focus on people's needs, problems, and potential (Boesen & Martin, 2007) to provide a framework for rebalancing social marketing systems through changing the power asymmetries between stakeholders, which lead to ethical tension and conflict.

As identified by Szablewska and Kubacki (2019), human rights process principles can be adapted to the context of social marketing, as they are amenable to achieving the social good, in particular when addressing complex issues and 'wicked' problems (Kennedy et al., 2017). In practice, following them in social marketing programming constitutes a good practice that strengthens the effectiveness and efficiency of social marketing strategies and increases their legitimacy. In that sense, they are a conceptually sound and practically achievable tool that can facilitate the process of addressing the conflicting interests of various stakeholders and the power asymmetry in a social marketing system.

Practical application of human rights principles allows for identifying the relevant stakeholders, what their interests are, and how their often-conflicting objectives can be addressed and ultimately negotiated for achieving the social good. As social marketing objectives are commonly underpinned by social justice, it is therefore important for social marketers to proactively advance the application of human rights principles within social marketing systems (e.g. through leadership and advocacy) to facilitate the resolution of the ethical tension and conflict resulting from the power asymmetry between stakeholders and their different roles as incumbents, challengers, and regulating agencies. Such principles provide a common standard for all stakeholders to meet society's expectations and achieve the social good.

It is not just ethically and morally right for all stakeholders to follow such principles; there is also strong evidence that human right principles can offer direct benefits to different stakeholders without jeopardising their business objectives (VEOHRC, 2008). For example, following the application of human rights principles, the UK Audit Commission (2003) identified improvements

36 *Krzysztof Kubacki et al.*

in the quality of service delivery across a wide range of social issues, including general healthcare, mental health, disability and carer services, housing, emergency services, and criminal justice. Similar findings were later reported by the UK Department of Health (Equality and Human Rights Group, 2008), which, among other benefits of adopting human rights principles, also indicated a reduced risk of complaints related to equality legislation, more-effective handling of complex issues, and better decision-making. Such principles also offer benefits to commercial organisations, including improved risk management, improved reputation and brand image, the facilitation of the recruitment and retention of staff, and the provision of opportunities for growth (Amis, Brew, & Ersmarker, 2005).

Finally, there are also important advantages for social marketers who follow human rights principles in stakeholder management. These principles provide a universal framework to build long-term stakeholder relationships based on building trust and mutual respect, engaging with vulnerable stakeholders, minimising the risk of potential reputational damage to a participating stakeholder, and providing an environment conducive to cultural change, which underpins all behavioural change (VEOHRC, 2008). For each individual stakeholder, the principles also provide an opportunity for self-reflection and assessment of the extent to which their organisational practices and policies satisfy the standards set by the principles.

Thus, following the principles allows social marketers to mobilise the (often-excluded and -marginalised) passive stakeholders to increase their capacity for active participation in the system by the redistribution of reward, coercive, legitimate, expert, and referent power. This approach not only offers an ethically principled practice to follow but also is pragmatic in achieving effective and efficient social marketing programmes that lead to the social good.

References

Amis, L., Brew, P., & Ersmarker, C. (2005). Human rights: It is your business. The case for corporate engagement. International Business Leaders Forum, January.

Audit Commission (2003). Human rights: Improving public service delivery. Retrieved from https://lx.iriss.org.uk/sites/default/files/resources/HumanRights-report.pdf.

Broberg, M., & Sano, H. O. (2018). Strengths and weaknesses in a human rights-based approach to international development – An analysis of a rights-based approach to development assistance based on practical experiences. *International Journal of Human Rights, 22*(5), 664–680.

Boesen, J.K., & Martin, T. (2007). Applying a rights-based approach: An inspirational guide for civil society. *Danish Institute for Human Rights.* Retrieved from https://gsdrc.org/document-library/applying-a-rights-based-approach-an-inspirational-guide-for-civil-society/.

Clulow, V. (2005). Future dilemmas for marketers: Can stakeholder analysis add value? *European Journal of Marketing, 39*(9–10), 978–997.

Cowan, K., Paswan, A.K., & Van Steenburg, E. (2015). When inter-firm relationship benefits mitigate power asymmetry. *Industrial Marketing Management, 48*, 140–148.

Domegan, C., Collins, K., Stead, M., McHugh, P., & Hughes, T. (2013). Value co-creation in social marketing: Functional or fanciful? *Journal of Social Marketing*, *3*(3), 239–256.

Duane, S., & Domegan, C. (2018). Social marketing partnerships: Evolution, scope and substance. *Marketing Theory*. doi: 10.1177/1470593118799810.

Eagle, L., Dahl, S., & Low, D. (2020). Ethical dimensions of social marketing and social change. In A. M. Kennedy (Ed.), *Macro-social Marketing Insights* (pp. 193–214). Abingdon: Routledge.

Equality and Human Rights Group (2008). *Human Rights in Healthcare: A Framework for Local Action* (2nd ed.). Department of Health. Retrieved from http://www.hscbusiness.hscni.net/pdf/Human_rights_in_healthcare_2nd_edition_DOH.pdf.

Freeman, R.E. (1984). *Strategic Management: A Stakeholder Approach*. Boston, MA: Pitman.

French, R.P., & Raven, B. (1959). The bases of social power. In D. Cartwright (Ed.), *Studies in Social Power* (pp. 155–164). Ann Arbor: University of Michigan Press.

Gaski, J. (1999). Does marketing ethics really have anything to say? A critical inventory of the literature. *Journal of Business Ethics*, *18*(3), 315–334.

Gregson, J., Foerster, S.B., Orr, R., Jones, L., Benedict, J., Clarke, B., ... Zotz, K. (2001). System, environmental, and policy changes: Using the social–ecological model as a framework for evaluating nutrition education and social marketing programs with low-income audiences. *Journal of Nutrition Education*, *33*(Supplement 1), S4–S15.

Handley, S.M., & Benton Jr., W.C. (2012). Mediated power and outsourcing relationships. *Journal of Operations Management*, *30*(3), 253–267.

Hastings, G., & Domegan, C. (2017). *Social Marketing: Rebels with a Cause*. London, UK: Routledge.

Jones, T.M., Felps, W., & Bigley, G.A. (2007). Ethical theory and stakeholder-related decisions: The role of stakeholder culture. *Academy of Management Review*, *32*(1), 137–155.

Kennedy, A.M. (2016). Macro-social marketing. *Journal of Macromarketing*, *36*(3), 354–365.

Kennedy, A.M., Kapitan, S., Bajaj, N., Bakonji, A., & Sands, S. (2017). Uncovering wicked problems' system structure: Seeing the forest for the trees. *Journal of Social Marketing*, *7*(1), 51–73.

Lacoste, S., & Johnsen, E. (2015). Supplier–customer relationships: A case study of power dynamics. *Journal of Purchasing & Supply Management*, *21*(4), 229–240.

Lefebvre, C. (2006). Partnerships for social marketing programs: An example from the National Bone Health Campaign. *Social Marketing Quarterly*, *12*(1), 41–54.

Luca, N.R., Hibbert, S., & McDonald, R. (2016). Midstream value creation in social marketing. *Journal of Marketing Management*, *32*(11–12), 1145–1173.

McHugh, P., Domegan, C., & Duane, S. (2018). Protocols for stakeholder participation in social marketing systems. *Social Marketing Quarterly*, *24*(3), 164–193.

Ministry of Justice (2008). *Human Rights Insight Project*. Ministry of Justice Research Series 1/08.

Niblett, G.R. (2005). Stretching the limits of social marketing partnerships, upstream and downstream: Setting the context for the 10th Innovations in Social Marketing Conference. *Social Marketing Quarterly*, *11*(3–4), 9–15.

Olsen, P.I., Prenkert, F., Hoholm, T., & Harrison, D. (2014). The dynamics of networked power in a concentrated business network. *Journal of Business Research*, *67*(12), 2579–2589.

Shand, D., & Arnberg, M. (1996). *Responsive Government: Service Quality Initiatives. Technical Report.* Paris: Organization for Economic Cooperation and Development.

Siemieniako, D., & Mitręga, M. (2018). Improving power position with regard to non-mediated power sources – The supplier's perspective. *Industrial Marketing Management, 70*, 90–100.

Smith, A.M., & Fischbacher, M. (2005). New service development: A stakeholder perspective. *European Journal of Marketing, 39*(9–10), 1025–1048.

Szablewska, N., & Kubacki, K. (2019). A human rights-based approach to the social good in social marketing. *Journal of Business Ethics, 155(3),* 871–888.

United Nations Global Compact (2015). A guide for business: How to develop a human rights policy (2nd ed.). Retrieved from www.unglobalcompact.org/docs/issues_doc/human_rights/Resources/HR_Policy_Guide.pdf.

United Nations Development Group (2011). UN common learning package on HRBA principles. Retrieved from https://undg.org/home/undg–mechanisms/undg–hrm/knowledge–management/about–the–un–practitioners–portal–on–hrba–programming–hrba–portal/english–learning–package/.

Universal Declaration of Human Rights (1948). U.N. G.A. Res. 217A (III). U.N. Doc A/810.

World Health Organization (2018). Global status report on alcohol and health. Retrieved from www.who.int/substance_abuse/publications/global_alcohol_report/en/.

Weiss, J.W. (2014). *Business Ethics: A Stakeholder and Issues Management Approach* (6th ed.). San Francisco, CA: Berrett-Koehler.

Victorian Equal Opportunity & Human Rights Commission (2008). *From Principle to Practice: Implementing the Human Rights Based Approach in Community Organisations.* State of Victoria.

Zolkiewski, J. (2011). Value, power, and health care services in the UK: A business-to-business services network perspective. *Journal of Marketing Management, 27*(3–4), 424–448.

4 Stakeholder involvement in social marketing anti-smoking interventions

V. Dao Truong, Quynh Pham, and Stephen Saunders

Introduction

The association between tobacco smoking and serious health conditions, disease, and death is well recognised. According to the World Health Organization (WHO, 2018), tobacco smoking is the leading cause of deaths from non-communicable diseases that annually kills more than seven million people worldwide. In addition, second-hand smoke is responsible for the death of 890,000 people (WHO, 2018). Tobacco smoking reportedly kills more people than tuberculosis, HIV/AIDS, and malaria combined (WHO, 2018).

In 2003, the WHO Framework Convention on Tobacco Control was adopted by the World Health Assembly, which created an international commitment to reduce tobacco smoking and made tobacco control a priority within the global health agenda. On this basis, in 2014 the WHO member states agreed to a worldwide 30% tobacco use reduction target by 2025 (Lindson-Hawley et al., 2016). Yet, predictions indicate that only 25% of countries worldwide may achieve a reduction in men's smoking, and only 52% of countries worldwide may achieve a reduction in women's smoking by 2025 (Lindson-Hawley et al., 2016). While tobacco use among adults has declined in some Western countries (Brown, Luckett, Davidson, & DiGiacomo, 2017), a large proportion of the annual smoking-related death toll is predicted to happen in low- and middle-income countries (WHO, 2018).

Worldwide, there have been widespread attempts amongst various stakeholders to encourage individuals to quit smoking, by primarily focusing on educational and regulatory measures. While education tends to target the demand side of the tobacco trade (e.g. education campaigns on social and public media to encourage people to quit) (Bala, Strzeszynski, Topor-Madry, & Cahil, 2013), regulation tends to target the supply side (e.g. policy implementation to ban illicit tobacco trade) (Jha & Peto, 2014). Although these attempts have achieved some success, high smoking rates suggest that further endeavours to change smoking behaviours are required. Recently, increased academic attention has been given to behavioural change mechanisms, such as social marketing, as a strategy for motivating individuals to quit smoking (Diehr et al., 2011; Duffy et al., 2012).

Social marketing makes use of commercial marketing techniques and methods to influence and promote behavioural change in a target audience to engender public good (Truong, 2014). Over the past 30 years, the most significant development in the social marketing field involves the shift from its traditional focus on (downstream) individual change to a broader conception of its role in promoting (upstream) institutional and organisational change (Saunders, Barrington, & Sridharan, 2015; Truong, Saunders, & Dong, 2019). This shift in focus was the result of robust academic debate, wherein many researchers argued that social marketing seeks to influence not only individual change but also broader institutional and organisational change including changes within stakeholders such as special-interest groups, activists, and policymakers (Lefebvre, 2013). More generally, this shift in view reflects a growing trend in the social sciences which recognises that broad social change requires more than individual behaviour change (Lefebvre, 2013).

Though social marketers recognise the need to target (upstream) institutional and organisational change, they tend to focus on influencing the behaviours of upstream stakeholder actors (e.g. policymakers) who implement a desired change through policy and regulation (Truong, 2017). To some extent, such a focus is appropriate, given that the ability of social marketing to influence behaviour change is subject to regulatory and sociotechnical structures that are interlinked at different levels. Yet, such ideas about broadening social marketing may not be broad enough, since they are only focussed on broadening the range of individuals who should adopt the proposed behaviour, rather than involve and engage relevant stakeholder actors in the social marketing process. As Lefebvre (2013, p. 5) states,

> understanding that both individual change and social change are the results of a marketplace of ideas and behaviours that are, in turn, constantly shaped by the activities of public, private, and civil society actors means also understanding that all of these actors must become part of sustainable, long-term solutions.

In other words, these actors can be viewed as relevant stakeholders because they can affect or are affected by the social marketing intervention.

The importance of broader stakeholders in social marketing has been explored in some prior studies, though often under different labels such as 'partners' (Hudson, Snawder, Esswein, & Striley, 2008), 'alliances' (Berger, Cunningham, & Drumwright, 1999), 'agencies' (Andreasen, 2006), and 'coalitions' (Singer & Kayson, 2004). The need to consider the involvement of relevant stakeholders in social marketing interventions has recently been stated explicitly (McHugh, Domegan, & Duane, 2018), with some reports published (Beierle, 2002; Gregson et al., 2001). However, there is a dearth of systematic studies of stakeholder involvement in social marketing interventions. Where stakeholder involvement has been reviewed (Buyucek, Kubacki, Rundle-Thiele, & Pang, 2016), little is known about the impact of stakeholder involvement on intervention outcomes.

This chapter examines the extent to which various stakeholders are involved in social marketing interventions from 2009 to 2018, when the aim of the intervention was to influence and encourage individuals to quit smoking. 'Stakeholders' refer to those who can affect or are affected by programme interventions. This chapter focuses only on tobacco/cigarette smoking, as it is the most common method for consuming tobacco (WHO, 2018). Specifically, this chapter seeks to answer four research questions: Who are the stakeholders involved in the identified interventions? At what stage of the intervention process are they involved? What are the modes and methods of stakeholder involvement? And what is the impact of stakeholder involvement on intervention outcomes? In the next section, marketing stakeholder theory is outlined as a theoretical foundation.

Marketing stakeholder theory

The term 'stakeholder' was first introduced in the management literature in 1963 (Freeman et al., 2010). Initially, literature only referred to institutional and organisational shareholders who owned stock and who were the primary beneficiaries of organisation activities. Thus, the stakeholder concept was limited to "those groups without whose support the organisation would cease to exist" (Freeman et al., 2010, p. 31). However, stakeholder theory views stakeholders as a broader set of individuals and groups who are not necessarily primary beneficiaries but can affect or are affected by an organisation's operations (Phillips, 2003). Further, stakeholder theory recognises that these individuals and groups have interrelated interests, and thus for the organisation to thrive it needs to maintain good stakeholder relationships through considering and balancing their relevant interests (Phillips, 2003).

Freeman (1984, p. iv) defined stakeholders as "any group or individual who can affect or is affected by the achievement of a corporation's purpose." This definition explains why the former (who can affect the firm) deserves attention, but it does not account for those who are affected by, but do not influence, an organisation's operations. Post, Preston, and Sachs (2002, p. 19) later defined stakeholders as "individuals and constituencies that contribute, either voluntarily or involuntarily, to its wealth-creating capacity and activities, and that are therefore [the organisation's] potential beneficiaries and/or risk bearers." However, the boundary line between who is a stakeholder and who is not is not always clear. As Phillips (2003, p. 82) argued, for now the theory is "unable to rule out *any* group from stakeholder status." Consequently, there exist various classifications of stakeholders: internal versus external, primary versus secondary, actual versus potential, or necessary versus contingent (Freeman et al., 2010). According to Friedman and Miles (2006), the main stakeholder groups include customers, employees, local communities, suppliers and distributors, and shareholders; whereas, secondary stakeholders include the media, the public, business partners, present and future generations, competitors, academics, NGOs, financiers, and governments/regulators.

42   V. Dao Truong et al.

Stakeholder theory has been examined in many disciplines, including marketing (Hillebrand, Driessen, & Koll, 2015). Nearly 60 years ago, Levitt (1960) labelled marketers' narrow focus on products as 'marketing myopia' and urged them to (re)define its focus more broadly in terms of customer needs. More recently, Smith, Drumwright, and Gentile (2010) argue that focusing on customer needs is also too restrictive as it fails to consider the broader social context wherein business decisions are made. They call on marketers to respond to the 'new marketing myopia' by shifting toward a marketing stakeholder orientation to create value through exchange relationships. Consequently, Hult, Mena, Ferrell, and Ferrell (2011, p. 44) defined stakeholder marketing as "activities and processes within a system of social institutions that facilitate and maintain value through exchange relationships with multiple stakeholders." Hence, stakeholder marketing generally recognises that the value of the firm is co-created by a range of stakeholders who form networks of relationships (Hillebrand et al., 2015). Kull, Mena, and Korschun (2016) view such networks of stakeholder relationships as a strategic resource that potentially improves competitive advantage and organisational performance. Yet, the extant marketing literature has not gone beyond observing the existence of multiple stakeholders for whom the organisation needs to care. Understanding that stakeholders are themselves interrelated in networks also means understanding that an organisation has to deal with different types of problems rather than just more of the same problems (Hillebrand et al., 2015). This may have significant implications for social marketing, in that individuals maintain relationships in networks, which are in turn influenced by the activities, interests, and concerns of each individual member. Consequently, social marketing efforts need to consider not only the target audience (main stakeholders) but also other people in their network and the relationships between them.

Smith et al. (2010) offer five guiding steps to stakeholder marketing, namely identifying stakeholders, determining stakeholder salience, studying stakeholder expectations, engaging with stakeholders, and integrating a stakeholder orientation into the marketing process. These steps are consistent with Laczniak and Murphy's (1993) four strategies of delineating who the stakeholders are, distinguishing the primary and secondary stakes each stakeholder group holds in the firm, deciding on the firm's responsibilities with each stakeholder group, and formulating strategies to address stakeholder conflicts. Such guidance is potentially useful in the social marketing context, wherein the target audience can be considered the main stakeholder group because they are arguably the most affected by the intervention. Whereas other stakeholders (e.g. community members) can be considered secondary stakeholder groups because they are arguably less affected by the intervention (Freeman et al., 2010). The next section describes the method used in this study.

Methods

This study focussed on anti-smoking (i.e. 'quit smoking') interventions that labelled themselves as 'social marketing.' A search was made of scholarly databases, including Google Scholar, Web of Science, Scopus, Proquest, Cochrane, Medline, PSYCINFO, Emerald, ScienceDirect, and Taylor & Francis (Truong, 2014). A number of key words were entered into these databases, namely 'quit smoking' or 'smoking cessation' or 'smoking prevention' or 'tobacco smoking' or 'cigarette smoking' and 'social marketing,' and 'smoking' or 'tobacco' and 'intervention' or 'campaign' or 'programme' or 'study.' The references for the identified articles were also examined to search for potential articles. In addition, prior reviews of social marketing interventions (e.g. Almestahiri, Rundle-Thiele, Parkinson, & Arli, 2017) were investigated to ensure inclusion of relevant interventions.

The search process was carried out from September 2018 to mid-April 2019, yielding 1,361 articles. To be eligible for inclusion in the study, identified articles needed to report on the design, implementation, or evaluation of 'quit smoking' social marketing interventions and be published in English-language scholarly outlets from 2009 to 2018 inclusive. Reports on closely related social marketing interventions were not included (e.g. anti-vaping). Reviews, conceptual, and methodological articles were also excluded. In total, 18 articles (reporting on 12 eligible interventions) were analysed.

The content and full-texts of the 18 identified articles were examined. An excel sheet was used to record information about authors, interventions, target audience and location, stakeholders involved, stages of the social marketing process involved, modes and methods of involvement, and impact of stakeholder involvement on intervention outcomes. Consistent with Freeman et al. (2010), smokers (target audience) were regarded as the main stakeholder group, whereas the other stakeholders were considered the secondary stakeholder groups. Stages of the social marketing process included design (formative research), implementation, and evaluation. Modes of involvement referred to the role of stakeholders in the intervention (e.g. consultants, investigators, staff) and the tasks they performed, while methods indicated the means by which they were involved (e.g. focus groups, interviews, surveys).

Results

The 12 social marketing anti-smoking ('quit smoking') interventions examined are summarised in Table 4.1. Half of these interventions took place in the United States, three in Australia, and one in the United Kingdom, Canada, and China, respectively. In terms of target audience, a large majority of the interventions targeted adults and young adolescents, while two focussed on pregnant women. Overall, 11 interventions had details of stakeholder involvement while one did not provide such information (i.e. *Break up with Tobacco*; Plant et al., 2017).

Stakeholder groups

Not surprisingly, smokers (the target audience and main stakeholder group) were the most frequently involved and engaged stakeholder group, with nine

Table 4.1 Stakeholder involvement in social marketing anti-smoking interventions (2009–2018)

No.	Intervention	Authors	Target Audience	Design	Implementation	Evaluation	Reported Modes and Methods of Stakeholder Involvement	Reported Impact of Stakeholder Involvement on Intervention Outcomes
1	Improving Life Chances for Children	Lowry et al., 2009	Pregnant women in Gateshead (UK)	Target audience, general public, health professionals	Not reported	Not reported	Design: Focus groups (audience, general public), interviews (health professionals)	Not reported
2	EX	McCausland et al., 2009; Vallone et al., 2010, 2011	Smokers aged 25–49 years in Baltimore, Grand Rapids, and San Antonio	Target audience, former smokers	State and local organisations, customers and employees of corporate and retail partners	Not reported	Design: Focus groups, interviews, surveys Implementation: Partners to disseminate messages	Not reported
3	I Am the Owner of Me	Schmidt, Kiss, & Lokanc-Diluzio, 2009	Adolescents 12 to 18 years old in Calgary	Youth, community partners, Health Canada and local health agencies	Youth	Youth	Design: Focus groups with youth to develop and test messages Implementation: Youth engaged in disseminating messages Evaluation: Stakeholder survey	Not reported
4	There is No Cigarette without Loss	Perusco et al., 2007, 2010	Arabic speakers in south-west Sydney (particular focus on older male smokers)	Health workers, a community representative, a consumer representative	Community workers, health workers, community educators, a social marketing consultant	Community workers, health workers, community educators	Design: Consultation forums and focus groups Implementation: Survey administration and dissemination of messages Evaluation: Survey administration	Stakeholder involvement reportedly ensured the cultural appropriateness of the intervention, but no specific impact was mentioned.

5	Tobacco Tactics	Duffy et al., 2012; Ewing et al., 2012	Inpatient smokers 18 years and older in six hospitals in Trinity	Smokers	A research nurse, master trainers, staff nurses, former smokers	Smokers	Design: Smokers survey Implementation: Research nurses provide training to staff nurse. Staff nurses provide counselling to smokers. Former smoker volunteers provide peer support to smokers. Evaluation: Smokers survey	Not reported
6	One Tiny Reason To Quit	Kennedy et al., 2013, 2014	Pregnant African–American women in Richmond, Virginia	Pregnant women, university researchers, local providers of health and social services, former service recipients, community volunteers, national experts	Community outreach workers, clinic and social-service agency staff	Outreach workers	Design: Interviews with researchers and service providers; focus groups with pregnant women; interviews with national experts Implementation: Dissemination of messages Evaluation: Tracking card data	Reported. Prior stakeholder relationships and trust resulted in smooth intervention operations. About 43 face-to-face contacts were made with the target audience and 145 copies of the poster delivered.
7	Get Healthy Philly	Parvanta et al., 2013	Low-income and African–American smokers in Philadelphia, focusing on those ready to quit	Smokers, Philadelphia Department of Public Health, an advertising agency, university researchers	Not reported	Not reported	Survey at formative stage to understand smokers' cessation	Not reported
8	Kick the Habit	Campbell et al., 2014	Aboriginal residents in New South Wales, Australia: 40 years and older (site 1), young people (site 2), and young parents (site 3)	Aboriginal Community Controlled Health Services, community members, a creative agency, local role models	Local health services staff, creative agency	Community members, local health services staff	Design: Workshop discussion, focus groups Implementation: Local health services staff and the creative agency helped launch local campaigns using local resources. Evaluation: Local health services staff (interviews) and community members (survey) as subjects	Not reported

(continued)

Table 4.1 (Cont.)

No.	Intervention	Authors	Target Audience	Design	Implementation	Evaluation	Reported Modes and Methods of Stakeholder Involvement	Reported Impact of Stakeholder Involvement on Intervention Outcomes
9	Social Branding	Ling et al., 2014	Young bar patrons in San Diego, California	Target audience, Rescue Social Change Group	Rescue Social Change Group, local artists, commune brand ambassador, opinion leaders (bartenders, DJs, journalists)	Target audience, key informants (bar owners, bartenders, DJs)	Design: Interviews, focus groups, survey. Implementation: Dissemination of messages through commune events. Evaluation: Survey (target audience), interviews (key informants).	Reported. Thanks to the involvement of local artists, commune events were felt as being "owned" by the community and the messages were coming from influential peers rather than outside marketers. Impacts measured in terms of number of events organised, flyers distributed, etc.
10	Community Intervention for Health	Lv et al., 2014 (see also Lv et al., 2011)	Individuals aged 18 to 65 years in Hangzhou (China)	Target audience	Staff of local Centres for Disease Control and Prevention, doctors of community health centres, community health assistants, school doctors, worksite clinic doctors	Target audience	Design: Survey. Implementation: Distribution of messages, medical consultation, organisation of community events, and training of local health professionals Evaluation: Survey	Not reported

No.	Intervention	Reference	Target audience			Target audience		
11	Give up Smokes for Good	Maksimovic et al., 2015	Aboriginal adult smokers aged 18–39 in South Australia	Aboriginal community members (practitioners, community leaders, people in the target group), tobacco social marketing experts, key health agencies	Aboriginal community members, tobacco social marketing experts, key health agencies		Design: Consultation. No specific methods mentioned. Implementation: Specific modes and methods of involvement not reported. Evaluation: Audience survey	Reported. The intervention success was due to close partnerships with local Aboriginal Health Services and community members. Visits to and talks with key staff and community members ensured that intervention materials were culturally appropriate. Indeed, more than 90% of post-intervention survey participants indicated that posters and radio ads were appropriate/very appropriate.
12	Break up with Tobacco	Plant et al., 2017	Lesbians, gays, and bisexuals in Los Angeles county	Not reported	Not reported	Not reported	Not reported	Not reported

of the 12 social marketing interventions reporting involvement and engagement with smokers (*Improving Life Chances for Children, EX, I Am the Owner of Me, Tobacco Tactics, One Tiny Reason to Quit, Get Healthy Philly, Social Branding, Community Intervention for Health*, and *Give up Smokes for Good*). This finding is consistent with that of Buyucek et al. (2016) who indicated that most social marketing interventions involved their target audience as the main stakeholder group at some stage during the social marketing process. Health organisations and health-expert stakeholder groups were the second most frequently involved and engaged groups, with eight of the 12 interventions reporting involvement and engagement with them. For example, *I Am the Owner of Me* involved the active participation of governmental health organisations such as Health Canada and the Alberta Alcohol and Drug Commission (Schmidt, Kiss, & Lokanc-Diluzio, 2009). Similarly, *Kick the Habit* involved and engaged staff from the Aboriginal Health and Medical Research Council (Campbell et al., 2014). This finding is also not surprising, given the importance of leveraging the professional skills and practical experiences of these stakeholder groups. For instance, the success of *Give up Smokes for Good* was in part attributed to the engagement of key local aboriginal health agencies who ensured intervention materials were culturally appropriate for aboriginal adult smokers (Maksimovic et al., 2015).

Community members (or the general public) were the third most frequently involved and engaged stakeholder groups, with six of the 12 social marketing interventions reporting involvement and engagement with them (*Improving Life Chances for Children, I Am the Owner of Me, There is No Cigarette without Loss, One Tiny Reason to Quit, Kick the Habit*, and *Give up Smokes for Good*). Other, less frequently involved and engaged stakeholder groups included former smokers (*EX, Tobacco Tactics*, and *One Tiny Reason to Quit*) and university researchers (*One Tiny Reason to Quit* and *Get Healthy Philly*). Other stakeholder groups that were not frequently involved and engaged included influential peers, the media, social marketing experts, community educators, and social-service providers.

Stage of the social marketing process

Regardless of which stakeholder groups were included, involvement and engagement were more common in the earlier (design) stage, rather than in later stages (implementation and evaluation), of the social marketing process. For instance, 11 of the 12 social marketing interventions that were analysed reported stakeholder involvement and engagement in the design stage of the social marketing process (i.e. the involvement of various stakeholder groups helping to identify the target audience, determine potential facilitators and barriers to behaviour change, and/or formulating and testing the appropriateness of messages). In addition, nine of the 12 social marketing interventions reported stakeholder involvement and engagement in the implementation stage of the social marketing process, while only eight included stakeholders during the evaluation stage. Furthermore, only eight of the 12 interventions reported stakeholder involvement and engagement across all three stages of the social marketing process. Interestingly, none of the interventions reported stakeholder involvement and engagement prior to the design stage, despite evidence that very early prior stakeholder engagement results in more effective outcomes (Concannon et al., 2014). The actual number of stakeholders tended to be higher in the earlier (design) stage than in later stages (implementation and evaluation) of the social marketing process. For example, at the design stage *One Tiny Reason to Quit* involved a wide number of stakeholder groups, including not only pregnant women smokers (target audience) but also university researchers, health and social-service providers, former smokers, community volunteers, and national (health) experts. But, at the implementation stage *One Tiny Reason to Quit* involved a much smaller number of stakeholder groups, including community outreach workers, and clinic/social-service agency staff. At the evaluation stage, only one stakeholder group was involved – outreach workers (Kennedy et al., 2013).

Modes and methods of stakeholder involvement

The modes and methods of stakeholder involvement differed across stakeholder groups and the various stages of the social marketing process. At the design stage, the majority of interventions tended to involve smokers (target audience) and other stakeholder groups as research participants (in focus groups, interviews, and surveys). The primary aim of the research was to understand and gain deeper insights into smoking behaviour and intentions to quit, to determine what social marketing communication tools and messages could be designed, developed, and tested (Lowry et al., 2009; Schmidt et al., 2009). Further, during the design stage, some stakeholder groups such as local health agency staff, health experts, and community members tended to be involved as consultants or advisers and were sometimes seen as co-planners or co-investigators (Maksimovic et al., 2015; Perusco et al., 2010).

In terms of methods, qualitative methods such as focus groups and in-depth interviews were used more often than quantitative methods such as structured surveys (which typically relied on validated measurement scales). In fact, structured surveys were predominantly used during the later evaluation stages of the social marketing process, when smokers (target audience) were asked to evaluate the social marketing intervention.

At the later implementation stage, the most prominent activity that stakeholder groups seemed to be involved in was the dissemination of social marketing communications and messages to smokers (target audience) – with six interventions reportedly engaged in these types of activities. In addition, some stakeholder group activities also included smokers (target audience) themselves, state and local organisations as partners (McCausland et al., 2009), or community outreach staff (Kennedy et al., 2013). Other activities performed by stakeholders at the later implementation stage included training (Duffy et al., 2012), medical counselling (Lv et al., 2014), and survey administration (Perusco et al., 2010).

50   V. Dao Truong et al.

Impact of stakeholder group involvement on intervention outcomes

Overall, the specific impact of stakeholder group involvement and engagement was not explicitly reported in any of the 12 eligible interventions. However, four of the interventions did attribute part of their success to the involvement of stakeholder groups. For example, both *There is No Cigarette without Loss* and *Give up Smokes for Good* stated that the involvement of key local health agencies and community members helped ensure the cultural appropriateness of their intervention approaches and materials. The explicit recognition of these stakeholders may be because they were somewhat culturally distinct populations – Arabic speakers in Sydney (Perusco et al., 2010) and aboriginal adults in South Australia (Maksimovic et al., 2015). In particular, during the later evaluation stage, *Give up Smokes for Good* reported that over 90% of their target audience (main stakeholder group) indicated that posters and radio ads were appropriate or very appropriate (Maksimovic et al., 2015) while *One Tiny Reason to Quit* stated that prior relationships and trust with its stakeholders groups helped ensure smooth intervention operations (Kennedy et al., 2013). For *Social Branding*, the involvement of influential peers (DJs, musicians) made smokers (target audience) feel that the social marketing processes were 'owned' by the community and that the social marketing communications and messages were delivered by an insider, whom they could respect and trust, rather than by an outsider (Ling et al., 2014).

Conclusion

Smoking kills millions of people worldwide every year (WHO, 2018). Recently, the social marketing literature has highlighted the potential for social marketing to effectively and efficiently influence and encourage individuals to quit smoking, particularly through the participation of a wide variety of stakeholder groups. Our study contributes to this literature by analysing the extent of involvement and engagement of the various stakeholder groups in the 12 'quit smoking' social marketing interventions. The results indicated that smokers (target audience) were the most frequently involved and engaged stakeholder group, followed by health organisations and health-expert stakeholder groups. Regardless of the stakeholder groups included, involvement and engagement were more common in the earlier (design) stage, rather than in later stages (implementation and evaluation), of the social marketing process. The modes and methods of stakeholder involvement also differed across stakeholder groups and the various stages of the social marketing process.

Given the on-going calls to broaden the focus of social marketing from downstream to upstream (Lefebvre, 2013) and from micro to macro (Truong, 2017), our study is significant in that it highlights how stakeholder theory can be used to consider the involvement and engagement of different stakeholder groups during the social marketing process. It argues that both social marketing scholars and practitioners may need to consider how social marketing interventions affect and/or are affected by relevant stakeholder groups (other than the target audience), if a comprehensive evaluation of all stages in the social marketing process (and its subsequent outcomes) is to be made. Importantly, stakeholder group involvement should be given relevant consideration at all critical stages of the social marketing process. At these critical stages, stakeholder groups may offer useful thoughts, ideas, and practices with respect to changes in the macro-environment and stakeholder relationships and offer insights into the effectiveness and efficiency of the social marketing process. For example, VicHealth (Australia) involves and engages key stakeholder groups throughout the social marketing process so that they can leverage stakeholder group learnings, expertise, experiences, support, and actions (VicHealth, 2018).

For now, it is impossible to conclude on any association between stakeholder involvement and improved intervention outcomes given that specific impacts of the former on the latter were not reported in most interventions analysed: only four interventions attributed (part of) their success to the engagement of stakeholders. This is because most intervention evaluations were limited to the target audience as mentioned. A second possible reason is that social marketing evaluations tend to be process-orientated (e.g. measured by the number of activities performed/posters delivered) rather than outcome-orientated (e.g. measured by actual behaviour change) (Truong, 2014). Perhaps, to facilitate analysis of the association between stakeholder group involvement and intervention outcomes, more reports of stakeholder involvement need to be published where practitioners and stakeholder groups share their 'successes and failures' and experiences.

A number of limitations to this study should be acknowledged. First, this study is only limited to scholarly articles available through online scholarly databases for the period 2009–2018, when it is quite common in the social marketing field to share information about social marketing interventions (particularly stakeholder group involvement) in other outlets such as field reports. Second, the searches were restricted to the English language, and thus further research is warranted into studies published in other languages. Third, the analysis was restricted to 'quit smoking' specific social marketing interventions. Future research may thus examine other social marketing interventions that were focussed on a broader wide range of positive social behaviours and outcomes that partly incorporated 'quit smoking.'

References

Almestahiri, R., Rundle-Thiele, S., Parkinson, J., & Arli, D. (2017). The use of the major components of social marketing: A systematic review of tobacco cessation programs. *Social Marketing Quarterly, 23,* 232–248.

Andreasen, A.R. (2006). *Social Marketing in the 21st Century*. Thousand Oaks, CA: Sage.

Bala, M.M., Strzeszynski, L., Topor-Madry, R., & Cahill, K. (2013). Mass media interventions for smoking cessation in adults. *Cochrane Database of Systematic Reviews, 6,* Cd004704.

52 *V. Dao Truong et al.*

Beierle, T.C. (2002). The quality of stakeholder-based decisions. *Risk Analysis, 22*, 739–749.

Berger, I.E., Cunningham, P.H., & Drumwright, M.E. (1999). Social alliances: Company/Nonprofit collaboration. *Social Marketing Quarterly, 5*, 49–53.

Brown, N., Luckett, T., Davidson, P.M., & DiGiacomo, M. (2017). Family-focussed interventions to reduce harm from smoking in primary school-aged children: A systematic review of evaluative studies. *Preventive Medicine, 101*, 117–125.

Buyucek, N., Kubacki, K., Rundle-Thiele, S., & Pang, B. (2016). A systematic review of stakeholder involvement in social marketing interventions. *Australasian Marketing Journal, 24*, 8–19.

Campbell, M.A., Finlay, S., Lucas, K., Neal, N., & Williams, R. (2014). Kick the habit: A social marketing campaign by aboriginal communities in NSW. *Australian Journal of Primary Health, 20*, 327–333.

Concannon, T.W., Fuster, M., Saunders, T., Patel, K., et al. (2014). A systematic review of stakeholder engagement in comparative effectiveness and patient-centred outcomes research. *Journal of General Internal Medicine, 29*, 1692–1701.

Diehr, P., Hannon, P., Pizacani, B., Forehand, M., et al. (2011). Social marketing, stages of change, and public health smoking interventions. *Health Education & Behaviour, 38*, 123–132.

Duffy, S.A., Ronis, D.L., Titler, M.G., Blow, F.C., et al. (2012). Dissemination of the nurse-administered Tobacco Tactics intervention versus usual care in six Trinity community hospitals: Study protocol for a comparative effectiveness trial. *Trials, 13*, 125–136.

Ewing, L.A., Karvonen, C.A., Noonan, D., & Duffy, S.A. (2012). Development of the Tobacco Tactics logo: From thump prints to press. *Tobacco Induced Diseases, 10*, 6–14.

Freeman, R.E. (1984). *Strategic Management: A Stakeholder Approach.* Boston, MA: Pitman.

Freeman, R.E., Harrison, J.S., Wicks, A.C., Parmar, B.L., & de Colle, S. (2010). *Stakeholder Theory: The State of the Art.* Cambridge: Cambridge University Press.

Friedman, A.L., & Miles, S. (2006). *Stakeholders: Theory and Practice.* Oxford: Oxford University Press.

Gregson, J., Foerster, S.B., Orr, R., Jones, L., et al. (2001). System, environmental, and policy changes: Using the social-ecological model as a framework for evaluating nutrition education and social marketing programs with low-income audiences. *Journal of Nutrition Education, 33*, S4–S15.

Hillebrand, B., Driessen, P.H., & Koll, O. (2015). Stakeholder marketing: Theoretical foundations and required capabilities. *Journal of the Academy of Marketing Science, 43*, 411–428.

Hudson, H., Snawder, J., Esswein, E., & Striley, C. (2008). Partnering and consumer orientation: Techniques that move occupational safety and health research into practice. *Social Marketing Quarterly, 14*, 99–104.

Hult, G.T.M., Mena, J.A., Ferrell, O.C., & Ferrell, L. (2011). Stakeholder marketing: A definition and conceptual framework. *AMS Review, 1*, 44–65.

Jha, P., & Peto, R. (2014). Global effects of smoking, of quitting, and of taxing tobacco. *New England Journal of Medicine, 370*, 60–68.

Kennedy, M.G., Genderson, M.W., Sepulveda, A.L., Garland, S.L., et al. (2013). Increasing tobacco quitline calls from pregnant African American women: The "One tiny reason to quit" social marketing campaign. *Journal of Women's Health, 22*, 432–438.

Kull, A., Mena, J.A., & Korschun, D. (2016). A resource-based view of stakeholder marketing. *Journal of Business Research, 69*, 5553–5560.

Laczniak, G.R., & Murphy, P.E. (1993). *Ethical Marketing Decisions: The Higher Road.* Needham Heights, MA: Allyn & Bacon.

Lefebvre, R.C. (2013). *Social Marketing and Social Change: Strategies and Tools for Improving Health, Well-being, and the Environment.* San Francisco, CA: Jossey-Bass.

Levitt, T. (1960). Marketing myopia. *Harvard Business Review, 38*, 57–66.

Lindson-Hawley, N., Hartmann-Boyce, J., Fanshawe, T.R., Begh, R., Farley, A., & Lancaster, T. (2016). Interventions to reduce harm from continued tobacco use. *Cochrane Database of Systematic Reviews, 10*, CD005231.

Ling, P.M., Lee, Y.O., Hong, J., Neilands, T.B., et al. (2014). Social branding to decrease smoking among young adults in bars. *American Journal of Public Health, 104*, 751–760.

Lowry, R.J., Billett, A., Buchanan, C., & Whiston, S. (2009). Increasing breastfeeding and reducing smoking in pregnancy: A social marketing success improving life chances for children. *Perspectives in Public Health, 6*, 277–280.

Lv, J., Liu, Q-M., Ren, Y-J., He, P-P., et al. (2014). A community-based multilevel intervention for smoking, physical activity and diet: Short-term findings from the Community Interventions for Health programme in Hangzhou, China. *Journal of Epidemiological Community Health, 68*, 333–339.

Maksimovic, L., Shen, D., Bandick, M., Ettridge, K., & Eckert, M. (2015). Evaluation of the pilot phase of the "Give up smokes for good" social marketing campaign. *Health Promotion Journal of Australia, 26*, 16–23.

McCausland, K.L., Allen, J.A., Duke, J.C., Xiao, H., et al. (2009). Piloting EX, a social marketing campaign to prompt smoking cessation. *Social Marketing Quarterly, 15*, 80–101.

McHugh, P., Domegan, C., & Duane, S. (2018). Protocols for stakeholder participation in social marketing systems. *Social Marketing Quarterly, 24*, 164–193.

Phillips, R. (2003). *Stakeholder Theory and Organisational Ethics.* San Francisco, CA: Berrett-Koehler.

Plant, A., Montoya, J.A., Tyree, R., Aragon, L., et al. (2017). The Break up: Evaluation of an anti-smoking educational campaign for lesbians, gays, and bisexuals in Los Angeles county. *Journal of Health Communication, 22*, 29–36.

Perusco, A., Rikard-Bell, G., Mohsin, M., Millen, E., et al. (2007). Tobacco control priorities for Arabic speakers: Key findings from a baseline telephone survey of Arabic speakers residing in Sydney's south-west. *Health Promotion Journal of Australia, 18*, 121–126.

Perusco, A., Poder, N., Mohsin, M., & Rikard-Bell, G., et al. (2010). Evaluation of a comprehensive tobacco control project targeting Arabic-speakers residing in south west Sydney, Australia. *Health Promotion International, 25*, 153–165.

Post, J.E., Preston, L.E., & Sachs, S. (2002). *Redefining the Corporation: Stakeholder Management and Organizational Wealth.* Palo Alto, CA: Stanford University Press.

Saunders, S.G., Barrington, D.J., & Sridharan, S. (2015). Redefining social marketing: Beyond behavioural change. *Journal of Social Marketing, 5*(2), 160–168.

Schmidt, E., Kiss, S.M., & Lokanc-Diluzio, W. (2009). Changing social norms: A mass media campaign for youth ages 12–18. *Canadian Journal of Public Health, 100*, 41–45.

Singer, B., & Kayson, S. (2004). Partnerships, alliances, and stakeholder communication. *Social Marketing Quarterly, 10*, 67–71.

Smith, N.C., Drumwright, M.E., & Gentile, M.C. (2010). The new marketing myopia. *Journal of Public Policy & Marketing, 29*, 4–11.

Truong, V.D. (2014). Social marketing: A systematic review of research 1998–2012. *Social Marketing Quarterly, 20*, 15–34.

Truong, V.D. (2017). Macro-social marketing programs in Vietnam: Outcomes, challenges, and implications. *Journal of Macromarketing, 37*, 409–425.

Truong, V.D., Saunders, S., & Dong, X.D. (2019). Systems social marketing: A critical appraisal. *Journal of Social Marketing, 9*, 180–203.

VicHealth (2018). *Stakeholder Engagement Framework 2018–23*. Retrieved 1 September 2019, from www.vichealth.vic.gov.au.

World Health Organization (WHO). (2018). *Tobacco: Key Facts*. Retrieved 1 April 2019, from www.who.int/news-room/fact-sheets/detail/tobacco.

5 MOSA

Addressing alcohol issues in Slovenia through an upstream multiple stakeholder approach

Tanja Kamin and Maja Roškar

Introduction

In Slovenia harmful and hazardous alcohol use are among the biggest public health problems (Lovrečič & Lovrečič, 2018; Roškar et al., 2018a). Every year, an average of 927 people die as a result of the harmful effects of alcohol use on health and in traffic accidents caused by drunk drivers (Lovrečič & Lovrečič, 2018; Ministry of the Interior, 2003–2017; Roškar et al., 2018a). Moreover, government funds are strongly affected by alcohol-related health costs, costs resulting from traffic accidents, crime, domestic violence, theft etc., which together presents a substantial burden for the Slovene state. It is estimated that alcohol-related costs account for 1 per cent of Slovene GDP (Sedlak, Zaletel, Kasesnik, Roškar, & Sambt, 2018). According to these figures, Slovenia needs a comprehensive social action to successfully combat the problem. Despite strict legal regulations regarding alcohol availability, like minimum legal purchase age; time and place restrictions for alcohol sales on and off premise; strict regulations regarding alcohol advertising; and increased number of public health campaigns addressing alcohol consumption-related behaviours (Kamin, 2005; OPA, 2017; Petrič, 2014), alcohol consumption remains a steadier problem in Slovenia than one would expect. There could be several reasons for that.

Among the main reasons we would expose, that alcohol is strongly imbedded in Slovene culture (Čebašek Travnik, 2006), that legal restrictions of alcohol-related behaviours are decent on paper but not accompanied with systematic and strict enforcement strategies that would encourage deliberate compliance with the law (Kamin & Kokole, 2016, and that implemented public (health) campaigns for tackling alcohol consumption had not been designed along criteria that would lead to effective behaviour and social change (Kamin, 2006). In addition, Slovenia is a wine-growing country; thus, alcohol production forms an important part of Slovene economy and culture (Ministry of Finance, 2019). This results in divergent, even competitive and contradictory attitudes to alcohol consumption and promotion in society also among policymakers. The Ministry of Health, for example, advocates for stricter policies to combat risky alcohol consumption, while the Ministry of Economy or Chamber of

56 *Tanja Kamin and Maja Roškar*

Commerce and Industry are more interested in loosening regulation. Thus, all possible strategies for solving alcohol-related problems take place in a complex social setting in a social system with various system participants, with different interests, and should be dealt with on the basis of systems thinking (Domegan et al., 2016) and with holistic approach with down-, mid-, and upstream interventions (Hoek & Jones, 2011).

MOSA: A social marketing approach to addressing alcohol-related problems

There are different approaches for tackling alcohol issues, but studies convincingly show that social marketing-based alcohol-related interventions achieve positive results in tackling alcohol-related harm: they have been found to create some immediate but also longer-term changes via attitude, behavioural intention, and/or raising awareness; some also achieved positive behavioural outcomes (Kubacki et al., 2015; Stead et al., 2007).

The majority of evaluated alcohol-related social marketing interventions published to date were oriented downstream (the target population was primarily young people, and the problem addressed was either alcohol consumption or drunk-driving); only a few interventions were oriented midstream (Kamin & Kokole, 2016; Kubacki et al., 2015; Stead et al., 2007), and not many were addressed upstream towards the biggest influencers and political decision makers. Similar to Jones (2014), we came to conclusions that for changing alcohol-related behaviours and reducing alcohol consumption among selected populations, we would need to approach the problem on various levels. This means that we would need to mobilise community to engage in addressing alcohol-related problems as a collective and to improve already existing efforts addressing the most vulnerable populations in order to be more effective. To ensure synchronised strategic actions a thorough and systematic stakeholder approach that would encourage different actors, who shape the physical and symbolic environment of alcohol consumption in the country, was needed. Slovenia had been lacking such an approach.

In this chapter we will present a case study of a stakeholder approach in addressing this gap, inspired by upstream and midstream social marketing principles. The project branded as MOSA, Mobilising community for responsibility towards alcohol,[1] was established in 2008 (www.infomosa.si) and is still running. At its core, MOSA aims to identify and connect the most important stakeholders that have been tackling alcohol-related problems in Slovenia, better synchronise their scattered efforts, elevate standards of interventions design and implementation according to social marketing principles, and develop valuable exchanges among various system participants: namely, the general population and the stakeholders.

In the first part of the chapter we will describe a process for identifying key stakeholders who shape the alcohol issue in Slovenia and expose some differences in their opinions about how alcohol-related problems should be addressed in the country. Understanding positions of different stakeholders with regard to solutions for solving these problems, we identified stakeholders that MOSA should first work with for achieving the biggest impact on ways how alcohol-related problems are dealt with. We aimed to focus on weaknesses and strengths of already existing system of stakeholders that are highly motivated to solve alcohol-related problems through decreasing alcohol consumption among various groups within the population and helped them to become more efficient in their activities and stronger in relation to stakeholders that are opposed or less eager to regulate alcohol consumption in the country.

The second part of this chapter presents stakeholders that MOSA focused on in the first stage of the project, namely NGOs, research institutions, and parties in the Ministry of Health, who are crucial in selecting, financing, designing, implementing, and evaluating interventions on micro, mezzo, and macro level for addressing alcohol consumption in Slovenia. Activities for capacity building of chosen stakeholders and establishment and maintenance of MOSA network will be discussed in more detail.

Stakeholder approach to tackling alcohol issues on a national level

A stakeholder approach has been widely used in social marketing interventions in the last decades (Buyucek, Kubacki, Rundle-Thiele, & Pang, 2016). Various theoretical views of strategic management were developed to improve performance of companies (Bonnafous-Boucher & Rendtorff, 2016; Donaldson & Preston; 1995; Freeman, 2010; Preble, 2005). These theories postulate that companies can only be effective if multiple stakeholders are involved. Research supports this notion, suggesting that success may be enhanced when numerous stakeholders are involved in planning and decision-making, which applies also to non-profit organisations (Buyucek, Kubacki, Rundle-Thiele, & Pang, 2016; Knox & Gruar, 2007). It has been argued that synergistic effects of multiple stakeholders provide supportive environments needed for individual behavioural and social change (Buyucek, Kubacki, Rundle-Thiele, & Pang, 2016; Knox & Gruar, 2007). While involvement of multiple stakeholders in intervention planning, implementation, and evaluation stages may enhance outcomes (Buyucek, Kubacki, Rundle-Thiele, & Pang, 2016), it is also true that identifying and managing complex interactions between multiple stakeholders are difficult and time consuming, which was experienced in the MOSA project.

The MOSA project's first essential step in the stakeholder approach to problem solving was stakeholder analysis. Understanding the needs, opinions, and influences of different stakeholder groups is crucial in gaining stakeholders' support, guiding stakeholders to a common goal, and thus achieving better outcomes (Buyucek, Kubacki, Rundle-Thiele, & Pang, 2016; Donaldson & Preston, 1995). By applying a stakeholder approach in managing alcohol-related problems in Slovenia, we do not imply that all stakeholders need to be evenly involved in decision-making (Donaldson & Preston, 1995). However, they should be identified, understood, and dealt with as competitors or possible

58   *Tanja Kamin and Maja Roškar*

partners in solving alcohol-related problems and in achieving desired social change. Stakeholder analysis does not only aim to identify stakeholders and their main characteristics but aims to understand stakeholders' interrelationships, conflicts of interests, and influences they bring to a decision-making process (Brugha & Varvasovszky, 2000; Bryson, 2004; Knox & Gruar, 2007; Preble, 2005). In the sphere of alcohol-related problems, stakeholders could be defined as individuals, groups, or organisations (Bryson, 2004; Freeman, 2010) who can affect or are affected by alcohol policy in a particular place and time. The broad definition of stakeholders from the public and non-profit management literature (Bryson, 2004) is useful, since it includes a wide array of stakeholders: not only those who have the power to change a phenomena, like government, but also those who are 'powerless,' like civil initiatives, communities, or groups of people, that can gain power in order to affect the phenomena.

Since not all stakeholders who hold a stake in certain phenomena or initiative are self-evident (Bunn, Savage, & Holloway, 2002; Reed et al., 2009), the first step of stakeholder analysis on the alcohol-related problems area should aim to identify all possible stakeholders: individuals, groups, governmental, and non-governmental organisations with a stake, interest, or influence in alcohol issues. Following harm chain thinking (Hastings, 2013), stakeholders related to alcohol issues could be grouped according to (1) those who consume alcohol; (2) those who cause harm, like places that serve or sell alcohol and promote drinking; (3) those who regulate alcohol consumption and can address harm, like government, alcohol industry, and national advertising association; and (4) those who influence alcohol policy and 'significant others,' like the media, health professionals, researchers, community groups, and non-governmental organisations (NGOs). These groups of stakeholders are likely to have differing attitudes to alcohol and services and behaviours related to it, different knowledge about alcohol-related problems, and different interests in production, distribution, consumption, and communication about alcohol. A stakeholder approach to solving alcohol-related problems in Slovenia should acknowledge these differences and commonalities of interests to encourage cooperation in addressing the alcohol issue. Since the first group of potential stakeholders is the most addressed by different downstream interventions in Slovenia (Kamin, 2006), the MOSA project aimed to identify potential stakeholders among the other three groups.

Stakeholder analysis

Based on literature review (Brugha & Varvasovszky, 2000; Bryson, 2004; Knox & Gruar, 2007; Preble, 2005) and knowledge gained concerning the alcohol-related situation in Slovenia, a systematic approach to stakeholder analysis, with consecutive research design, was conducted within the MOSA project. Results of each research step determined the research focus of the next step, aiming to narrow down selection of the potential upstream and midstream stakeholders that would become the key stakeholders in the MOSA network. The analysis was conducted in four consecutive steps, as described in Table 5.1.

MOSA: *Addressing alcohol in Slovenia* 59

Table 5.1 Steps of stakeholder analysis

Research question	Data collection	Data analysis
1st stage Who are potential upstream and midstream stakeholders in the alcohol area in Slovenia?	Desktop analysis (databases, such as the registry of societies, organisations entitled to donations, list of organisations co-financed through public tenders, registry of humanitarian organisations, and others), telephone and face-to-face informative interviews with the most visible individuals working on the area of alcohol-related problems, and semi-structured face-to-face interviews with representatives from the Ministry of Health (three members of Division for health promotion and prevention of non-communicable diseases), two representatives of National institute of public health that work on alcohol area, and three NGO employees working on alcohol harm prevention.	Categorisation of actors according to their focus in alcohol issue in Slovenia, their field of work, their target populations, founders and their assessed influence on shaping alcohol policy and solutions for addressing alcohol-related problems in Slovenia.[1] Collection of interventions (programmes, projects, and campaigns) aiming to prevent hazardous and harmful drinking in Slovenia.[2]
2nd stage What are the commonalities and differences in potential upstream and midstream stakeholders' views on alcohol issues in Slovenia?	Survey research among main categories of stakeholders in Slovenia: Government organisations, professional organisations (e.g. Institute of public health, University, healthcare providers, professional associations), non-governmental organisations (NGOs), the media, and alcohol industry. 173 potential stakeholders completed the questionnaire (Radoš Krnel & Kamin, 2010; Radoš Krnel, Kamin, Košir, & Markič, 2010).	Mapping commonalities and differences in stakeholders' views on the alcohol issues in Slovenia (Radoš, Krnel, & Kamin, 2010; Radoš, Krnel, Kamin, Košir, & Markič, 2010).
3rd stage What are stakeholders' interests and influences in solving alcohol issues in Slovenia?	Data gathered in the first and the second stage.	Categories of stakeholders according to their interest to solve alcohol-related issue or their interest to improve alcohol policy and by their power to influence alcohol policy.

(continued)

60 *Tanja Kamin and Maja Roškar*

Table 5.1 (Cont.)

Research question	Data collection	Data analysis
4th stage What are opportunities and obstacles for NGOs in addressing alcohol-related problems in Slovenia?	Survey research and interviews with NGOs that work on the alcohol area. (Zorko, Košir, Kamin, Radoš, Krnel, & Zupančič, 2010)	Opportunities and barriers for NGOs in scoping, developing, implementing, and evaluating interventions (Zorko, Košir, Kamin, Radoš, Krnel, & Zupančič, 2010)
5th stage How are downstream campaigns designed for tackling alcohol-related problems in the country?	Collection of interventions (programmes, projects, and campaigns) aiming to prevent hazardous and harmful drinking in Slovenia	Analysis of campaigns against social marketing benchmark criteria

[1]All actors as possible stakeholders are listed and described in the MOSA database: www.infomosa.si/baze_podatkov/akterji/seznam.html; [2]Interventions are listed and described in the MOSA database: www.infomosa.si/baze_podatkov/preventivni_programi/seznam.html.

Stakeholder identification and categorisation

We identified five categories of potential upstream and midstream stakeholders that work in the alcohol area in Slovenia: (1) governmental organisations, (2) professional organisations (e.g. the Institute of public health, academic research organisations, healthcare providers, professional associations), (3) NGOs, (4) the media, and (5) alcohol industry. Since understanding the needs, opinions, and influences of different stakeholder groups is crucial in gaining stakeholders support and essential in guiding them to a common goal (Buyucek, Kubacki, Rundle-Thiele, & Pang, 2016), we conducted a survey among these groups of stakeholders to measure commonalities and differences in stakeholders' views on alcohol issue in Slovenia (Radoš Krnel & Kamin, 2010; Radoš Krnel, Kamin, Košir, & Markič, 2010). The data revealed diverse opinions on the scope of alcohol-related problems in the country between the five groups of stakeholders. Groups of stakeholders hold different, sometimes even contradictory ideas for the solutions to alcohol-related problems (Radoš Krnel & Kamin, 2010; Radoš Krnel, Kamin, Košir, & Markič, 2010), a finding which is common in other countries across the European Union (Anderson & Baumberg, 2006).

The biggest discrepancies in stakeholders' attitudes towards alcohol consumption-related regulation were between alcohol industry and all the other stakeholder groups. The alcohol industry evaluated measures like minimal pricing and advertising regulations that would affect it the most, as the least important for solving alcohol-related problems in Slovenia. Unsurprisingly, the alcohol industry was the keenest for measures which transfer responsibility for alcohol-related problems on individual consumers; therefore they mostly support downstream solutions, like campaigns for encouraging responsible alcohol consumption (Radoš Krnel, Kamin, Košir, & Markič, 2010).

The greatest difference in interests between the governmental organizations and the industry was, as expected, with regard to regulation. More attuned were different stakeholders with regard to education measures. Governmental organizations too considered education policies as important and as rather effective measures for reducing the harm done by alcohol (Radoš Krnel, Kamin, Košir, & Markič, 2010). Considering the government invests plenty of money in campaigning directly to citizens or through funding downstream programs and interventions that NGOs or other institutions design and implement for reducing alcohol-related harm (Kamin, 2006), one would expect even higher opinion about education measures among governmental organisations. The number of promotional and prevention interventions (programmes, projects, and campaigns) aiming to prevent hazardous and harmful drinking in Slovenia has clearly increased after 2006 (Roškar et al., 2018b). Systematic collection of data by the MOSA project identified 70 of such interventions; most of them target adolescents and adults and mainly include informing consumers about the harmful implications of alcohol use and about safe driving. In recent years, alcohol-related prevention activities have increased in coverage and scope, for example through the development of programmes for the responsible serving of alcohol, raising awareness about alcohol use during pregnancy, and interdisciplinary and comprehensive treatment of hazardous and harmful drinkers (Roškar et al., 2018b).

Despite the government's strong favour for legislative restrictions of alcohol availability and consumption, the government needs to be aware that legislative restrictions for managing alcohol have its limitations and can receive good results only with good enforcement and, more importantly, with established social consensus about the need and usefulness of such legislation (Kamin & Kokole, 2016). For achieving consensus in society about social usefulness, for example, of the minimum drinking age law, campaigns and social marketing interventions prove to be beneficial, if they are done well (Kamin & Kokole, 2016). However, in Slovenia there has been a lack of evidence about the effectiveness of public health campaigns (Kamin, 2006); thus scepticism about their potency among public health authorities and government is not unforeseen.

This insight affected further focus of the MOSA project: advocating for changes with two groups of stakeholders, one is the Ministry of Health, who is the main actor in shaping alcohol-related policy and distributes funds to other organisations for designing and implementing interventions for solving alcohol-related problems in the country, and the other are organisations who compete for these funds and design as well as implement and evaluate interventions for solving alcohol-related problems. A reliable systematic overview over what is being done in Slovenia on alcohol-related field and with what effects would

62 *Tanja Kamin and Maja Roškar*

be needed and better criteria for designing, implementing, evaluating, and funding should be introduced.

Deriving from this data, the MOSA stakeholder approach further focused on stakeholders that have been already addressing alcohol problems, but not as efficient as they could. Therefore, further research activities were focused on these stakeholders, namely governmental organisations, research institutes, and NGOs.

We conducted a survey with the NGO stakeholder group (Zorko, Košir, Kamin, Radoš Krnel, & Zupančič, 2010) and interviews and group discussions with selected NGO representatives to deepen understanding of their work – opportunities and barriers in addressing alcohol-related problems in the country. In addition, we gathered more detailed information about 55 interventions in the area of alcohol issues in Slovenia[2] and analysed them against social marketing benchmark criteria (clear behavioural objective, formative research before intervention, segmentation, consideration of competition, marketing mix, exchange, evaluation).

The data revealed that existing interventions (programmes, projects, and campaigns) aiming to prevent hazardous and harmful drinking in Slovenia were not designed and evaluated in a way that would provide financers of those programs with reliable and convincing evidence about their success; interventions were undoubtedly done with good intentions, a lot of enthusiasm, based on the idea that constant presence of the topic in the public is important and good enough on itself. The majority of interventions aimed at preventing harmful consequences of alcohol and promoting healthy lifestyle of youth, including their parents. The majority of interventions were not developed with respect to formative research, which would help clearly define behavioural problems, behavioural goals, and specific segments of population groups that need intervention. Thus, evaluation, when existed, was focused more on process evaluation than on evaluation of effectiveness and efficiency.

NGOs working on the area of alcohol had been lacking knowledge and resources for designing evidence-based interventions. Besides, they had been in majority acting as isolated islands, often ad hoc, not being aware of other organisations' work, neither competitors' nor those who could become partners in designing and implementing interventions. The most concerning finding was that many NGOs had not seen a need or opportunity to collaborate with others (other NGOs or research institutions); many were not included in any of the Slovenian networks on the field, and even less so in the international networks (Zorko, Košir, Kamin, Radoš Krnel, & Zupančič, 2010). An important finding was that a lot of key figures in NGO stakeholders' group were lacking knowledge about strategic design, implementation, and evaluation of interventions but were keen to learn and strengthen their capacities (Zorko, Košir, Kamin, Radoš Krnel, & Zupančič, 2010).

A summary stage of stakeholder analysis was stakeholder assessment according to their interests and influences, as many authors suggest (Bryson, 2004; Knox & Gruar, 2007; Reed et al., 2009; Varvasovszky & Brugha, 2000; Varvasovszky &

MOSA: *Addressing alcohol in Slovenia* 63

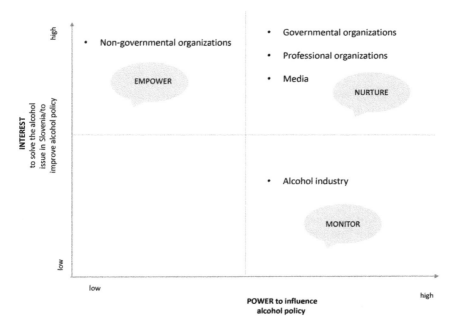

Figure 5.1 MOSA Interest-Power Matrix.

Mckee, 1998). Figure 5.1 presents our main stakeholder categories arranged according to their interest to solve alcohol-related issue in Slovenia or their interest to improve alcohol policy in Slovenia (vertical axis) and by their power to influence alcohol policy (horizontal axis).

As evident from Figure 5.1, alcohol industry was assessed as the stakeholder with high power to influence alcohol policy, but with low interest in resolution of alcohol issue in Slovenia or improvement of alcohol policy. Reed and others define these sorts of stakeholders as context setters, which may represent high risk to the phenomenon under investigation; thus, they should be carefully monitored (Reed et al., 2009).

On the other hand NGOs were assessed as those with high interest for the resolution of alcohol issue but low-medium power to influence alcohol policy, which describes them as supportive stakeholders eager to gain power (Reed et al., 2009). Our analysis of NGOs (Zorko, Košir, Kamin, Radoš Krnel, & Zupančič, 2010) pointed to the lack of synergy and strategic activities between NGOs in solving alcohol-related problems and/or influencing alcohol policy. However, NGOs could become influential by gaining more knowledge, skills, organisational support, and opportunities for forming alliances with other stakeholders (other NGOs, research institutions, or alike) to more efficiently address alcohol issue not only in downstream interventions but also in

64 Tanja Kamin and Maja Roškar

midstream interventions towards stakeholders like advertising association, the media, and alcohol and entertainment industry.

MOSA stakeholder network for enhancing empowerment processes and capacity building

According to our analysis, NGOs presented a group of stakeholders with great potential for pushing alcohol-related social change forward. Thus, MOSA project placed its biggest focus on this group of stakeholders and designed activities that could influence empowerment processes of NGOs through networking and knowledge exchange.

Before we carry on describing empowerment processes, it has to be noted that stakeholder analysis is beneficial and crucial, especially when dealing with issues requiring involvement of multiple stakeholders, whose views and interests differ or even contrast. On the other hand, stakeholder analysis needs to be carried out carefully, since it can also induce or deepen existing conflicts between various stakeholders. Furthermore, results of the stakeholder analysis need to be interpreted with caution, bearing in mind ethical concerns when revealing data on others (Reed et al., 2009). For example, NGOs primarily compete for the same budget divided for interventions by the Ministry of Health. Nevertheless, stakeholder analysis itself, given that stakeholders are involved in the analysis, can minimise differences or even unify opinions. In our case, later became evident across several stakeholder roundtables and meetings, where they had the chance to discuss the role of governmental and NGOs and research organisations in the resolution of alcohol issue in Slovenia (Zorko, Košir, Kamin, Radoš Krnel, & Zupančič, 2010).

MOSA network was set as an 'agent' of empowerment processes (Zimmerman, 1995), since it creates opportunities for the network members (crucial stakeholders) to broaden knowledge, develop skills, expand their social support, and gain other important resources necessary when dealing with alcohol-related issues. MOSA experts can be understood as facilitators of MOSA network users' empowering processes via practices such as sharing up-to-date data on alcohol research, knowledge about strategic development, implementation and evaluation of interventions, raising awareness about current alcohol problem in Slovenia and effects of alcohol policy, enabling and supervising the exchange of stakeholder's expertise, and supporting the development of cooperative relationships between crucial MOSA stakeholders: NGOs, the Ministry of Health, National Institute of Public Health, research institutes, and health professionals working with alcohol-related problems.

We based facilitation of empowerment processes in the MOSA network on two pillars, as it is demonstrated in Figure 5.2: (1) One was building and updating systematic, accurate, and publicly accessible databases of activities on alcohol issue in Slovenia and was designed as a pull strategy; (2) the other was based on push strategy, including engaging key stakeholders in active networking, encouragement for knowledge exchange, attendance in social marketing workshops, data sharing, and discussions and collaboration on joint projects.

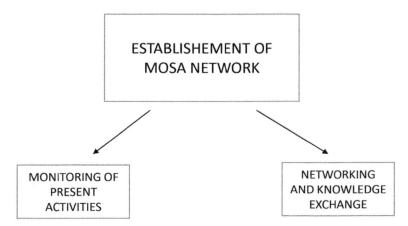

Figure 5.2 Two pillars of the MOSA network.

Activities in the first pillar were offering a clear picture of who is who on the alcohol area in Slovenia, what are their activities, what are the most common approaches, and where are gaps and opportunities for future action. They were also showing opportunities for possible strategic alliances between different stakeholders that are on the quest of solving alcohol issue in Slovenia. It should be noted that NGOs rarely cooperated, primarily because they compete for the same funds. This is a huge obstacle in forming strategic alliances between stakeholders and was one of the crucial challenges for MOSA to overcome. Strategic alliances between NGOs, for example, can facilitate efficiency savings and improve their competitiveness (Hastings, 2013; Morgan & Hunt, 1994) against factors that influence problematic alcohol-related behaviours, like cultural acceptability of alcohol consumption and alcohol industry's marketing activities. They can also help to prioritise issues and join forces in competition for public attention in a cluttered communication environment. Relationships between NGOs and the Government could lead to better set objectives of interventions, long-term financing of successful interventions, and short- and long-term evaluations, which could inform policy decision-making. With better cooperation between crucial

66 *Tanja Kamin and Maja Roškar*

stakeholders, NGOs could also better influence setting and implementation of media and policy agenda and thus influence faster change of environment and alcohol–related social norms.

The MOSA project documented all activities in the network and gradually built databases and analyses that provided the Ministry of Health, who is the main actor in shaping alcohol-related policy and distributes funds to other organisations for designing and implementing interventions for solving alcohol-related problems in the country, reliable systematic overview over what is being done in Slovenia on alcohol-related field and with what effects.

Changes introduced by MOSA stakeholder approach

MOSA started as a project, funded by the Ministry of Health in 2008 and managed to get included in the system of public health, as a national program, in 2017, thus ensuring its sustainability (Figure 5.3).

To foster networking and knowledge exchange, the MOSA interactive webpage (www.infomosa.si, www.infomosa.si/en/) with open-access databases has been established and remains regularly updated. It has been primarily

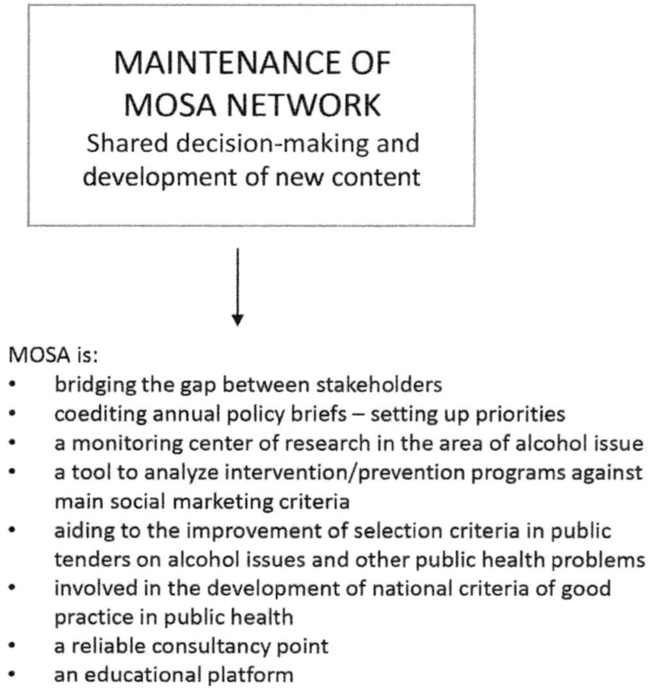

> ## MAINTENANCE OF
> ## MOSA NETWORK
> Shared decision-making and
> development of new content

MOSA is:
- bridging the gap between stakeholders
- coediting annual policy briefs – setting up priorities
- a monitoring center of research in the area of alcohol issue
- a tool to analyze intervention/prevention programs against main social marketing criteria
- aiding to the improvement of selection criteria in public tenders on alcohol issues and other public health problems
- involved in the development of national criteria of good practice in public health
- a reliable consultancy point
- an educational platform

Figure 5.3 MOSA network sustainability.

MOSA: Addressing alcohol in Slovenia   67

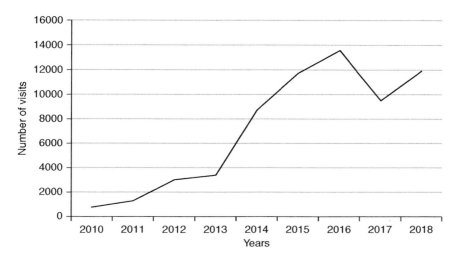

Figure 5.4 MOSA interactive webpage with number of visits.

designed as a platform for the key stakeholders, but it gradually included information about procedures and sources of help, in case of individual alcohol-related problems, for general public. In ten years, the page recorded 47,000 visits (in comparison, the MOSA stakeholder database comprises of 303 units); the number which is steadily growing ever since (Figure 5.4).

MOSA serves as a networking umbrella and monitoring centre and as an educational platform. It delivers knowledge through lectures and workshops covering different themes (e.g. social marketing approach to the development of promotion and prevention, the planning process of preventive programmes, how to perform evaluation, characteristics of effective prevention, effective alcohol policy measures) and different target groups (students, youth organisations, NGOs, professionals). Thus, MOSA has been contributing to crucial stakeholders' capacity building. Part of capacity building consists also of regular meetings entitled 'MOSA market' on regional and national level (as satellites to regional conferences and biannual national alcohol policy conferences). 'MOSA markets' not only aim to promote collaboration between NGOs and other stakeholders, but they also aim to familiarise different actors with existing prevention programs in Slovenia. This exchange is crucial in order to foster cooperation, common development, and to avoid duplication of interventions. In the last couple of years, we have witnessed better cooperation between NGOs, especially in terms of several common actions when advocating effective prevention and policy measures, but also in joint applications for designing more holistic and evidence-based interventions for addressing alcohol-related problems, where NGOs cooperate with research and public health institutions. The evaluation of 'MOSA markets' showed that stakeholders see MOSA as a valuable platform for networking and sharing experiences about designing, implementing, and evaluating interventions (NIPH, 2018).

Through collaboration with different stakeholders, MOSA is constantly developing new content and identifying gaps in tackling different areas of the alcohol issue in Slovenia. MOSA became a monitoring centre of research in the area of alcohol issue in Slovenia and serves as a tool to analyse interventions against main social marketing criteria.

As such, MOSA became a reliable national monitoring centre and consultancy point for finding strategic solutions for solving alcohol issue in the country. The Ministry of Health and other stakeholders are acknowledging MOSA findings while setting up priorities. MOSA for instance aided the improvement of selection criteria in public tenders on alcohol issues and other public health problems; criteria that are more in line with social marketing principles and criteria that encourage bids with cooperation of multiple stakeholders with complementary expertise. MOSA is also actively involved in the development of national criteria of good practice in public health (Radoš Krnel, Kamin, Jandl, Gabrijelčič Blenkuš, Hočevar Grom, Lesnik & Roškar, 2020) and aims to establish a connection between MOSA and publicly financed intervention through obligatory reporting to existing MOSA prevention database. This is a mechanism for elevating standards of designed interventions on the alcohol area in the country, which is already visible in the way, how the Ministry of Health is shaping bids, how organisations prepare intervention proposals, and how proposals are assessed and chosen by expert evaluators.

Conclusion

In this chapter we presented MOSA as an upstream social marketing approach to addressing alcohol-related problems in Slovenia. MOSA started as a collaborative project between the University of Ljubljana and the National Institute of Public Health that competed for financial support from the Ministry of Health in 2008. It was established as a meta-organisational entity to provide transparent, dynamic, clear, and easily accessible information about alcohol issues and to encourage various directly or indirectly involved actors working on the area of alcohol-related problems towards more efficient and effective interventions, based on principles of social marketing. MOSA itself was designed in accordance with principles of social marketing and focused on systematic capacity building of the most important stakeholders, aiming to encourage strategic alliances between them and elevating standards of interventions for tackling alcohol-related problems in Slovenia.

Gradually, MOSA became recognised as a project of strategic importance, and in 2017 it was included in the system of public health, as a national program, thus granted its sustainable maintenance and growth.

MOSA was the first case of such strategic, long-term-oriented stakeholders' approach to solving problems in the public health area in Slovenia. As such it

MOSA: Addressing alcohol in Slovenia 69

was acknowledged as a good practice to follow on other public health fields in Slovenia.

Acknowledgements

The authors would like to thank Vesna Kerstin Petrič from The Ministry of Health for her investment in the formation and development of MOSA and Sandra Radoš Krnel, National Institute of Public Health, Marko Kolšek, University of Ljubljana, Medical Faculty, Mojca Gabrijelčič, National Institute of Public Health for their input and support.

Notes

1 The leading organisation of MOSA is the Centre for Social Psychology at the Faculty of Social Sciences, University of Ljubljana. MOSA partners are National Institute of Public Health and Department of Family Medicine, Faculty of Medicine, University of Ljubljana. MOSA is financed by the Ministry of Health of the Republic of Slovenia; Faculty of Social Sciences, University of Ljubljana; National Institute of Public Health and Faculty of Medicine, University of Ljubljana.
2 Interventions are listed and described in the MOSA database: www.infomosa.si/baze_podatkov/preventivni_programi/seznam.html.

References

Act Restricting the Use of Alcohol (OPA). *Official Gazette of RS*, Nos. 15/03 and 27/17. Retrieved from http://pisrs.si/Pis.web/pregledPredpisa?id=ZAKO3130#.
Anderson, P., & Baumberg, B. (2006). Stakeholders' views of alcohol policy. *Nordic Studies on Alcohol and Drugs, 23*, 393–414.
Bonnafous-Boucher, M., & Rendtorff, J.D. (2016). *Stakeholder Theory: A Model for Strategic Management.* Cham: Springer International.
Brugha, R., & Varvasovszky, Z. (2000). Stakeholder analysis: A review. *Health Policy and Planning, 15*(3), 239–246.
Bryson, J.M. (2004). What to do when stakeholders matter. Stakeholder identification and analysis techniques. *Public Management Review, 6*, 22–53.
Bunn, M.D., Savage, G.T., & Holloway, B.B. (2002). Stakeholder analysis for multi-sector innovations. *Journal of Business & Industrial Management, 17*(23), 181–203.
Buyucek, N, Kubacki, K., Rundle-Thiele, S., & Pang, B. (2016). A systematic review of stakeholder involvement in social marketing interventions. *Australasian Marketing Journal, 24*, 8–19.
Čebašek Travnik, Z. (2006). Alkohol in druge droge kot javnozdravstveni problem. *Delo + varnost: Revija za varstvo pri delu in varstvo pred požarom, 51*(3), 24–25.
Domegan, C., McHugh, P., Devaney, M., Duane, S., Hogan, M., Brome, B.J.,... Piwowarczyk, J. (2016). System thinking social marketing: Conceptual extensions and empirical investigations. *Journal of Marketing Management, 32*(11–12), 1123–1144.
Donaldson, T., & Preston, L.E. (1995). The stakeholder theory of the corporation: Concepts, evidence, and implications. *Academy and Management Review, 20*(1), 65–91.

70 Tanja Kamin and Maja Roškar

Freeman, E. (2010). *Strategic Management: A Stakeholder Approach.* Cambridge: Cambridge University Press.

Hastings, G. (2013). *Social Marketing. Why Should the Devil Have All the Best Tunes?* New York: Taylor & Francis.

Hoek, J., & Jones, S.C. (2011). Regulation, public health and social marketing: A behaviour change trinity. *Journal of Social Marketing, 1*(1), 32–44.

Jones, S. (2014). Using social marketing to create communities for our children and adolescents that do not model and encourage drinking. *Health & Place, 30,* 260–269.

Kamin, T., & Kokole, D. (2016). Midstream social marketing intervention to influence retailers' compliance with the minimum legal drinking age law. *Journal of Social Marketing, 6*(2), 104–120.

Kamin, T. (2005). Management of health risk visibility and construction of a healthy citizen. *Medijska istraživanja, 11*(1), 77–95.

Kamin, T. (2006). *Zravje na barikadah. Dileme promocije zdravja.* Ljubljana: Fakulteta za družbene vede.

Knox, S., & Gruar, C. (2007). The application of stakeholder theory to relationship marketing strategy development in a non-profit organization. *Journal of Business Ethics, 75*(2), 115–135.

Kubacki, K., Rundle-Thiele, S., Pang, B., & Buyucek, N. (2015). Minimizing alcohol harm: A systematic social marketing review (2000–2014). *Journal of Business Research, 68*(10), 2214–2222.

Lovrečič, B., & Lovrečič, M. (2018). *Poraba alkohola in zdravstveni kazalniki tvegane in škodljive rabe alkohola. Slovenija, 2016.* Ljubljana: Nacionalni inštitut za javno zdravje.

Ministry of Finance of the Republic of Slovenia. *Obrazložitev splošnega dela proračuna Republike Slovenije za leto 2019.* Retrieved from https://www.gov.si/assets/ministrstva/MF/Proracun-direktorat/Drzavni-proracun/Sprejeti-proracun/Rebalans-2019/Obr-splosni-del-in-politike/Obrazlozitev-splosnega-dela.pdf.

Ministry of the Interior of the Republic of Slovenia. *Policija. Letna poročila o delu policije 2003–2017.* Retrieved from www.policija.si/index.php/en/statistika.

Morgan, R.M., & Hunt, S.D. (1994). The commitment-trust theory of relationship marketing. *Journal of Marketing, 58*(3), 20–38.

NIPH – National Institute of Public Health. (2018). *Evalvacija 4. Nacionalne conference o alkoholni politiki. Zadovoljstvo z vsebino MOSA tržnice.* (Unpublished).

Petrič, V.K. (2014). Razvoj alkoholne politike. In M. Zorko, T. Hočevar, A. Tančič Grum, V.K. Petrič, S. Radoš Krnel, M. Lovrečič, & B. Lovrečič (Eds.), *Alkohol v Sloveniji. Trendi v načinu pitja, zdravstvene posledice škodljivega pitja, mnenja akterjev in predlogi ukrepov za učinkovitejšo alkoholno politico* (pp. 26–33). Ljubljana: Nacionalni inštitut za javno zdravje.

Preble, J. (2005). Toward a comprehensive model of stakeholder management. *Business and Society Review, 110*(4), 407–431.

Radoš Krnel, S., & Kamin, T. (2010). Stakeholders' opinions on the alcohol policy measures in Slovenia. *European Journal of Public Health, 20*(S1), 201.

Radoš Krnel, S., Kamin, T., Jandl, M., Gabrijelčič Blenkuš, M., Hočevar Grom, A., Lesnik, T., & Roškar, M. (2020). *Merila za vrednotenje intervencij na področju javnega zdravja.* Ljubljana: Nacionalni inštitut za javno zdravje.

Radoš Krnel, S., Kamin, T., Košir, M., & Markič, M. (2010). Stakeholders' interests through their opinions on the alcohol policy measures in Slovenia. *Zdravstveno varstvo, 49*(2), 86–98.

MOSA: Addressing alcohol in Slovenia 71

Reed, M.S., Grave, A., Dandy, N., Posthumusc, H., Hubacek, K., Morris, J.,… Stringer, L.C. (2009). Who's in and why? A typology of stakeholder analysis methods for natural resource management. *Journal of Environmental Management*, *90*(5), 1933–1949.

Roškar, M., Blažko, N., Petrič, V.K., Serec, M., Hovnik Keršmanc, M., Lovrečič, M., … Makarič, S. (2018a). *Alkoholna politika v Sloveniji: Priložnosti za zmanjševanje škode in stroškov ter neenakosti med prebivalci.* Ljubljana: Nacionalni inštitut za javno zdravje.

Roškar, M., Kamin, T., Serec, M. (2018b). *MOSA – Mobilizing Community for Responsibility towards Alcohol. Report on the Drug Situation … of the Republic of Slovenia.* Ljubljana: National Institute of Public Health Retrieved www.nijz.si/sites/www. nijz.si/files/publikacije-datoteke/np_2018_zadnja.pdf.

Sedlak, S., Zaletel, M., Kasesnik, K., Roškar, M., & Sambt, J. (2018). *Ekonomske posledice tveganega in škodljivega pitja alkohola v Sloveniji v obdobju 2012–2014.* Ljubljana: Nacionalni inštitut za javno zdravje. Retrieved from www.nijz.si/sites/ www.nijz.si/files/publikacije-datoteke/ekonposledicealko2012-2014_koncnanijz_ 1_0.pdf.

Stead, M., Gordon, R., Angus, K., & McDermott, L. (2007). A systematic review of social marketing effectiveness. *Health Education*, *107*(2), 126–191.

Varvasovszky, S., & Brugha, R. (2000). How to do (or not to do) … A stakeholder analysis. *Health Policy and Planning*, *15*(3), 338–345.

Varvasovszky, S., & Mckee, M. (1998). An analysis of alcohol policy in Hungary. Who is in charge? *Addiction*, *93*(12), 1815–1827.

Zimmerman, M. (1995). Psychological empowerment: Issues and illustrations. *American Journal of Community Psychology*, *23*(5), 581–599.

Zorko, M., Košir, M., Kamin, T., Radoš Krnel, S., & Zupančič, A. (2010). *Involvement of Civil Society Organizations, Working in the Area of Alcohol, in the Research Process: STEPS Project: Report from Slovenia.* Ljubljana: National Institute of Public Health. Retrieved from www.infomosa.si/doc/STEPS_report.pdf.

6 Challenges in conducting social marketing-based alcohol prevention trials in schools

Christiane Stock, Timo Dietrich,
Lotte Vallentin-Holbech, and Sharyn Rundle-Thiele

Introduction

There is a growing awareness of the need to deliver evidence for alcohol and other interventions delivered in schools to ensure desired outcomes are achieved. Evidence-based interventions are those that are empirically supported and substantiated with controlled research findings that demonstrate beneficial, desired, and predictable outcomes (Forman et al., 2009). In many countries the use of evidence-based interventions has been mandated through national policies. In Denmark, the national policy on alcohol is advising municipalities to apply evidence-based alcohol prevention in schools (National Board of Health, 2012). In addition, there exists a legal obligation for alcohol education in schools (Promulgation of the law on the Danish public school, chapter 2 §7). Although not mandatory, the use of evidence-based and experiential learning in alcohol education is strongly recommended in Australia. The Australian Curriculum, Assessment and Reporting Authority (ACARA) provides direction for health and physical education and state and territory curriculum (ACARA, 2018), but utilisation of recommended approaches is not mandated, and state jurisdictions further complicate implementation. As a result, Australian states have a variety of programmes in place.

Examples of evidence-based alcohol prevention approaches targeting adolescents include limiting the availability and legal age for purchase and use of alcohol through legislation, limiting advertisements for alcohol, and education. This chapter concentrates on alcohol prevention programmes delivered in school settings. Alcohol and drug programmes have been conducted since the late nineteenth century, and professional evaluations of these programs began to emerge in the mid-1960s (Beck, 1998). Alcohol and drug education in schools has evolved from simple information-based approaches in the 1960s featuring didactic delivery to more complex social influence and multi-component approaches extending delivery beyond students to parents and the wider community (Ellickson & Bell, 1990; Foxcroft & Tsertsvadze, 2012; Hurley, Dietrich, & Rundle-Thiele, 2019). From a research perspective, there has been a call for greater rigour when it comes to designing programmes and evaluating their effectiveness (Foxcroft & Tsertsvadze, 2012), yet progress in

Challenges in alcohol prevention 73

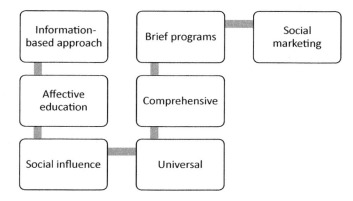

Figure 6.1 Evolution of alcohol and drug education.

the field is slow. Alcohol programmes delivered in school settings have evolved over time, and while the development has not been perfectly linear, the graphic summary in Figure 6.1 depicts development and different alcohol programme approaches for interventions delivered in school settings.

The evolution of alcohol programmes has resulted in an increasing literature base featuring effective school-based alcohol programmes (for example see Foxcroft & Tsertsvadze, 2012; Teesson et al., 2012; Tobler & Stratton, 1997; White & Pitts, 1998). Best practice components for effective alcohol education have been identified in meta-analyses, systematic reviews, and umbrella reviews (e.g. Botvin & Griffin, 2004, 2007; Cuijpers, 2002; Dusenbury & Falco, 1995; DuMcBride, 2003; Midford et al., 2002; Nation et al., 2003; Roche et al., 2010; Stigler et al., 2011; Tobler & Stratton, 1997). For example, it is recommended that programmes be interactive (featuring discussions, role-play, group activities, online activities), theory-based (guided by comprehensive theoretical frameworks), developmentally appropriate (programme is designed for age group), culturally sensitive (relevant language and context), normative in approach (correct information regarding alcohol and drug usage), foster personal and social resistance skills (build resilience skills and self-confidence), incorporate booster sessions (reinforce messages), and include a teacher training component (briefing manuals and/or workshops) (Botvin & Griffin, 2004, 2007; Cuijpers, 2002; Foxcroft & Tsertsvadze, 2012; Onrust et al., 2016; Tobler & Stratton, 1997; Roche et al., 2010; Stigler et al., 2011). Effective programmes show sustained change outcomes for periods as long as 24–32 months when programmes are delivered over an entire semester and/or over multiple years (McBride et al., 2004). However, many programmes are not sufficiently resourced and as such are criticised for their failure to attain enduring effects following programme participation (Hastings, Stead, & MacKintosh, 2002; Stead et al., 2007). The application of social marketing to alcohol education programmes in high-school settings has more recently received attention

74 *Christiane Stock et al.*

with innovative programmes focusing on experiential learning and gamified program components delivering promising short-term effects (Dietrich et al., 2019; Rundle-Thiele et al., 2013; Rundle-Thiele et al., 2015). Further programme development is needed to achieve semester or multiple year deliveries to understanding long-term efficacy that can be achieved with social marketing programmes. Wider involvement of stakeholders and extended application of theory have been identified as additional avenues to enhance programme outcomes (Hurley et al., 2019).

Many school-based alcohol and drug programmes have not been tested using optimal research designs such as RCT (Botvin & Griffith, 2007). There is no doubt that high-quality research is needed in order to extend our understanding of alcohol programmes delivered in school settings. The health field has been the most assiduous in its emphasis on evidence-based practice using a randomised control trial research design. Several initiatives have aimed to increase the internal validity of RCTs, such as the Consolidated Standards of Reporting Trials (CONSORT, 2012). However, there is also a growing concern that effectiveness tested in RCTs may be compromised in real-world settings (Green & Glasgow, 2006). This concern about the lack of external validity of RCTs has led to the development of the generalisability, applicability, and predictability (GAP) criteria for assessing the external validity of trials (Fernandez-Hermida et al., 2012). While RCTs are regarded as the gold standard for establishing the effectiveness of interventions (Foxcroft & Tsertsvadze, 2012), these can be difficult to achieve given factors such as survey fatigue are experienced within controlled settings where no treatment is afforded.

The demand for effectiveness studies with high internal and external validity has many implications for research practice. Researchers increasingly strive to adhere to quality standards when planning, conducting, and reporting about alcohol programmes trailed in schools. A recent review of programmes targeting parents identified significant room for improvement in study quality with Effective Public Health Practice Project (EPHPP) assessments indicating that ten out of the 13 identified programmes were considered to be of 'weak' quality. According to Hurley et al. (2019), blinding assessors and reducing selection bias through increased use of RCTs are avenues that can be pursued to enhance study quality. Enhanced study quality will continue to be affected by a number of real-life factors, such as limited funding resources, school access, and other practical conditions. Among the practical conditions the involvement of stakeholders within school settings, namely school principals, executive assistants, teachers, and students, who impact both the implementation of the programme and the quality of the research for measuring programme effects are a critical issue.

Sharing information and knowledge about RCT research designs and implementation processes is an important step towards improving research practice in prevention and intervention research. Publishing articles on study design enables the sharing of specific information on adequate research designs for alcohol education among researchers. However, design articles provide only limited information about potential challenges and barriers with respect to conducting the actual trial as planned in the school context. It is widely accepted that quantity and quality of the implementation of programmes determine how effective prevention programmes are and that there are superior outcomes occur when the programme has been implemented with high fidelity (Dusenbury et al., 2003; Lisha et al., 2012). In fact, in one of the largest meta-analyses of school-based substance abuse prevention programmes, Tobler and Stratton (1997) concluded that problems related to programme implementation have the largest impact in terms of decreasing programme effectiveness.

However, relatively little attention has been directed towards implementation problems related to the conduct of implementation and research activities themselves, such as collecting the data as planned in the research protocol within the intended group of trial participants. There is a lack of information on failures, challenges, practical problems – differentiating general challenges of RCTs and specific challenges for conducting alcohol prevention trials in schools. The difficulty of recruitment, implementation, and evaluation of large-scale RCTs in schools is poorly documented and warrants research attention. Thus, summarising and communicating experiences and insights for improvement of research practice in general and specifically in alcohol prevention and intervention trials is an important undertaking. Communicating such experience is needed in order to plan and develop trial designs that have the ability to create confidence for researchers and schools. Schools are frequently approached to participate in numerous research projects, and they are faced with increasing curriculum demands leaving them with less flexibility and room to implement extracurricular programs. Consequently, it is naïve for the research community to expect entry into schools, and understanding is needed to ensure that researchers can communicate clear benefits of involvement in programme evaluations.

This chapter aims to describe experiences of stakeholder involvement from two case studies involving three cluster RCTs that have been conducted in Australia and Denmark. Knowledge exchange regarding factors facilitating and hindering the conduct of RCTs in the context of school-based alcohol prevention was facilitated through a partnership between the Unit for Health Promotion Research (Denmark) and Social Marketing @ Griffith (Australia). The case studies describe research and development projects in which the authors of this chapter themselves were involved. The selection of the case studies therefore follows the criterion of first-hand experience. This chapter has three objectives. First, it seeks to summarise challenges regarding stakeholder involvement for conducting RCTs in schools. Second, it describes specific challenges for alcohol prevention trials and considerations for how researchers can respond to these. Third, recommendations to enhance stakeholder involvement in research practice are outlined.

76   *Christiane Stock et al.*

Case description of the two programs and three cluster RCTs

The Blurred Minds project (Australia)

The first case study described in this chapter summarises the research team's experience with stakeholders for the *Blurred Minds* project. *Blurred Minds* V1 was initially developed and evaluated using an RCT (see Rundle-Thiele et al., 2015 for detail on the initial *Blurred Minds* programme) across one state in Australia. Process and outcome evaluation results informed the development of version 2 of *Blurred Minds*. *Blurred Minds* V2 was evaluated using a stratified RCT (intervention: 9; control: 5) in 2017 (Dietrich et al., 2019). *Blurred Minds* V2 featured five core lessons, focusing on the effects of alcohol, the science of alcohol, myths and norms, legalities and advertising as well as a resilience building component. All lessons were developed using game design elements to enhance programme engagement. Gamification has previously been used to effectively influence health and well-being behaviour (Johnson et al., 2016), and *Blurred Minds* V2 (www.blurredminds.com.au) contained a suite of gamification activities (e.g. virtual reality, online games and practical activities).

Guided by the Theory of Planned Behaviour (TPB) *Blurred Minds* V1 was designed to maintain, and where appropriate, change key variables, namely adolescent attitudes, social norms, self-efficacy, and behavioural intention, towards binge drinking. The TPB states that together attitudes, subjective norms, and perceived behavioural control are related to intentions which, in turn, explain behaviour (Ajzen, 2011). A TPB informed evaluation was employed using a repeated measure design research design where students were surveyed at two time points: (1) prior to their participation in the programme and (2) immediately after completion using the TPB main constructs. Intentions to perform the behaviour (Fishbein and Ajzen, 2011; Norman and Conner, 2006), social norms, and perceived behavioural control (Fishbein and Ajzen, 2011; Norman and Conner, 2006) were measured using unipolar scales from 1 (strongly disagree) to 7 (strongly agree). A total of 1,257 students (intervention: 615; control: 642) completed surveys, and positive effects were observed for TPB constructs (Rundle-Thiele et al., 2015).

Blurred Minds V2 included five chief investigators, one research fellow, and two PhD students. The design of the trial was driven by the research team, and the content of the programme was based on feedback from earlier programme iterations (Dietrich et al., 2015; Rundle-Thiele et al., 2013 & 2015) and user involvement in program co-design (Dietrich et al., 2016; 2017). *Blurred Minds* features a long-term partnership with the team's key industry partner, which has developed over more than ten years and is underpinned by trust and commitment to application of social marketing in alcohol programmes. Despite this trusting relationship with the State Catholic administrative authority, access to schools is subject to ethical and Diocese approval and individual approaches to schools who have to agree to participate in the trial. A complicating factor is individual school autonomy and competing alcohol programmes already running in schools, which creates an access barrier. In order to overcome these contextual difficulties a two-step approach to individual school recruitment was pursued. First, the key stakeholder partner sent a personalised communication to principals of the 36 randomly selected schools utilising a visually appealing school information flyer. Second, trained research assistants were employed to follow up with each school to further liaise with principals, executive assistants, and respective teachers who were in charge of the health and physical education curriculum. The most important factor was flexibility towards the schools' teaching curriculum, and schools were free to select delivery dates according their requirements. Previous relationships with key stakeholders at schools were not as helpful as key project staff changed responsibilities or moved positions between the trials indicating a capacity to building lasting relationships in this sector is difficult. Overall, recruitment rates in the second trial of 50% were achieved which was significantly lower than rates attained in the earlier RCT where individual school recruitment rates of 60% were achieved.

The GOOD Life project (Denmark)

The second case study from which data regarding stakeholder involvement and challenges are derived is *The GOOD Life* project. In brief, *The GOOD Life* is a social norms-based programme to reduce alcohol and other drug use among pupils in eighth and ninth grade. *The GOOD Life* was implemented in public schools in the Region of Southern Denmark. The intervention programme *The GOOD Life* was composed of three social norms elements representing three different communication channels, namely face-to-face communication led by a trained moderator with high levels of interaction and engagement with pupils (normative feedback session), print communication (posters), and interactive media (web application involving a quiz to test individual norm perceptions). The intervention period of eight weeks began with the normative feedback session conducted either in single classes or whole grades according to school preferences, followed by the posters with social norms messages displayed in the classroom, and lastly by inviting pupils to visit the web-based application. In all three elements *The GOOD Life* provided normative feedback through social norms messages, which were specific for each participating school. Using survey data on personal drug use behaviour and perceptions of peer norms, social norms messages were phrased to challenge potential overestimations of peer behaviour and attitudes towards alcohol and other drug use. Additional details of the programme and trial design are published elsewhere (Stock et al., 2016).

The effectiveness of *The GOOD Life* programme to reduce alcohol and other drug use was tested in a cluster-randomised controlled trial (Vallentin-Holbech et al., 2018). The intervention period was preceded and followed by data collection, with the follow-up taking place three months after baseline. Public schools in the Region of Southern Denmark with grades 8 and 9 were invited

78 *Christiane Stock et al.*

to participate in the study, and participating schools were randomly allocated to either intervention or control schools. In total, 39 schools were included in the trial, and the sample comprised approximately 1,400 pupils. Alcohol, tobacco, and marijuana use as well as the perceived frequency of use among peers of their own grade was measured in an online questionnaire at baseline and at three-month follow-up. Data from the baseline survey were used to develop social norms messages specifically for each school. Primary outcomes of the trial were binge drinking (five or more units at one occasion) and perceived frequency of binge drinking among peers, while smoking, marijuana use, and alcohol-related harm were analysed as secondary outcomes. The trial is registered at Current Controlled Trials with study ID ISRCTN27491960.0.

In regards to stakeholder involvement the study, *The GOOD Life*, established a steering committee consisting of the principal investigator, one PhD student, a school principal with experience and interest in health promotion programmes at schools, a consultant from the governmental organisation responsible for implementing the national public health policy in the local municipalities, a representative for the prevention network of schools, and the police conducting drug prevention programmes within schools. The intended design of the trial and the content of the intervention were discussed primarily with the school principal who provided important information on the feasibility of the study in the context of the political environment at Danish schools at the time of the study. The context for conducting randomised trials at schools was difficult, because during the year in which we started the recruitment of schools, a major school reform was implemented in Denmark. The school reform introduced afternoon teaching and many other changes in school organisation impacting the work–life balance of teachers, which made schools hesitant to participate in the research project. To overcome this challenge, the school principal advised the researchers to adjust both the intervention itself and the trial design to better meet the needs of schools. The most important factor was limiting the amount of work for teachers and to minimise the teaching time required for the intervention. The steering group was also involved in discussing the results of the trial and its relevance for future prevention work in the Region of Southern Denmark. The research group learned from listening to stakeholders and practitioners how to disseminate the findings of the trial for practitioners and the type of information for inclusion in a written handbook about the program *The GOOD Life*.

Challenges and implications of stakeholder involvement

As described above, both projects have involved a set of stakeholders in the implementation process of the alcohol prevention programmes and incorporated stakeholders in order to collect data relevant for the cluster RCT as evaluation design. There were a number of challenges related to the stakeholder involvement in the various phases of the research projects such as: (1) ethical approval; (2) study design, recruitment, and randomisation; (3) length of the follow–up

Challenges in alcohol prevention 79

period, incentives for participation, implementation of the trial, and communication with stakeholders.

Ethical approval

The two case studies collected important information concerning the interaction between researchers and stakeholders related to ethical approval. In most countries, ethical approval by one or more ethics committees is required prior to beginning experimental research with human participants. Further, many journals also require ethical approval. The challenge here is that most ethical protocols have been developed for clinical trials, and fitting these to school settings is very difficult. Some ethical committees require standard phrases in the informed consent form that have been developed for clinical trials but may arouse unnecessary concern among parents during programme implementation (e.g. a statement on the potential negative side effects of the intervention). Since most pupils are underage, ethical requirements require written parental consent, and research teams need to rely on schools for forms to be administered. A key challenge therefore is that in practice many students do not have informed consent prior to programme implementation, and this proves impractical given students wish to participate and schools do not provide adequate supervision for students who cannot participate placing them at risk of harm. Non-participation in the programme reduces sample sizes and has implications for trial evaluations. School recruitment is impacted when active consent mechanisms are required. Ethical processes and procedures imposed on research teams do not reflect ethical challenges arising for research teams. Within *Blurred Minds* which has now been administered to more than 4,000 students an ethical complaint has yet to be received. Adjustments to ethical processes are needed to optimise RCT and other field trial outcomes. A better alternative is to allow passive consent procedures to ensure that participation numbers can be increased. Passive consent mechanisms involve the research team advising parents and students about the programme, including any risks associated with programme participation, and parents and students who do not wish to participate are invited to opt out of programme participation. In Australia, additional challenges arose, and school education authorities required additional ethical approval prior to recruitment and programme roll out. Completion of multiple ethical applications imposes unnecessary cost burdens on project teams, and simplification is needed moving forward such that one ethical body will accept an approved application from another governing body to avoid unnecessary duplication of effort.

In *The GOOD Life* study the written material delivered to adolescents and their parents as well as the consent forms were discussed with the teachers or school principals in order to include their feedback in the formulations of the information material. Teachers did not have any problems with collecting the forms, as they were informed about the process and got clear information about their task and involvement. To receive as many signed forms as possible

80 *Christiane Stock et al.*

from pupils we recommended that a coordinator be appointed at each school. It is best that this coordinator is not the principal or secretary, as teachers have closer relationships with students and are able to remind students on a daily basis about the returning of forms. Also, the information material about the project and consent should be tailored to each school including listing of the school contact in addition to research team contact information.

Study design, recruitment, and randomisation

Interaction with stakeholders from schools is required when it comes to defining the study design of alcohol and drug prevention trials. In such trials, interventions can consist of complex and costly combinations of educational activities (e.g. face-to-face, internet, and print communication), and large sample sizes and a high number of clusters (schools) need to be enrolled in the trial to ensure adequate evaluation can be undertaken. Strategies such as two-arm designs where interventions are tested against a control (no programme) or a traditional programme condition are attractive alternatives. In practice, it is difficult to convince school principals to participate in a trial when there is a high chance their school can randomly be assigned to the control condition. Therefore, some trials leave out randomisation (e.g. Shaping the Social study). Such non-RCTs recruit a number of intervention schools and thereafter recruit matching control schools. Since randomisation is methodically preferred to ensure high-quality assessment, a wait-list design can be used to overcome recruitment problems. In both, *The GOOD Life* and the *Blurred Minds* studies, researchers offered control schools the intervention after completion of the follow-up data collection. This was advised by the school principal in *The GOOD Life* steering group and helped to increase the recruitment rates substantially to achieve the 39 schools needed for the trial. However, the disadvantage is that a second follow-up was not possible, because it was inappropriate to offer the intervention one year after the data collection. The corresponding classes would no longer benefit from the programme, given their graduation to the following year level.

Any governmental obligations for schools to assure health and drug education increase the likelihood of participation in trials. Schools that have a school hour scheduled for extracurricular activities are more likely to participate. These factors mainly depend on governmental policies and are difficult to influence as a researcher, but if such a policy exists researchers can build this as a key feature into communication strategies with schools as an additional selling point for programme involvement. However, once alcohol and drug education components are mandatory and schools start to develop, use existing or purchase external programmes, they may be less likely to have additional capacity to trial innovative research programmes.

With regards to timing school invites it is recommended to avoid busy times for school administrators, such as the beginning of school term. In *The GOOD Life* study, we received better response and acceptance when the invitation

Challenges in alcohol prevention   81

was provided late in the term or in the semester before summer break, when principals were planning their strategies for the next semester/year. In *Blurred Minds*, the recruitment period occurred over two terms, starting in the last term of the year before the summer break and resuming in the first term of the New Year for schools that were not able to commit at the end of the previous year. The process is lengthy, and it takes multiple attempts to get definitive answers. Once the commitment is received, however, scheduling can also take several additional weeks.

Length of follow-up period

Follow-up periods need to be agreed with school stakeholders. Follow-up periods of 6, 12, or 18 months provide strong evidence of long-term effectiveness of the intervention. However, several or long follow-up periods are difficult to realise in schools, because research preferences often do not match with school term organisation and availability of pupils at the desired follow-up time points. Also, surveys do not provide schools with the feeling of a value add, and pupils are usually bored and annoyed with surveys. There remains little incentive and interest for schools to complete long-term follow-up data collection initiatives. The first follow-up after the intervention needs to be carefully planned in order to fit into one annual school calendar. A period of 3–4 months between baseline and first follow-up is a realistic time frame for short duration interventions. Since many consumption measures indicate a timeframe of alcohol/drug use in the last 30 days, follow-up directly after the intervention period is finished is not advised, because measurable effects occur later. For longer interventions the period needs to be prolonged – e.g. six months. Any follow-up data collection should keep at least one-month distance from New Year's Eve, which is a heavy drinking occasion that may bias the data. A second follow-up is best conducted after 6, 12, or 18 months. However, pupils in senior grades inevitably leave school or change schools, which limits their availability for long-term follow-up. Linkage with registry data (if available in the country) may enable measurement of long-term effects.

In *The GOOD Life* it was decided to limit the follow-up period to three months from the initially planned six months after consultation with school principals. This limitation was needed in order to find time periods for data collection where most pupils were available, that do not conflict with school breaks or exam periods. In addition, a second follow-up was not possible due to utilisation of a wait-list design. In *Blurred Minds V2*, plans for a six-month follow-up data collection point were in place, and this was negotiated with schools. However, similar to the *Blurred Minds V1* research trial (Rundle-Thiele et al., 2015), schools struggled to complete longitudinal data collection due to survey fatigue, competing curriculum demands as well as teachers simply not executing the data collection despite numerous reminders. Moving forward, data collection needs to be sold as a value add so that it is not perceived as a nuisance by the school staff. The value add could come in form of tailored reports

82   *Christiane Stock et al.*

delivering diagnostic data and shareable information for teachers, parents, and potentially the wider community in easy-to-access forms (e.g. infographics).

The role of incentives

In order to increase participation of schools, school classes, and pupils we recommend that trials should budget for use of incentives. Participation in quantitative data collections (online survey) is higher when incentives are provided (e.g. large-value lotteries). Teacher feedback in *The GOOD Life* study indicated that incentives for teachers or school classes had a limited effect on motivation/ participation in the intervention. We recruited pupils to take part in focus group interviews as part of the process evaluation, and we asked teachers for semi-structured interviews. Our experience showed that offering incentives for pupils increased the likelihood of finding interviewees for the qualitative data collection that are representative and not only those who are very positive about the intervention. The *Blurred Minds* program did not use incentives to recruit schools or encourage survey completions. Similar to *The GOOD Life* study, the research team found that schools were either interested in participating or not. Schools that already had alcohol programmes in place were less likely to participate while schools that had basic programmes or no programmes in place were more likely to partake.

Implementation of trials

Similar to the recruitment phase, the implementation phase requires interaction with and involvement of stakeholders. The amount of involvement of stakeholders and the connected challenges depend on who is delivering the program. In *The GOOD Life* trial, the programme was delivered by staff of the research team which limited stakeholder involvement. However, the baseline and follow-up data collection via an electronic questionnaire was delivered by teachers across two teaching sessions, and this led to problems in data collection and limited our sample size and data available for effect analyses. Similarly, *Blurred Minds* was delivered by a team of trained researchers who had experience in delivering alcohol prevention programmes. This reduced fidelity issues and was a key selling point in recruiting schools to participate in the trial.

In *Blurred Minds* an electronic questionnaire was accessed by students. Each school was provided with an electronic link attached to an email received by the school coordinator. The link provided access to the survey web page where each student then would be assigned a unique URL that would serve as their response ID. However, in some school classes the exact same URL was copied and used by all students causing the responses to be overwritten, resulting in only one completed questionnaire for an entire class resulting in loss of data for the research team. For future surveys, it is recommended that an electronic link is directly distributed to the students through mechanisms that can protect student anonymity. Within the *Blurred Minds* evaluation online surveys employing a unique 13-digit identifier code (letter of first name, date of birth, letter of mothers and fathers' first name, school code) were utilised with surveys matched following data collection. The lengthy identifier code reduced matching errors significantly compared to our previous trial and allowed schools to simply administer the survey via one link. At the start of each survey, students entered their unique code.

When implementing the programme or campaign it is also essential to make sure that teachers do not interfere with the content of the programme and therewith decrease the fidelity of the programme delivered. For example, in *The GOOD Life* trial, teachers added messages. Since *The GOOD Life* programme is entirely based on providing normative feedback to pupils and presenting positive behavioural messages of the moderate consumption of the majority of pupils, it does not contain any information on alcohol- or drug-related risks. Adding such risk information from the school teacher side does interfere with the trial objectives. Therefore, we communicated clearly that the effectiveness of the program will only be given, and the research aims could only be fulfilled, if no additional drug education was provided by teachers. Within *Blurred Minds* – a gamified programme where students have a lot of fun – teachers would occasionally try to participate and share fear-based stories or negative experiences, which also impacted the fidelity of the trial.

Communication with stakeholders

Communication with teachers and school principals about the alcohol and drug prevention programme is essential in order to receive their approval and support for conducting the trial in their school or class. Several potential problems can occur in communication, especially when the programme or social marketing intervention is dealing with alcohol and drugs. A common issue that might come up is that stakeholders have a different perspective on the need for an alcohol and drug programme. Although school health surveys show that the consumption level among adolescents at the local and national levels is high to hazardous, stakeholders from schools often have the opinion that their school is different. Although it is known from multi-level studies that school differences exist, this opinion is seldom based on data but relies on assumptions, opinions, and observations of students' habits and may therefore be understood as an optimistic bias. Denying the need for a programme can be motivated by the fear that making alcohol and drug use a target of intervention at their school might diminish the reputation of their school. If communicating with stakeholders, researchers need to be aware that others might not share their data-driven perspective of the problem. If local data are available the presentation of risk profiles might help to overcome resistance. Another communication strategy might be to acknowledge school differences and the assumption that the particular school could be better off than others, but to stress the argument that even low-risk schools would benefit from the programme and that having a drug prevention programme at their school shows positive engagement

84 *Christiane Stock et al.*

in pupils' health and social development. Moreover, teams can communicate benefits of programme delivery by reminding schools that delivery of alcohol programmes in their school is a protective factor that can further inoculate their students. Research indicates that pro alcohol messages outnumber prevention and moderation messages by 1 to 238 (Rundle-Thiele et al., 2013). Given that pupils are exposed to pro alcohol drinking messages 365 days a year an opportunity for students to receive moderate or non-drinking messages within the school setting can help to win over sceptical schools. Finally, we have found that executive assistants or personal assistants of the principal act as 'gatekeepers' who need to be convinced first of the value of the research programme. They are in most cases the one key stakeholder who will nudge and urge the principal to decide and therefore need to be approached in the first instance with a strong sell on programme benefits for the school.

Conclusions and recommendations

School-based programmes remain a cost-effective way to prevent alcohol-related harm in adolescents (Foxcroft et al., 2012). Stakeholder theory implies that involvement of stakeholders in intervention planning, implementation, and evaluation stages may enhance programme outcomes (Buyucek et al., 2016). Freeman (1984) stated that "any group or individual who can affect or is affected by the achievement of a corporation's purpose" (p. iv) is a stakeholder. Stakeholder theory contends that organisations that understand the "needs and concerns" of stakeholders have better survival rates given they are more able to gain the support of those groups with the ultimate aim of sustaining and improving their performance (Bryson, 2004). Positive correlations between company success and the number of stakeholders that are considered during planning and decision-making processes have been identified (Donaldson and Preston, 1995). Following a review of interventions aiming to reduce problem alcohol use, Buyucek et al. (2016) called for broader involvement of stakeholders in all intervention stages. Guided by stakeholder theory, we contend that consideration of stakeholders is an important feature of programme planning that can serve to increase programme uptake by schools.

Key stakeholder groups

Given that stakeholders are critical to deliver the support needed to implement and subsequently evaluate programmes, understanding the needs and concerns of each stakeholder group must be the starting point for any project. Teachers function as one important stakeholder group that is essential throughout the design and implementation process, given they serve as gatekeepers who select programmes and can impact fidelity based on implementation practices. School administrators are frequently the first communication point, and gaining their support is crucial to access key decision makers who determine whether a programme becomes implemented within the school. Finally, consideration of all support staff and students is needed to optimise intervention and evaluation outcomes. Careful management of all stakeholders involved is needed to assure both successful programme delivery and optimal completion of evaluations.

Identifying facilitating factors

Careful consideration of stakeholder needs can assist project teams to increase the number of schools electing to participate in a trial. We recommend researchers develop informative materials for schools that outline benefits that arise for their students (e.g. project outcomes such as changes in knowledge and attitudes towards drinking) while simultaneously de-emphasising commitment required by a school (e.g. time and staff). Highlighting both the benefits of the programme and possible objections might increase programme uptake by schools. By understanding that a control only-condition is a significant imposition on any school community, alternate research designs can be employed by programme teams in research funding applications to better meet the needs of school communities. For example, research teams are encouraged to offer wait-list control designs which ensure the intervention is delivered to control schools after follow-up data collection.

Stakeholder theory as a guiding framework for programme planning

Stakeholder theory is a management theory that was the result of work aiming to improve the survival probabilities of corporate companies in a competitive market economy through understanding the 'needs and concerns' of stakeholder groups and to gain the support of those groups with the ultimate aim of sustaining and improving performance (Buyucek et al., 2016). By applying stakeholder thinking to intervention planning, implementation, and evaluation, researchers can ensure more effective management of school communities. Schools are communities comprised of staff (managers, administrators, and front-line teaching and support staff), students, parents, and other concerned community members. By understanding school operations, researchers can plan project timing to ensure project needs are aligned to school community needs. For example, research teams can avoid sending out invitations to schools during extremely busy times (before and after school breaks); they can make sure that the data collection is finished before the school year ends to avoid loss to follow-up due to change in student composition in the next school year; they can avoid key reform periods; and they can avoid exam times. Sensitivity to and careful consideration of school operations will ensure that project teams understand scheduled exam weeks, other special activities (e.g. school camps), enabling project planning to work around key school dates.

Giving back to stakeholders

Research teams need to change orientation and planning to give more consideration to the communities served by the research project. Historically, researchers have focused on attaining project outcomes but often fail to

86 *Christiane Stock et al.*

communicate research outcomes to the communities who made the research possible. Researchers need to extend reporting beyond funding bodies and academic stakeholders to ensure that the people supporting or participating in the research are informed about outcomes. Therefore, it is recommended that researchers employ personal communication with teachers and school principals ensuring effective two-way communication. Research teams should not rely on email contact and where possible in-person communication is recommended to build a strong supporting network. Additionally, establishing newsletters for community members served in the research programme ensures that research teams communicate outcomes of the project. Key initiatives that project teams must incorporate into project design include reports for school communities to provide direct feedback to classes, schools, or other groupings on student outcomes within the cohort measured, and communication about availability and access to intervention materials. This provides direct feedback and value to the schools and students ensuring that research teams build supporting communities who in turn are willing to provide further support and advocate on behalf of the research team.

References

ACARA. (2018). Health and Physical Education (HPE), accessed 30 January 2018 at: www.acara.edu.au/curriculum/learning-areas-subjects/health-and-physical-education.

Ajzen, I. (2011). *The Theory of Planned Behaviour: Reactions and Reflections.* Taylor & Francis.

Beck, J. (1998). 100 Years of "Just Say No" Versus "Just Say Know". *Evaluation Review, 22*(1), 15–45.

Botvin, G., & Griffin, K. (2004). Life skills training: Empirical findings and future directions. *Journal of Primary Prevention, 25*(2), 211–232. doi:10.1023/B:JOPP.0000042391.58573.5b.

Botvin, G., & Griffin, K. (2007). School-based programmes to prevent alcohol, tobacco and other drug use. *International Review of Psychiatry, 19*(6), 607–615. doi:10.1080/09540260701797753.

Bryson, J.M., 2004. What to do when stakeholders matter. *Public Management Review, 6*(1), 21–53.

Buyucek, N., Kubacki, K., Rundle-Thiele, S.R., & Pang, B. (2016). A systematic review of stakeholder involvement in social marketing interventions. *Australasian Marketing Journal, 24*(1), 8–19.

Cuijpers, P. (2002). Effective ingredients of school-based drug prevention programs: A systematic review. *Addictive Behaviors, 27*(6), 1009–1023. doi:10.1016/s0306-4603(02)00295-2.

CONSORT. (2012). Consolidated Standards of Reporting Trials, Library for health research reporting www.equator-network.org/resource-centre/library-of-health-research-reporting/.

Dietrich, T., Rundle-Thiele, S., Kubacki, K., Durl, J., Gullo, M., Arli, D., & Connor, J.P. (2019), Virtual reality in social marketing: A process evaluation. *Marketing Intelligence and Planning, 37*(7), 806–820.

Dietrich, T., Trischler, J., Schuster, L., & Rundle-Thiele, S. (2017). Co-designing services with vulnerable consumers. *Journal of Service Theory and Practice, 27*(3), 663–688.

Dietrich, T., Rundle-Thiele, S., Schuster, L., & Connor, J. (2016). Co-designing social marketing programs. *Journal of Social Marketing, 6*(1), 41–61.

Dietrich, T., Rundle-Thiele, S., Schuster, L., Drennan, J., Russell-Bennett, R., Leo, C., Gullo, M., & Connor, J. (2015). Differential segmentation responses to an alcohol social marketing program. *Addictive Behaviors, 49*, 68–77.

Donaldson, T., & Preston, L.E., (1995). The stakeholder theory of the corporation: Concepts, evidence, and implications. *Academy of Management Review,* 20 (1), 65–91.

Dusenbury, L., & Falco, M. (1995). Eleven components of effective drug abuse prevention curricula. *Journal of School Health, 65*(10), 420–425.

Dusenbury, L., Brannigan, R., Falco, M., & Hansen, W. (2003). A review of research on fidelity of implementation: Implications for drug abuse prevention in school settings. *Health Education Research, 18*(2), 237–256. doi:10.1093/her/18.2.237

Ellickson, P., & Bell, R. (1990). Drug prevention in junior high: A multi-site longitudinal test. *Science, 247*(4948), 1299–1305.

Fishbein, M. and Ajzen, I. (2011). *Predicting and Changing Behavior: The Reasoned Action Approach.* Taylor & Francis.

Foxcroft, D., & Tsertsvadze, A. (2012). Universal school-based prevention programs for alcohol misuse in young people (Review). *Evidence-Based Child Health, 7*(2), 450–575.

Forman, S.G., Olin, S.S., Hoagwood, K.E., Crowe, M., & Saka, N. (2009). Evidence-based interventions in schools: Developer's views of implementation barriers and facilitators. *School Mental Health,* 1, 26–36.

Fernandez-Hermida, J.R., Calafat, A., Becoña, E., Tsertsvadze, A., & Foxcroft, D.R. (2012). Assessment of generalizability, applicability and predictability (GAP) for evaluating external validity in studies of universal family-based prevention of alcohol misuse in young people: Systematic methodological review of randomized controlled trials. *Addiction,* 107(9) , 1570–9.

Freeman, R.E., (1984). *Stakeholder Management: Framework and Philosophy.* Pitman.

Green, L.W., & Glasgow, L.E. (2006). Evaluating the relevance, generalization, and applicability of research: Issues in external validation and translation methodology. *Evaluation and the Health Professions,* 29(1), 126–153.

Hastings, G., Stead, M., & MacKintosh, A. (2002). Rethinking drugs prevention: Radical thoughts from social marketing. *Health Education, 61*(4), 347–364.

Hurley, E., Dietrich, T., & Rundle-Thiele, S. (2019). A systematic review of parent based programs to prevent or reduce alcohol consumption in adolescents. *BMC Public Health, 19,* 1451. Retrieved from https://doi.org/10.1186/s12889-019-7733-x.

Johnson, D., Deterding, S., Kuhn, K., Staneva, A., Stoyanov, S., & Hides, L. (2016). Gamification for health and wellbeing: A systematic review of the literature. *Internet Interventions, 6,* 89–106.

Lisha, N., Sun, P., Rohrbach, L., Spruijt-Metz, D., Unger, J., & Sussman, S. (2012). An evaluation of immediate outcomes and fidelity of a drug abuse prevention program in continuation high schools: Project Towards No Drug Abuse (TND). *Journal of Drug Education, 42*(1), 33–57.

McBride, N. (2003). A systematic review of school drug education. *Health Education Research, 18*(6), 729–742.

McBride, N., Farringdon, F., Midford, R., Meuleners, L., & Phillips, M. (2004). Harm minimization in school drug education: Final results of the School Health and Alcohol Harm Reduction Project (SHAHRP). *Addiction, 99*(3), 278–291.

Midford, R., Munro, G., McBride, N., Snow, P., & Ladzinski, U. (2002). Principles that underpin effective school-based drug education. *Journal of Drug Education, 32*(4), 363–386.

Nation, M., Crusto, C., Wandersman, A., Kumpfer, K., Seybolt, D., Morrisey-Kane, E., & Davino, K. (2003). What works in prevention; principles of effective prevention programs. *American Psychologist, 58*(6/7), 449–456.

National Board of Health (2012). Forebyggelsespakke alkohol (Danish prevention policy on alcohol). National Board of Health.

Norman, P., & Conner, M. (2006). The theory of planned behaviour and binge drinking: Assessing the moderating role of past behaviour within the theory of planned behaviour. *British Journal of Health Psychology, 11*(1), 55–70.

Onrust, S., Otten, R., Lammers, J., & Smit, F. (2016). School-based programmes to reduce and prevent substance use in different age groups: What works for whom? Systematic review and meta-regression analysis. *Clinical Psychology Review, 44*, 45–59.

Roche, A., Bywood, P., Hughes, C., Freeman, T., Duraisingam, V., Trifonoff, A., ... Steenson, T. (2010). *Final Report to the: Australian Government Department of Education, Employment and Workplace Relations.* National Centre for Education and Training on Addiction.

Rundle-Thiele, S., Schuster, L., Dietrich, T., Drennan, J., Russell-Bennett, R., Leo, C., & Connor, J. (2015). Maintaining or changing a drinking behavior? GOKA's short-term outcomes. *Journal of Business Research, 68*(10), 2155–2163.

Rundle-Thiele, S., Russell-Bennett, R., Leo, C., & Dietrich, T. (2013). Moderating teen drinking: Combining social marketing and education. *Health Education, 113*(5), 392–406.

Stigler, M., Neusel, E., & Perry, C. (2011). School-based programs to prevent and reduce alcohol use among youth. *Alcohol Research & Health, 34*(2), 157–162.

Stead, M., Stradling, R., MacNeil, M., MacKintosh, A., & Minty, S. (2007). Implementation evaluation of the Blueprint multi-component drug prevention programme: Fidelity of school component delivery. *Drug and Alcohol Review, 26*(6), 653–664.

Stock C., Vallentin-Holbech L., Rasmussen B.M. (2016). *The GOOD life:* Study protocol for a social norms intervention to reduce alcohol and other drug use among Danish adolescents. *BMC Public Health, 16*, 704.

Teesson, M., Newton, N., & Barrett, E. (2012). Australian school-based prevention programs for alcohol and other drugs: A systematic review. *Drug and Alcohol Review, 31*(6), 731–736.

Tobler, N., & Stratton, H. (1997). Effectiveness of school-based drug prevention programs: A meta-analysis of the research. *Journal of Primary Prevention, 18*(1), 71–128.

Vallentin-Holbech, L., Rasmussen, B.M., & Stock, C. (2018). Effects of the social norms intervention *The GOOD Life* on norm perceptions, binge drinking and alcohol-related harms: A cluster-randomised controlled trial. *Preventive Medicine Reports, 12*, 304–311. doi: 10.1016/j.pmedr.2018.10.019.

White, D., & Pitts, M. (1998). Educating young people about drugs: A systematic review. *Addiction, 93*(10), 1475–1487.

7 Engaging dissensus
Innovating social change

Marie-Louise Fry, Linda Brennan, and Josephine Previte

Introduction

Alcohol and its consumption across western societies occupies contested space. On the one hand, alcohol signifies leisure, pleasure, and acceptance when consumed in moderation. In fact, the majority of Australians consume alcohol within acceptable limits (AIHW, 2017). Yet when consumed excessively, alcohol signifies condemnation, unacceptability, and disorder. These tensions reflect continual dissent about whether or not alcohol is consonant with health or well-being, what needs to be done, and with whom it needs to be done, or for. Resulting from this contestation is a bifurcated alcohol social change landscape dominated by institutionalised norms that both legitimise and delegitimise potential change opportunities (Kennedy, 2015). For example, alcohol industry 'responsible drinking' campaigns targeting moderate drinking are contested by health stakeholders who question such approaches as credible solutions or a relevant road map for creating a more positive future to a safe drinking culture.

The debate is further exacerbated by the denotation of alcohol, and related consumption activities, as a wicked problem. Wicked problems are highly complex, multifaceted social problems that have human relationships and interactions at their centre (McGregor, 2012). Wicked problems possess multi-layered, incomplete, and contradictory interdependencies making it difficult to define the problem and identify who to target (Kennedy, 2015). Furthermore, the alcohol change landscape comprises multiple and diverse stakeholders who have radically different interpretations for understanding the focal problem and approaching potential solutions (Conklin, 2006). The diversity of interpretations, in turn, results in contestation among stakeholders as to the legitimacy of the goal solution (e.g. addressing moderation or minimising alcohol misuse). Wicked problems are unstructured issues possessing no definitive, stable problem; a definition which suggests that any given solution is merely the best that can be done at the time and will generate further issues (Conklin, 2006). As such, solutions to wicked problems are neither verifiably right or wrong, nor are they complete (CoA, 2012). Additionally, as many stakeholders often perpetuate the problem, or are involved in developing solution opportunities

90 *Marie-Louise Fry et al.*

across multiple levels of influence (including industry, political, legal, health), tackling the problem is beyond the capacity or scope of any *one* organisation to understand and respond (CoA, 2012).

In this chapter, we illustrate how a multisectoral alcohol social change partnership engages a participatory collective intelligence approach to innovate solution opportunities for the wicked problem of alcohol. Collective intelligence offers an approach to engage dissensus across varied stakeholders and decision-makers, each with conflicting values and viewpoints of potential solution opportunities, by encouraging consensus-based logic and reflective negotiations to bring about a collective consciousness to address a complex issue (McCauley et al., 2019). This chapter begins with an overview of key arguments within alcohol social change and then briefly overviews collective intelligence as a collaborative methodology, innovating wicked problem solution opportunities. The participatory research context is then explored using Willis et al.'s (2016) six-phase multisectoral partnership collective intelligence framework. The chapter concludes with reflection on the participatory process harnessing dissensus to innovate alcohol social change.

Dissensus in alcohol social change

The role of the alcohol industry as part of the alcohol solution, rather than as a singular causal factor producing a societal level alcohol problem, occupies contested space. The divide is played out on two sides: those adopting the hard line that industry, as the supplier of alcohol, is the 'tainted enemy' and those who take a more moderate stance towards participatory collaborations of shared understanding to manage and reduce alcohol-related harm (Herrick, 2011). Herein lies the conundrum. While alcohol is a legal product in many countries, no major alcohol industry player can survive in the long term if its reputation becomes linked with the downside of alcohol misuse rather than with the upside of responsible consumption and alcohol enjoyment (Geiger & Cuzzocrea, 2017). Furthermore, the alcohol industry has capability to play a crucial role in limiting the damage caused by alcohol via its investment in corporate social responsibility efforts (Herrick, 2011). Such efforts include commitments to addressing under-age drinking, drink-driving, and harmful drinking, as well as strengthening codes of practice and guiding consumers on responsible consumption (Mialon & McCambridge, 2018).

Public health advocates argue that alcohol industry responsible drinking programs represent no more than another form of self-promotion (Pettigrew et al., 2016), yet both public health advocates and industry responsible drinking programs have been found to share several interrelated assumptions (Pantani et al., 2012). First, there is the assumption that responsible drinking can be learned. Second, how people drink, and in what circumstances, determines whether their experiences are positive or negative. Third, despite well-identified risks, alcohol can also provide benefits to society, including pleasure, enjoyment, celebration, and group bonding (Fry et al., 2014). In this frame, alcohol industry 'responsible drinking' initiatives appreciate that alcohol consumption represents an individual choice: a choice that occurs within a messy social and cultural context (Herrick, 2011).

Third-party organisations, comprising multisectoral partnerships, offer collaborative opportunities to reducing alcohol-related harm by helping people make better choices about their drinking. Multisectoral alcohol change partnerships, such as the International Alliance for Responsible Drinking (UK), the Foundation for Advancing Alcohol Responsibility (USA), Drinks Initiatives (EU), DrinkAware (UK), and DrinkWise (Australia), are non-profit organisations, typically funded at least partially by alcohol organisations, yet are governed independently to address alcohol social change and alcohol education (Pantani et al., 2012). Inherently, these partnerships represent a collective of diverse stakeholder groups (such as police, medical/health, education, politics, as well as food, hospitality, and alcohol sectors), each with conflicting goals and values, yet who are equally equipped and interested in building synergies to co-create new, alternate possible solution opportunities (McGregor, 2012). Yet, the legitimacy of these multisectoral organisations to contribute to alcohol social change is premised on their inclusion of industry as a key stakeholder, and in turn alcohol industry's ability to be trusted.

While not a substitute for individual actions, government responsibilities, and commitments, these partnerships are instrumental for alternate solution outcomes for 'better drinking,' 'responsible drinking,' and 'drinking properly.' By engaging a collective intelligence philosophy, multisectoral partnerships in the alcohol consumption space are transitioning beyond existing programs. Existing programs are constrained by the typologies of risk and harm. The transition is toward previously unexplored solutions – opportunities that can only stem from the diverse collective 'sitting at the table' to discuss, debate, and interrogate the social issue (McCauley et al., 2019). It is clear the extant framing of responsible drinking is at odds and conflicts directly with public health's conceptualisation and positioning of drinking as harmful. Nonetheless, responsible drinking is a credible and relevant alcohol consumption entity which many individuals enact to enjoy the positive, pleasurable, and sociable aspects of this product (Fry, 2011).

Additional dissent concerns alcohol industry influence in alcohol policy development, with critics arguing excessive industry lobbying aims to serve their own political and economic interests (e.g. deterring minimum pricing standards) rather than the health and welfare of society (Mialon & McCambridge, 2018). Interestingly, recent developments at the World Health Organization (WHO) challenge the boundaries of participatory involvement with organisations of a commercial or profit-making nature. Traditionally, WHO has had a long-standing official policy of non-engagement with business interest groups. Yet, more recently, WHO has relaxed this position with development of the Framework of Engagement with Non-State Actors (FENSA) (WHO, 2018) which advocates for stronger private-sector involvement. The framework rules specifically permit non-state actors, that is 'business interest groups' such as the private-sector entities, non-government organisations, philanthropic organisations, and academic institutions, to participate in the governance of and policy development at the WHO albeit with specific guidelines regarding the interaction process. WHO recognises the global health landscape has become more complex, with a significant increase in players in the global health arena who have capability and capacity to contribute to protect and promote public health.

As discussed earlier, tackling wicked problems is beyond any one organisation to either understand and/or respond, including the alcohol industry, public health advocates, government institutions, and other relevant stakeholders. To claim precedence in decision-making and to be 'all knowing' is problematic from a system's perspective. One 'small' change by one protagonist may instigate multiple system-wide changes in consequence. Additionally, alcohol solution opportunities are neither verifiably right nor wrong, nor are they complete (CoA, 2012), suggesting that there is room for positioning 'responsible drinking,' 'drinking properly,' and/or 'better drinking' alongside government risk/harm solutions. Garsten and Jacobsson (2013) argue that corporate actors (in this instance alcohol industry producers, retail outlets, and by default alcohol multisectoral partnerships) are necessary partners of the alcohol wicked problem solution rather than only being considered as the cause of a wide variety of social problems. Garsten and Jacobsson argue for political battles between corporate and wider social interests to be replaced by a post-political consensus-based discourse where corporate/industry actors work together towards a common goal.

Engaging dissensus: Harnessing collective intelligence

Engaging with wicked problems inherently entails examining embedded, complex sets of interactions within an ambiguous, dynamic environment. Wicked problems affect different societal actors and thus by definition require a collective perspective across corporate, public and non-profit stakeholders, and their active involvement in the focal problem discussion, as well as solution opportunities (Camillus, 2008). Collective intelligence represents a methodology that brings together relevant stakeholders from different backgrounds and sectors to work collaboratively, and importantly engage in a process of critical learning, reflection, and argumentation, to reach consensus on how to best address a complex issue (McCauley et al., 2019). Deliberative discussions and reflective negotiations underpin collective intelligence. Stakeholders are required to evaluate their views, consider alternative perspectives, and critically to identify known and 'unknown' knowledge gaps. Collective intelligence harnesses dissensus by encouraging engagement in consensus-based logic and reflective negotiations to bring about collective consciousness to innovate wicked problem solution opportunities (McCauley et al., 2019). Collective intelligence, as such, is founded on the principle of mutual value where

Engaging dissensus 93

collective intelligence across diverse entities is far greater than intelligence of independent stakeholders.

Undertaking to solve wicked problems is to embrace social complexity which requires new understandings across all relevant stakeholders and influencers to be included in solution decision-making, whether they are key players or peripherally involved (Conklin, 2006). It is not whether the team comes up with the right answer, but whose buy-in they have, and which perspectives are at the table that really matters. Thus, without including all key stakeholders in the decision-making process, solution opportunities remain biased in favour of a specific solution agenda, and importantly unchallenged, by not engaging a dialogue inclusive of all potential parties associated with the wicked social issue. Worse, a lack of inclusion in decision-making ensures that parties can become antagonistic to each other, conducting the equivalent of social warfare where mutually exclusive solutions become more and more impossible to achieve.

DrinkWise *How to drink properly*: Challenging the alcohol social change space

This qualitative case study illustrates how a multisectoral partnership – DrinkWise and their *How to drink properly* (HTDP) initiative – engages participatory collective intelligence processes to innovate alcohol social change opportunities. This case study was informed by a range of HTDP secondary data provided by DrinkWise (qualitative and quantitative market research evaluations), as well as interviews conducted with members of the DrinkWise Board, commissioned advertising agency personnel, market research organisations, and DrinkWise employees (with direct excerpts from board members denoted in italics). A significant body of literature also underpins the research. This case study explores the tensions the multisectoral DrinkWise partnership had to address, and continues to address, to legitimise themselves as an alcohol social change organisation. Additionally, the case study explores the collective intelligence process underpinning development of the HTDP initiative.

The case study analysis is underpinned by Willis et al.'s (2016) collective intelligence framework for multisectoral partnerships involving the six phases of: (a) prioritising needs, (b) evidence mapping, (c) using relevant methods and tools, (d) analysing and synthesising data, (e) feedback to multisectoral partners, and (f) taking action. Willis' framework is used because it is relatively 'simple' to convey, and it encapsulates the necessary phases of a collaborative enterprise. It also incorporates elements of meso- and micro-level decision-making that permit consideration of upstream and downstream social marketing strategy development. Importantly, Willis' work reviewed thousands of articles on key success factors in multisectorial partnerships, and the resultant framework is both theoretically well founded and practically useful. There are other excellent collective intelligence frameworks extant in the social marketing discipline such as that emerging from the Sea Change theme of research by Domegan, McHugh, and others (2013–2019 cited elsewhere in this chapter). Those

94 Marie-Louise Fry et al.

frameworks operate at a macro-societal level of change; consequently, the Willis framework was adopted for this meso–micro-level case study.

Prioritising needs

Prioritisation refers to refining multisectoral partnership needs and aims. The process of prioritisation validates the road map for social change, ensuring accountability, engagements, and shared understanding guiding social change opportunities.

Given industry inclusivity embodies a controversial alcohol social change model, DrinkWise recognised the need to manage tensions between legitimacy as an alcohol social change operator and criticism as a 'puppet of the alcohol industry', with various strategies enacted. The DrinkWise Board of Directors possess expertise and skill across influential alcohol change sectors inclusive of *regulating agencies* (e.g. law enforcement, government, education, health, and occupational health and well-being), as well as *challenger organisations* (e.g. alcohol industry member trade associations and alcohol producers) (McHugh et al., 2018).

Ensuring internal governance accountability, DrinkWise's Board constitutionally requires fourteen members, with eight representing community/regulator interests (e.g. health, law, policy, research) and six representing industry/challenger interests (e.g. alcohol producers, alcohol retailers, peak body representatives). Consequently, the governance structure controls the power of voices whereby an industry view can never prevail if, or when, there is conflict with the community view. This Board structure provides for a multisectoral perspective on identifying what key priorities exist within the alcohol social change space. DrinkWise regularly commissions academic and market research to ensure that there is consistent tracking of 'market' dynamics, as well as (re) calibration of priorities according to changes in the environment. In addition, DrinkWise continually monitor health and well-being research, such as that provided by the Australian Institute of Health and Welfare (AIHW), the Australian Bureau of Statistics, the Foundation for Alcohol Research and Education, and the Australian Drug Foundation, to ensure that DrinkWise's priorities align with societal expectations and current trends.

Navigating the tension of an industry-funded organisation, DrinkWise identifies its board's expert diversity as a strength. Industry/challenger representation not only enables industry to positively contribute to their social responsibility to "do something about addressing alcohol abuse and that's an ongoing responsibility, not a short-term fix" but enables DrinkWise to leverage industry acumen, capabilities, and perspectives in the context of alcohol social change with comprehensive understanding of "those consumers who are audiences for our core branding messages who are, of course, also the same audience for DrinkWise messages." Community/regulator members, while recognising potential risks of their membership, strongly believe arguments suggesting that "industry has no part in [alcohol change] is a simplistic idealistic approach" and as "governments alone are not going to solve the problem." DrinkWise has capability to address alcohol social change in ways that government cannot.

Engaging a diversity of viewpoints, values, and perspectives acknowledges mutual dissensus as a natural part of DrinkWise's alcohol social change decision-making culture. Yet, any tensions that may exist are reconciled by a governance structure ensuring accountability, engagement, and shared understanding to guide alcohol social change innovations to:

(a) Bring about a healthier, safer Australian drinking culture
(b) Address generational change in the way Australians consume alcohol
(c) Address behaviour change over long periods of time across diverse groups (see Figure 7.1)
(d) Engage a sustained, multifaceted, and inclusive approach to bring about positive change.

Thus, regardless of independent interests and influence (e.g. regulator versus challenger), DrinkWise represents a cooperative multi-stakeholder setting which over time has resulted in an ongoing process of learning and meta-reflections, evaluating risk and benefit potentials to build shared value and collegial approach to innovating alcohol social change.

Evidence mapping

Evidence mapping refers to prioritising key areas of the wicked issue to address. The prioritisation is underpinned by robust understanding of the alcohol issue (e.g. young adult's drinking, parent's influence on children's drinking). DrinkWise constitutionally requires all initiatives be developed from a broad, yet relevant, evidence base to harness deep insight into the behavioural ecology of drinking – values, attitudes, behaviours, and cultural drivers – influencing the alcohol consumption issue under investigation. Integrating a behavioural–ecological perspective enables DrinkWise to view individuals as actors within a complex social system and of behaviour change as operating as a social interaction between actors within a dynamic and interactive market system. Importantly, the value of embedding behavioural–ecological evidence mapping to developing initiatives enables DrinkWise to "find a space that it could legitimately play in first, but also wasn't cluttered and where DrinkWise can play its most influential role." For example, the HTDP initiative came about as a result of broad research and the realisation that young people's alcohol behaviours were being addressed by social media campaigns; however, many of the current approaches were largely ineffectual. The DrinkWise scope sits squarely on addressing alcohol consumption issues yet does so within a governance structure that guides relational agency to bring about positive alcohol social change. In this way, DrinkWise positions safe and healthier drinking practices within a cultural space that aims to empower rather than disempower young drinkers in making more positive alcohol consumption choices.

96 Marie-Louise Fry et al.

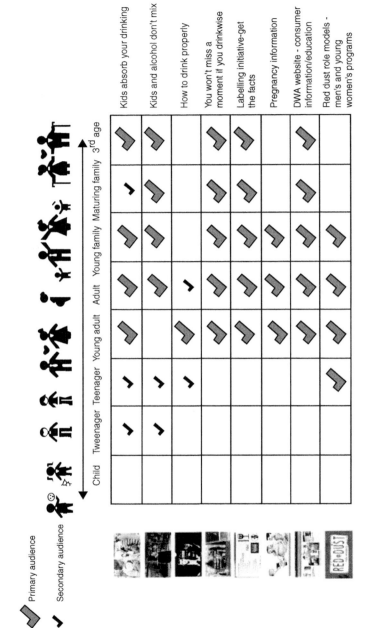

Figure 7.1 DrinkWise target audience matrix.

Engaging dissensus 97

Table 7.1 Multiple stakeholders informed the design of the HTDP campaign

Stakeholder	Source
Health	Expert panel, board members
Community	Board members, market research
Policing	Board members
Individuals	Market research
Government	Expert panel, board members
Industry	Board members
Anti-alcohol campaigners	Academic research and position papers
Media	Market research

DrinkWise draws on a variety of evidence across the system, ranging from commissioned research to academic reviews, as well as evidence reported from entities such as Australian Institute of Health and Welfare (AIHW), Alcohol and Drug Foundation (ADF), and Foundation for Alcohol Research and Education (FARE). In extending organisational resources to manage and map the breadth of insight used to inform its social change approach and campaigns, DrinkWise also has an expert advisory panel in addition to the multisectoral board membership. The expert advisory panel draws evidence from a variety of resources and stakeholders to guide alcohol social change initiatives. For the HTDP campaign, research with young people was an integral component in design and development. The system of stakeholders in the behaviour ecology consulted for this case study is presented in Table 7.1.

Methods and tools

Methods and tools refer to gathering relevant data. For HTDP, methods involved a multi-pronged behavioural–ecological approach, gathering information at various levels across the alcohol behavioural ecology (see, for example, Brennan, Previte, & Fry, 2016).

While national statistics yield evidence about alcohol trends, DrinkWise identified scant evidence examining sociocultural and group socialisation influences on young adults' alcohol consumption. Searching for an innovative space to position a responsible drinking campaign, DrinkWise commissioned external research to harness understanding of the social realities of a young adult's drinking journey.

An Australian market research organisation, with expertise in behavioural and cultural trend analytics, was commissioned to conduct HTDP formative and impact evaluation research. The formative research integrated qualitative and quantitative methods, as well as leveraging key attitudinal and behavioural insights into young Australian's drinking behaviour. Topics included: (i) perceptions of self–identity, role of social groups, and drinking environments in self-regulating binge-drinking behaviours; (ii) deep understanding of current

98 Marie-Louise Fry et al.

attitudes and behaviours; segmentation based on attitudes to drinking excessively; (iii) exploring attitudes towards getting drunk, irresponsible drinking, and responsible drinking; and (iv) evaluating types of messaging that could be leveraged to better target young adults' attitudes to irresponsible drinking. Campaign impact evaluation research assessed campaign outcomes on completion of HTDP phase 1 and HTDP phase 2.

While attitudinal and behavioural research provided valuable insight into individual alcohol behaviour, what was missing was nuanced insight into the sociocultural drivers associated with young adults' drinking journeys and the influence of friendship groups on alcohol decision-making. A bespoke consumer insights agency was commissioned to examine the social realities of young adult's alcohol consumption within and among friendship groups. Particular attention was directed to uncover an insight into how drinking decisions are influenced by people's frame of mind, the people they inherently are (identities), and interaction with their environment. The goal was to identify key influencers, understand the underlying trigger points of irresponsible and responsible decision-making, and detect fundamental phases of behaviour by exploring and deconstructing the journey of a 'night out.' The objective of the research was to understand core emotional and environmental prompts that might present opportunities to disrupt binge-drinking behaviours of 18- to 24-year olds.

The research method utilised triangulation; integrating qualitative ethnographic exploration among friendship triads, non-friendship triads, as well as individual in-depth interviews. Triangulating multiple data points to capture the realities of alcohol consumption was pivotal for the bespoke consumer insights agency to "get to the crux of the issue" ensuring harnessing of "sensitive insight with multiple social, environmental and personal layers." For example, integrating an

> ethnographic lens examining personal factors and social factors allowed us to truly understand what is happening in the moment identifying core environmental drivers. Friendship triads allowed us to explore through the lens of peer group dynamics uncovering social dynamics and influences, as well as understanding relevance of message platforms to shift behaviour. Group discussions were used to explore the topic and messaging territories from individual perspectives.

The strategic integration of the behavioural–ecological mapping process facilitated DrinkWise in adopting a more holistic view of behaviour change where the sociality of consumption is central to transforming behaviour and where individuals are viewed as actors in a complex market system.

Analysing and synthesising data

Analysing and synthesising data refers to harnessing *insight* or discovery of deep meaning from consumer's experiences, networks of interactions, co-created

Engaging dissensus 99

outcomes, and practices in relation to the social issue. Fundamentally, insight is that 'pivotal piece of understanding' into the target audience – that 'aha' or 'eureka' moment – that enables discovery of what moves and motivates people. Insight leads to specific opportunities for leveraging exchange value (French et al., 2010). Synthesising the HTDP behavioural–ecological mapping evidence of the social realities of young adult's drinking journeys uncovered the following key insights:

- Reputational risk and personal standing within a peer group is paramount; too much forgiving of irresponsible drinking leads to eventual isolation due to peer group rejection and exclusion. That is, it is not OK to get drunk. It is not OK to encourage others to get drunk either. Such behaviours will eventually lead to exclusion from the group.
- Young adults have a good understanding of responsible and irresponsible drinking behaviour. A *responsible drinker* is 'self-aware,' 'mature,' and 'balanced'; knows limits and controls their drinking (e.g. consumes water, pre-sets limits) ensuring they do not cross a self-imposed 'point of no return.' An *irresponsible drinker* is 'careless,' 'embarrassing,' and 'immature'; gets 'messy, sloppy, out of control'; does not care about drinking limits and continues to drink even if others have suggested they stop drinking.
- Alcohol socialisation is tribal; influenced and contextualised within and across friendship groups; peers act as a barometer for drinking behaviour and as a justification for drinking habits (excessive and moderate drinking behaviour).
- It is not that young adults do not know about moderate drinking or do not desire to do so, but rather that they do not have the social permission to moderate.
- Drinking messages need to identify a better way to drink rather than say 'stop' drinking.

These insights were evaluated by DrinkWise throughout the development of the campaign. First, the expert advisory panel was consulted as to their position on a potential messaging strategy that was counter to existing campaigns and likely to be very controversial. Second, the funding for such a campaign was substantial and required board decision-making before embarking on design elements. Third, market research with key audiences (see Table 7.1) was undertaken to ensure authentic representation of perspectives. Subsequently, insights from these stakeholder groups were used to iterate, via multiple conversations, the proposed solution in consultation with community, board members, and academic experts. The outcome was then prototyped and tested for effectiveness and veracity with young adults before being 'launched.' Important to this process was the number of people willing to provide permission to others to do something different and to be personally uncomfortable as a result. By listening to insights from others and sharing the collective's perspectives, stakeholders shifted their own perspectives away from non-controversial but relatively

100 *Marie-Louise Fry et al.*

ineffective fear-based campaigns using traditional media towards a highly controversial and relatively more effective social media campaign.

Feedback to multisectoral partners

The HTDP evidence mapping process was conducted over an 18-month period. During this period, DrinkWise staff participatory interactions entailed an ongoing process of feedback learning and meta-reflections, evaluating risk and potential benefits of the evidence data, and commissioning further research as required. Implicit during this learning process is the 'continual learning' philosophy (Willis et al., 2016), involving a circular process of synthesising the diversity of evidence to shape and understand the alcohol issue.

Coincident with the synthesis of existing evidence was the alignment of new learning and requests for new evidence as key gaps in 'understanding' emerged, all of which, as a consequence, shifted the direction in thinking about how to innovate alcohol social change. The stakeholder interactions were undertaken discursively, according to the evidence base. The market research interactions and advertising specialist exchanges yielded a learning process that expanded extant patterns of thinking. These interactions employed a collaborative approach which centred on addressing organisational aims and which generated meta-insights for DrinkWise. These meta-insights allowed the development of an alcohol social change strategy targeting 'drinking properly' based on three key territories:

- *Loading and control* signifies knowing personal limits and avoiding out of control states.
- *Reputation and belonging* refers to the 'consequences' and 'social risk' of binge drinking.
- *Empowerment* which enables young adults to make responsible drinking choices resulting in group acceptance and inclusion in future social occasions.

During the interaction process, stakeholders became increasingly aware of how they could contribute their stakeholder resources and capabilities to cooperatively develop an innovative alcohol social change opportunity. For example, industry use of digital spaces presented an insight into consideration of social media opportunities. A key outcome of stakeholder participatory interactions was the development of shared agreement regarding the alcohol social change innovation (e.g. creative imagery, media strategy, use of artificial intelligence in message development). Yet, this process was not without tensions, with community stakeholder perspectives requiring an ongoing process of reconciliation given the unconventional nature of HTDP. For example, the use of profanity and radical creative executions necessitated challenging and robust debates and discussions among board members evaluating market and reputational risks of the campaign itself and for the organisation DrinkWise.

Action

Action refers to aligning new learning into practice and performance, which for HTDP involved: (1) creating the *'drinking properly'* brand and (2) influencing change within the actual drinking context –that is, within the social ecology of the behaviour.

Creating the 'drinking properly' brand: The creative challenge for HTDP was to empower young adults to make positive, informed alcohol consumption choices; stem intoxication by breaking entrenched habits and influence social attitudes towards responsibility, and especially to 'speak with' young adults, rather than 'talk at' them. This required acceptance that young adults' social ecology and therefore their lived experiences include alcohol consumption. The HTDP campaign addresses the "presence of thinking about what you do" when drinking rather than "absence of drinking."

After testing multiple message concepts, HTDP imagery was positively evaluated, as it maintained a tone of 'knowing wisdom' that does not slip into prohibitionist nagging, and at the same time leveraged a relevant, compelling, aspirational, yet mature behaviour of 'drinking better, not hard.' The central character exudes James Bond sophistication, is charming, and interweaves sophistication yet with a touch of vernacular crass (Figure 7.2). The classic black-and-white execution leverages the semiotics of classiness, simultaneously creating marketplace differentiation from other anti-alcohol messages. Video clip background music, commissioned specifically, contributed a sophisticated funky, cool jazz element. The fluid script typeface signifies an ongoing conversation, interjected with a bold call out to specific words.

Building on the insights from the behavioural research mapping, HTDP integrated controversial language relevant to the cohort's everyday vernacular, especially when socialising with peers, to heighten message cut-through. Language integration was carefully considered to ensure maximum effect. There was deliberate selection of profanities in current usage by the cohort.

Figure 7.2 How to drink properly character and tag line.

102 Marie-Louise Fry et al.

Table 7.2 HTDP print creative examples

"DRINK PROPERLY. It's Classy as Fuck" (t-shirt)	DIGNITY. Learn how to keep it. (poster)
ORDER YOUR SCOTCH WITH A SIDE OF WATER. Because it's classy as fuck. (bar mat)	Learn how to drink AND MAINTAIN YOUR AIM. (Bathroom)
Drink CLASSY, bitches.	There's a time for SLOPPY DRINKING. It's called never. (coaster)
Sober can be classy, A VOMIT BEARD cannot.	Might I recommend A WATER before reapplying that eyeliner. (bathroom)

Figure 7.3 Drinks coaster.

Thus, while HTDP language maybe viewed as controversial, and even radical by some (see Table 7.2), its application is strategic, for example, see Figure 7.3.

Influencing social change within the drinking context: HTDP was specifically designed as a social media campaign. The choice of social media leveraged the behavioural environment, acknowledging young adults' transition to social media as a primary form of social communication. Social media enables in-situ, real-time communications enabling individuals to respond immediately to stimuli within their immediate sphere and within the drinking context. Rather than simply targeting one media channel, HTDP integrated multiple channels (YouTube, Facebook, Twitter, Snapchat, Instagram) to engage the audience with different messages across different platforms at different times throughout the drinking journey night. This required significant investment in advertising personnel uploading content contemporaneously with young people socialising. The shareability potential of social media for behaviour change has immense capacity to promulgate consumer-to-consumer exchanges, spreading and diffusing content that peaks interest among young adults, their peers, and ultimately between peer groups at rapid speed.

Ensuring cohesion between social media channels was critical, especially considering audience engagement across multiple channels at any one time. Consequently, a multifaceted, continuing process of developing bespoke content for particular channels was undertaken evidencing commitment to planning, constant interrogation ensuring the creative 'hits the mark,' as well as alignment of content across integrated social media channels. Additionally, the uniqueness of messages to particular channels engaged interest in HTDP initiative across channels while simultaneously assisted in reducing message wear-out.

At each stage of the campaign, multiple partners were involved in co-creating value, from initiation (prioritisation) and design to execution (action) and evaluation (feedback). The formative research (evidence mapping) provided the foundation for recognition of the unique capabilities of DrinkWise within the complex and contested alcohol consumption space (analysis and synthesis). That is, what could DrinkWise do that might not, or could not, be done by others (e.g. government, alcohol producers, or anti-alcohol campaigners)? Prioritising young people using social media with humorous profanity (methods and tools) was highly contentious and engaged significant stakeholder debate, concurrently sharing learnings (feedback) and developing respect for alternative points of view.

Moving forward

Multisectoral partnerships for complex health issues are not new, yet our understanding of these types of partnerships is limited. While the role of industry in policymaking is an issue fraught with power imbalance implications, the role of industry in resolving problems that they participate in creating is, as yet, effectively unexplored. As Dibb (2014) argues, industry involvement in the development of alcohol change opportunities represents a shift in how complex social problems are solved, particularly as private-sector collaborations have value in their capability to inject large amounts of capital, to contribute exceptional managerial skills, and ability to take a long-term business approach.

Nonetheless, the question remains: are alcohol industries a valid partner within the alcohol social change space? The current entrenched and bifurcated divide suggests not. This chapter does not argue that there is no place for articulation of the harms and risks of alcohol consumption, but it does argue there is a place for alcohol industry to further develop and reinforce a responsible drinking culture. Particularly, as in a free-choice environment, such as the adult use of alcohol, choice architects need to be cognisant of the right to autonomy, self-determination, and the reflexivity of citizens (Esmark, 2017), which are highly valued by participants. Efforts to engender social change that do not account for free choice are unlikely to succeed.

104   *Marie-Louise Fry et al.*

As a solution, this chapter presents a participatory collective intelligence social change framework to innovate alcohol social change opportunities. Underpinning the collective intelligence process is a partnership philosophy (McHugh et al., 2018). Participatory collective intelligence involves the engagement of all the entities and people that contribute to a problem, as well as those who are in a position to invest their capabilities and resources into seeking potential alternatives and implementing and evaluating solutions. Collective intelligence approaches present opportunities to co-create new ways of being, ways in which bifurcated ideological warfare does not form the basis of engagement with the issue. The approach does not necessarily involve consensus decision-making, although it does seek harmonious interactions between actors in the co-creation system. Participatory collective intelligence requires the creation of safe dialogic spaces, whereby stakeholders feel that they are actively creating a new and better future and that they are being heard. The management of imbalanced power relations is a critical component in creating a safe conversation environment for dissensus decision-making (McHugh et al., 2013). This requires harnessing (encouraging, exploiting, and applying) the dissent of all parties in order to create a consensual outcome. This also means being open to, listening to, and making accommodations for different perspectives and positions, regardless of ideology. Importantly, participatory collective intelligence necessitates granting permission for all affected parties within the system to engage with solution finding – something that is currently missing in the alcohol consumption debate. In participatory collective intelligence, permission to participate in problem solving does not imply capitulation or acquiescence by any of the parties but rather implies partnership in the journey to creating a better future.

DrinkWise extends alcohol social change strategic thinking beyond dyadic exchanges towards systems collaborations where multiple, disparate partners at various levels of the alcohol system share knowledge, experiences, expertise, and mobilise value co-creating communities to shape the social context of alcohol behaviour change. Working in multisectoral partnerships, beyond traditional silos, enables new insight and perspectives on previously held assumptions, ideas, and values enabling opportunity to co-create, co-discover, and co-deliver innovate social change opportunities (Domegan et al., 2013). In turn, these social change innovations have capability, over time, to influence institutional, cultural, and individual norms (Kennedy, 2015).

Critically, a natural element of multisectoral partnerships is the existence and engagement of dissensus – engaging with the tension or conflict – between partners. The more parties involved in a collaboration, the more different those parties are, the more diverse, and the more socially complex. As such, the greater the potential for the collective intelligence to result in understandings of shared dissensus, alongside points of shared consensus. Prioritising social change protocols ensures a road map for stakeholder participation guiding the social change innovation while simultaneously enabling contribution of diverse insights, expertise, and experiences. Engaging dissensus is to encourage debate, meta-reflections, and continuing dialogue between partners enabling a voice at the social change table, rather than suppression of tension. As a result, a process of aligning new learning enables solution opportunities based on joint resolution with positive benefit yet may not be perfect across individual stakeholders. The right to dissent is deeply embedded in the concept of collective intelligence. A safe space to challenge and be challenged is necessary for co-created outcomes. The acknowledgement of other points of view is a necessary first step in finding a compromise position. This is said bearing in mind that a compromise might mean that no one is happy with the final outcome, but that everyone can live with an arrangement if it means that the 'war is finally over.'

Despite decades of alcohol research, alcohol misuse remains on the agenda as a seemingly intractable wicked problem. Rather than continuing to effect social change within a disparate conflictual landscape, we argue the future of effective alcohol social change lies in harnessing dissensus by valuing the contribution from and within multisectoral partnerships where a collective intelligence social change framework innovates social change opportunities. Industry has been characterised as a pathogen inserted into an ecological system (Wymer, 2011). Yet this is not quite the right metaphor for alcohol as people welcome alcohol into their lives and experience positive associations from its consumption. Inclusion of alcohol industry as an alcohol social change partner will, of necessity, require uncommon, or at least infrequent conversations in the social marketing domain because key thought leaders such as Gerard Hastings (2007) shape such conversations, or social change planning, as 'dancing with the Devil.' However, this chapter argues that at least understanding the Devil's perspective might be necessary if we want to shift the lens from individual behavioural change to broader understanding of market systems social change. Compartmentalising alcohol change stakeholders into 'good' and 'bad' limits the ability to develop collaborative co-created solutions to wicked problems. All stakeholder views are necessary inputs in creating positive, mutually agreed, system-wide outcomes. This inescapably creates a conundrum for social marketers as in order to effect systemic change there need to be a shift in nomenclature from behaviour change to social change. Specifically, we argue for a reflexive and collective turn inclusive of industry as a relevant and necessary alcohol social change partner.

References

Australian Institute of Health and Welfare (2017). *National Drug Strategy Household Survey 2016: Detailed findings*. Drug Statistics series no. 31. Cat. no. PHE 214. Canberra: AIHW.

Brennan, L., Previte, J., & Fry, M.-L. (2016). Social marketing's consumer myopia: Embracing a systems view of social change markets. *Journal of Social Marketing*, 6(4), 219–239.

Camillus, J.C. (2008). Strategy as a wicked problem. *Harvard Business Review*, 86(5), 98–106.

CoA, Commonwealth of Australia (2012). *Tackling Wicked Problems: A Public Policy Perspective*, accessed 15 March 2019, available at www.apsc.gov.au/tackling-wicked-problems-public-policy-perspective.

Conklin, J. (2006). *Dialogue Mapping. Building Shared Understanding of Wicked Problems.* New York: Wiley.

Dibb, S. (2014). Up, up and away: Social marketing breaks free. *Journal of Marketing Management,* 30(11–12), 1159–1185.

Domegan, C., Collins, K., Stead, M., McHugh, P. & Hughes, T. (2013). Value co-creation in social marketing: Functional or fanciful? *Journal of Social Marketing,* 3(3), 239–256.

Domegan, C., McHugh, P., Biroscak, B. J., Bryant, C., & Calis, T. (2017). Non-linear causal modelling in social marketing for wicked problems. *Journal of Social Marketing,* 7(3), 305–329.

Esmark A. (2017). Nudging as a policy instrument. How choice architects pursue health, wealth and happiness in the information age. *ICCP3 Innovative governance and the governance of change.* Singapore: International Public Policy Association, 1–31. Available from: www.ippapublicpolicy.org/file/paper/594bba19efb01.pdf.

French, J., Blair-Stevens, C., McVey, D., & Merritt, R. (2010). *Social Marketing and Public Health: Theory and Practice.* Oxford: Oxford University Press.

Fry, M.L., Drennan, J., Previte, J., White, A., & Tjondronegoro, D. (2014). The role of desire in understanding intentions to drink responsibly: An application of the Model of Goal Directed Behaviou. *Journal of Marketing Management,* 30(5–6), 551–570.

Fry, M.L. (2011). Discourses of consumer's alcohol resistant identities. *Journal of Nonprofit and Public Sector Marketing,* 23(4), 348–366.

Garsten, C., & Jacobsson, K. (2013). Post-political regulation: Soft power and post-political visions in global governance. *Critical Sociology,* 39(3), 421–37.

Geiger, B.B., & Cuzzocrea, V. (2017). Corporate social responsibility and conflicts of interest in the alcohol and gambling industries: A post-political discourse. *The British Journal of Sociology,* 68(2), 254–272.

Hastings, G. (2007). *Social Marketing: Why Should the Devil Have All the Best Tunes?* London: Routledge.

Hastings, G., & Domegan, C. (2013). *Social Marketing: From Tunes to Symphonies.* Oxford: Butterworth-Heinemann.

Herrick, C. (2011). Why we need to think beyond the "industry" in alcohol research and policy studies. *Drugs: Education, Prevention and Policy,* 18(1), 10–15.

Kennedy, A.M. (2015). Macro-social marketing. *Journal of Macromarketing,* 36(3), 354–365.

McCauley, V., McHugh, P., Davison, K., & Domegan, C. (2019). Collective intelligence for advancing ocean literacy. *Environmental Education Research.* https://doi.org/10.1080/13504622.2018.1553234.

McGregor, S.L.T. (2012). Complexity economics, wicked problems and consumer education. *International Journal of Consumer Studies,* 36(3), 310–321.

McHugh, P., & Domegan, C. (2013). From autocratic governance to collaborative empowerment: A social marketing approach to the co-creation of policy. *Contemporary Issues in Social Marketing.* England: Cambridge Scholars, 78–94.

McHugh, P., Domegan, C., & Duane, S. (2018). Protocols for stakeholder participation in social marketing systems. *Social Marketing Quarterly,* 24(3), 164–193.

Mialon, M., & McCambridge, J. (2018). Alcohol industry corporate social responsibility initiatives and harmful drinking: A systematic review. *European Journal of Public Health*, 28(4): 664–673.

Pantani, D., Sparks, R., Sanchez, Z.M., & Pinsky, I. (2012). Responsible drinking programs and the alcohol industry in Brazil: Killing two birds with one stone. *Social Science and Medicine*, 75, 1387–1391.

Pettigrew, M., Fitzgerald, N., Durand, M.A., Knal, C., Favoren, M., & Perry, I. (2016). Diago's "Stop out of control drinking" Campaign in Ireland: An analysis. *PLOS ONE*, doi: 10.1371/journal.pone.0160379.

WHO (2018, World Health Organization). Engagement with non-State actors (FENSA): Report by the Director General. Retrieved from www.who.int/about/collaborations-and-partnerships/who-s-engagement-with-non-state-actors.

Willis, C.D., Greene, J.K., Abramowicz, A., & Riley, B.L. (2016). Strengthening the evidence and action on multi-sectoral partnerships in public health: An action research initiative. *Health Promotion and Chronic Disease Prevention in Canada*, 36(6): 101–111.

Wymer, W. (2011). Developing more effective social marketing strategies. *Journal of Social Marketing*, 1(1): 17–31.

8 Stakeholder analysis in a systems setting

An Active Travel case study in Ireland

Christine Domegan, Patricia McHugh, Dmitry Brychkov, and Fiona Donovan

> Four young fish were swimming across the lake one day, when they met an older fish swimming in the other direction. The old fish nodded at the youngsters as he passed and said 'Good morning, boys, the water is lovely today, isn't it?' The four young fish were well raised, so politely replied 'Yes the water is lovely, sir, thank you'. They swam on in silence for a couple of minutes, then one young fish looked over at another and asked; 'What the hell is water?'

Introduction

David Foster Wallace first wrote his fish story in 2008. Wallace explains that the point of his fish story is that the most ubiquitous and powerful influences on our behaviours are those closest to us – the ones we take for granted, do not even realise are there and cannot discuss or describe. Our immediate environment and the stakeholders around us are to us as the water is to the young fish, and it has an equally powerful impact on our lives whether we realise it or not. However deep we dig in our bid to understand the current and desired behaviour change in social marketing, we will not get a full picture unless we recognise the importance of all of the stakeholders in the systems we are living in with all its political, cultural, social, technological, and economic characteristics. All of us are influenced by the circumstances in which we find ourselves. We constantly react to the individuals and people in organisations that we meet in our daily lives. All sorts of stakeholders in the various systems we engage with throughout any given day influence us and our behaviours. Importantly for social marketers, stakeholders influence the success of behaviour change interventions in a system. It is as important to

Stakeholder analysis in a systems setting   109

think about wider-scale change, organisational and stakeholder transformation as it is to think about individual citizen behaviours. Change co-creation has to be multifaceted, multilevel, and involve multiple stakeholders when it comes to complex wicked problems, challenges of the tragedy of the commons, and global-to-local sustainability issues. This chapter presents the application of systems thinking to analyse stakeholders in a systems setting to go beyond the usual stakeholder tools and descriptive insights. Using classic stakeholder theory augmented with macromarketing and systems thinking, this chapter illustrates how an understanding of the dynamics of stakeholders is important to address the stakes of stakeholders who are involved in the system. Using an Irish Active Travel case study, the results highlight the need for holistic approaches to complex and wicked problems, involving multiple stakeholders at multiple levels. This chapter also highlights the key research tasks to co-ordinate and integrate societal stakeholder and public engagement to move towards the collective identification of needs and development of consensus-based solutions, based on multicausal assumptions, paradigms, methods, and methodologies.

The importance of stakeholders in a systems setting

Stakeholders in a systems setting have never been more important due to the increasingly interconnected nature of the world. Many complex problems that social marketers tackle "encompass or affect numerous people, groups and organizations ... where no one is fully in charge ... instead many individuals, groups and organizations are involved or affected or have some partial responsibility to act" (Bryson, 2004, pp. 23–24). This holds for wicked problems such as obesity, smoking, alcohol, and HIV/AIDS in health and air/water quality, conservation, species extinction, and climate action in the environmental domain.

The classic and most commonly used definition of stakeholders comes from Freeman's (1984) seminal work *Strategic Management: A Stakeholder Approach*. Here, stakeholders are "any group or individual who can affect or is affected by the achievement of the organization's objectives" (Freeman, 1984, p. 46). When originally conceived by Freeman, the concept applied to a firm or corporation and included employees, suppliers, shareholders, and trade unions for example. Freeman (2017) in his recent writings strongly advocates for the gravitation of stakeholder theory towards a societal perspective. Managing for stakeholders not shareholders encompasses social values, aspects of ethics, and morality. Freeman is not alone (note some argue that Freeman's prime focus is still the business organisation and the evolution of capitalism). That said, there is an explosion in stakeholder literature in numerous social value domains such as macromarketing, social marketing, and systems thinking, for example, Peterson (2013); Laczniak and Murphy (2012); Werhane (2008; 2011); and Geels (2004,

2005). The call is for a move away from an organisation-centric stakeholder analysis with its goods-dominant logic where stakeholder analysis is descriptive, and stakeholders are treated as operand resources to be managed. Based on the foundation laid by Freeman, the movement is towards a holistic orientation that embraces the multiplicity of diverse stakeholders. In practice, this understanding of stakeholders has evolved to the point where it translates into a system of stakeholders; a dispersed spectrum of individuals; and/or groups with common and not so common interests across geographical, political, resource, or social boundaries and across subsystems. This is akin to the service-dominant logic where every stakeholder (or actor) is an operant resource (associated with human skills and knowledge) and 'producer of effects' in a system (or service ecosystem) (Vargo and Lusch, 2018).

To understand stakeholders in a system, let us briefly turn our attention to the concept of a system and its meaning. The word 'system' derives from the Greek word *sistema* meaning *syn* ('together') and *histanai* ('to set'), giving us 'to set together.' This encourages a holistic lens not a reductionist one that recognises the interrelationships and the interdependences of the parts or elements of a system (Senge, 1990).

Systems can be biological (e.g. digestive or circularity system in the body), physical (e.g. a car or plane), or social (e.g. a family or organisation). From a social marketing perspective, a system is made up of networks of stakeholders, connected in a *structure (markets, governance, rules, organisation)* and engaged in *processes (value-based exchange, relationships, trust, conflict, communication)*, which allows for the performance of specific *functions (delivery, services, technology, partnerships)* in an *environment (context, country)* outside the *system boundary* (Figure 8.1). The system boundary is permeable to *inputs* from and *outputs* to the environment (Bossel, 1999).

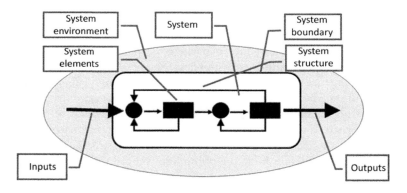

Figure 8.1 A system of stakeholders.
Source: Bossel (1999).

Stakeholder analysis in a systems setting 111

For example, a national transport system will consist of an extensive set of infrastructural elements, including roads, links, routes, corridors, areas, networks, (air)ports, and other facilities for multimodal transportation (e.g. car, bus, rail, plane, riverboat, ship, etc.) (Australian Transport Council, 2006). It will include private and public operators as well as commercial and non-commercial customers. A city transport system will incorporate cycle lanes and walkways to complement the road, rail, bus, airport, and port networks. Each of these transport networks form subsystems in their own right, meaning there are networks of stakeholders embedded within other stakeholder subsystems or higher order systems; systems and their stakeholders can be a part of another system or connected to adjacent systems (e.g. transport and land use are closely related systems).

A broadened holistic stakeholders system perspective assembles a top-down/bottom-up collective, (e.g. policy makers, regulators, local authorities, representatives of industry, professional associations, sectorial groups, consumer, and civil associations), bringing together different groups of people to generate value (Kennedy et al., 2017; Brennan, Previte, & Fry, 2016; Kennedy and Parsons, 2012). This type of stakeholder interrelatedness acknowledges the macro–micro multiple webs and chains of stakeholder groups simultaneously affect and are affected by the efforts of other stakeholders in a system (Hillebrand et al., 2015; Buyucek et al., 2016).

Whether examining a large- or small-scale system, the associated stakeholders and their networks operate under the principle of holism. Holism means a whole-oriented vision of the system under which the parts of this whole – the *structure, processes, function,* and *environment* – stand out and are understood at the same time, that is simultaneously and not in isolation (Gharajedaghi, 2011; Skyttner, 2005). In essence, the whole is greater than (or different from) the sum of the parts.

Apart from holism, a systemic vision of stakeholders implies dynamism, which reflects shifts in stakeholder roles, types, attributes, and relationships (Mitchell et al., 1997). Stakeholders in any given system also operate under the principle of dynamics, when change, evolution, fluctuations, and variation characterise the very essence of system's operation, including on the level of the system inputs and outputs. Sometimes, these changes are minute and are not highly visible such as product weight adjustments or minor price increases. On other occasions, the changes are significant and disruptive, as is often the case with technology developments. Regardless of the degree of change, disruption, innovation, or creativity in the system, stakeholders constantly alter their strategies and dynamics within the system. Causes and effects in the structure, processes, function, and environment are not close in time or space; multiple causality is more likely; and complex feedback mechanisms manifest as stakeholders act and react to each other over time (Weaver, 1948; Senge, 1990; Domegan et al., 2019). Innate system's dynamism may be coupled with the social mechanisms of path dependence and inertia, when the activities of stakeholders maintain system stability, lock-in, and self-reproduction.

112 *Christine Domegan et al.*

Despite the 40 years of progress in stakeholder studies in various fields, including management science, macromarketing, social marketing and systems thinking, theoretical difficulties, research challenges, and practical limitations remain surrounding the concept of stakeholders, especially about stakeholders in a systems setting. Our findings from over 15 years of stakeholder work in Europe and further (McHugh et al., 2018 and Domegan et al., 2019) highlight that stakeholder analysis demands complexity and dynamics research underlying the multiple stakeholders, their stakes and structure, processes, function, and environment.

To undertake such research with a range of stakeholders in any focal system, key tasks for the social marketer include the identification of the system boundaries, classification of all of the stakeholders, a power analysis, and the mapping of stakeholder dynamics. Stakeholder analysis in a system setting gathers and synthesises multiple stakeholder perspectives, at the macro, meso, and micro levels, for the issues at hand. This information is best integrated with 'expert' perspectives and the existing evidence base.

The chosen stakeholder analysis is best designed and implemented in a manner that ensures all the stakeholder voices are heard in the system. The stakeholder systems analysis has to be mindful that the perspectives of those who 'want to be at the table,', the self-identified, definitive, or dominant stakeholders are often prioritised, often to the neglect of the non-recognised, discretionary, or dormant majority for whom these issues are of low priority but are of undoubted significance (Hastings & Domegan, 2017). Over time, the stakeholders in a system change, new stakeholders can emerge while existing ones can cease to exist or be interested.

As social systems are characterised by the innate humanity, driven by the fundamental human urge to exchange value with one another, the role of stakeholders in a systems setting is paramount. Stakeholders affect each dimension of a system (Gharajedaghi, 2011). It is here stakeholder analysis is pivotal for understanding how systems originate, operate, and develop.

An Active Travel case study in Ireland

The context for this case study research is set by the Department of Health in Ireland and its aim to "increase the proportion of people who are healthy at all stages of life" through the implementation of the Healthy Ireland Framework (Healthy Ireland, 2013, p. 6). As part of this national policy, a 20% increase is sought in those engaging in regular physical activity (Healthy Ireland, 2013). One option to contribute to this goal is Active Travel. The Institute of Public Health in Ireland (2011, p. 3) defines Active Travel as "journeys that use physical activity, such as walking and cycling, instead of motorised means to move between locations." As a result, the National Physical Activity Plan (Healthy Ireland, 2016, p. 24) aims to "develop and promote walking and cycling strategies in each Local Authority area." In this case, the local authority area selected was Galway city (Figure 8.2). Galway is a harbour city with a population of

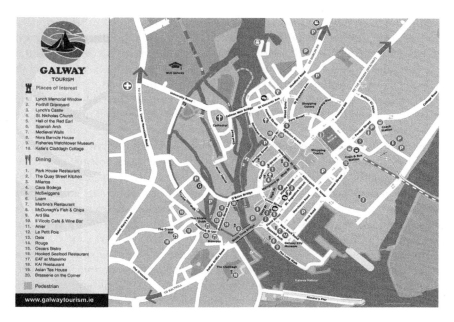

Figure 8.2 Map of Galway city.
Source: Galway Tourism (2019). www.galwaytourism.ie/UserFiles/Image/galway-tourist-map.pdf?pdf=Galway-Map.

79,934 on Ireland's west coast. Nested between the wild Atlantic Ocean and the Corrib river, Galway comes from the Irish name *Gaillimhe*, its earliest walled settlement, *Dún Gaillimhe or* 'Fort Gaillimh.' The city also bears the nickname 'City of the Tribes' because of the 14 merchant families called the 'tribes of Galway' who led the city in its medieval period.

Step 1 – Conduct a focal system boundary analysis

The first stakeholder analysis task is to establish the focal system you are working in to later identify and classify who the stakeholders are in the system and what they are doing in relation to the problem in hand. This is a 'system boundary analysis' – the systematic mapping of potentially influential elements, that is, stakeholders within a system of interest, who can affect or be affected by your social marketing intervention. These might include suppliers, trade unions, charities, policymakers, commercial firms, special interest groups, governments, banks, the media, and many others. System boundary analysis is important because the relevant stakeholders live and operate in the system, controlling assets, information, communications, networks, and influencing what the target groups value or do not value and what can and cannot be exchanged.

114 *Christine Domegan et al.*

In many situations, the support of the stakeholders in a focal system is central to implement change, and occasionally, they can be the problem or barrier to the transformation you want to achieve. They can represent direct opposition to change. A stakeholder boundary analysis will therefore ensure that all existing and potential groups and individuals who may be affected by Active Travel in Galway city are considered. A stakeholder boundary analysis also involves identifying what is realistically achievable and what is not achievable within the current parameters of the system. For all of us working in social marketing, we hope to see a lot of change. However, no one offering or organisation can do it all on their own. A focal stakeholder boundary analysis as the initial step in any stakeholder understanding allows us to think about what is possible and what is not possible within the resources and timeframe available. In effect, a stakeholder boundary analysis is about understanding the system and its stakeholders *before* dropping yourself into the system as a social marketer who wants to affect the stakeholders in the system and may want to collaborate with and/or form partnerships with some of the stakeholders.

Importantly from a social marketing perspective, a system, however large or small, will have delivery, product or service, communication, cooperation, trust, pricing, governance, and exchange elements, all of which will have associated stakeholders. A system of stakeholders from a social marketing perspective will also consist of various stakeholders exercising differential power and sometimes conflicting interests with the potential to assist a behavioural change intervention or block it from being effective.

Any analysis of stakeholders in social marketing depends on how we demarcate the boundaries of the focal system. The dominant approach is to be as inclusive as possible (Bryson, 2004) since system boundary demarcation is an arbitrary process (Kleidon, 2016). Such arbitrariness should not omit but specifically include a stakeholder orientation along the micro, meso, and macro dimensions. However small the focal system, system boundary demarcation with its ensuing stakeholder analysis needs to take into consideration multiple webs of top-down and bottom-up interactions between the following levels of actors: micro (individuals), meso (e.g. community, workplace, service and social capital) and macro (e.g. policy, structures, power relations and markets). For best practice, the boundary demarcation should be also inclusive of subsystems that are adjacent and complementary to the focal system, as well as embedded into it.

To start the system boundary and stakeholder analysis, create a social marketing working group (SMWG). The SMWG consists of three to five members whose task is to complete the stakeholder analysis activities in relation to your social marketing plan. The working group would best include some of the following people: a topic expert, a sectoral expert, a social marketing expert and governance, media, and/or NGO agencies. This small but diverse working group of people are tasked with the job of ensuring that a wide variety of stakeholders from different backgrounds are considered, discussed, and examined.

Stakeholder analysis in a systems setting 115

For our Active Travel case, the working group consisted of one Healthy Ireland expert, one social marketing expert, one transport expert, and one community association expert. The working group defined the Active Travel focal system of interest to consist of walking, cycling, skateboarding, and scooters around Galway city. However, the case study focused mostly on cycling. Table 8.1 presents the analysis of the boundaries of the focal system (i.e. the cycling system in Galway) with a categorisation of stakeholders subject to micro, meso, and macro levels. Adjacent systems embraced the traditional car and bus transport modes within the city, with outdoor clothing and festivals as complementary.

With this initial step being descriptive in nature, literature reviews and key informant interviews are important research tools to uncover the detailed complexity behind the stakeholders in the focal system. Brainstorming becomes important here to get beyond the obvious or accepted stakeholders – the SMWG should identify *all groups or individuals* who can affect or are affected or potentially affected by Active Travel in Galway city. The group work together listing potential stakeholders in the Active Travel focal system. After some time, the group can stop and discuss each suggestion, adding more stakeholders as they arise.

Task one member of the working group with integrating a list of stakeholders based on the groups' suggestions. You may want to get more ideas from stakeholders as you identify them – you could contact some of the stakeholders who are on your list and ask them to identify any stakeholders that the group may have overlooked. The goal is to identify the individual, community, and governance/policy bigger picture of the system. Then have the SMWG look at adjacent systems that might influence the focal system of interest.

Step 2 – Classify the focal system stakeholders

The next task for the SMWG is to classify the individual (micro), community (meso), and macro stakeholders in the focal system and adjacent systems. It is important *not* to confine yourself to one classification method, such as macro, meso, and micro. Make sure to try other stakeholder classification approaches to deepen your insights and learning. Why? Stakeholders will have multiple roles in a system, and it is inevitable there will be overlap (see Table 8.1). The overlap arises as a result of stakeholder roles which in turn depend on the strategic focus at a point in time and the problem at hand. An organisation/stakeholder group can be 'for an issue' in general, for example, cycling but on specific occasions in a specific context, against a cycle route, for example, because of a conservation area the cycling path plans to go through. Take our case study – a cycling system in Galway city. If we take a group of farmers in one of the satellite areas, away from the city boundary. Does this group belong to the focal or adjacent systems with respect to the cycling system in the Galway city? With our system boundaries as Galway city, the farmer stakeholders are geographically classified as part of the adjacent system. However, if the city decides to build a cycling

116   *Christine Domegan et al.*

Table 8.1 Active Travel stakeholders boundary analysis

Focal System	Adjacent and Complementary Systems
Individual/Micro Stakeholders Residents of Galway: • Galway City Centre • Outer Neighbourhoods • Extended Commuter Towns Elderly or Physically Disadvantaged Families Bicycle Owners Primary School Pupils Students: • NUIG www.nuigalway.ie/ • GMIT www.gmit.ie/ • GTI www.gti.ie/ • City secondary schools; Salerno, Taylor's, Mary's, The Bish, Endas, The Jez and Our Lady's College Workers in Galway: • Regular Active Commuters • <30-min walk to Workplace • 30 min–1-hour walk to Workplace • >1-hour walk to Workplace Visitors to Galway: • Tourists • Business/Work Trips • Other Visitors	**Individual/Micro Stakeholders** Regular Car Commuters/Travellers Bus Drivers Taxi Drivers Car Owners Bus Pass/Leap Card Owners
Community/Meso Organisations Cycling Clubs: • Galway Cycling www.facebook.com/GalwayCycling/ • Galway Cycle Bus www.facebook.com/Galwaycyclebus/ • Galway Bay Cycling Club Walking Clubs: • Galway Walking www.facebook.com/Galway-Walking-1740686799515392/ • Galway Walking Club Running Clubs: • Galway City Harriers • Galway City Meet and Train Group • Corofin Athletic Club • Maree A.C. Galway Bike Rental Scheme: • Coca Cola Zero Sugar Bikes Scheme Local Media: • Galway Advertiser • Galway Bay FM • Connacht Tribune • City Tribune	**Community/Meso Organisations** Commercial System: • Clothing and Outdoor Gear Stores (i.e. Call of the Wild, Mountain Warehouse, Outback Jacks, etc…) • Cycle Stores (i.e. Kearney Cycles, West Side Cycles, Halfords, etc…) • Car Dealerships Transport Systems: • Taxi Associations (Galway Taxis, City Taxis, Big O, MyTaxi App) • Aran Island Ferries • CityLink • GoBus • Bus Eireann • City Direct • Park and ride Education System: • NUI Galway • GMIT and GTI • Private Schools • Public Schools • Green Schools https://greenschoolsireland.org/

Stakeholder analysis in a systems setting 117

Table 8.1 (Cont.)

Focal System	Adjacent and Complementary Systems
• Galway Daily • Flirt FM (NUI Galway) Social Media Influencers: • This is Galway • Galway Tourism • Galway 2020 • Affiliated with Get Ireland Walking Business Districts: • Galway Central • Parkmore • Ballybrit • Mervue Engineering, Planning and Transport Firms • Arup Group • Systra Group	Health System: • Croi Heart & Stroke Charity www.facebook.com/CroiHeartStroke/?tn=%2Cd%2CP-R&eid=ARAjmqpBdR2kqhbLuxc9gr1qx3MxOv YoxiVahu7fWjODAxfp84e-xysKgWNntN9V86KLEGRYX-HrS_gT • University Hospital • Galway Clinic • Merlin Hospital • Bons Secours Festival and Event System: • Galway Races • Galway Arts Festival Hospitality System: • Hotels and B&Bs • Tour Guiding Agencies • Galway Walking Tour • Tribes 'Free' Walking Tour Religious System: • Church Groups Med-Tech Industry: • Medtronic • Boston Scientific Chamber of Commerce
Macro Decision-Makers Galway City Council County Council Healthy Ireland Government of Ireland Department of Transport, Tourism and Sport National Transport Authority: • Smarter Travel Workplaces • (www.smartertravelworkplaces.ie) Transport for Ireland (www.transportforireland.ie)	**Macro Decision-Makers** Galway 2020 Cultural Capital Committee Festival Committees European Environment Agency National Media: • RTE (Television and Radio Broadcaster) (www.rte.ie) • TheJournal.ie • Irish Times Department of Health; Institute of Public Health (IPH) www.publichealth.ie;

route, not only as a greenway, but as a part of Galway city commuter transportation system, their status immediately changes if this stakeholder group decides to oppose this route (for different reasons). This farming community becomes part of the focal system.

In our Active Travel context, we used Freeman's conventional stakeholder classification method. This involves segmenting stakeholders in primary,

118   *Christine Domegan et al.*

Table 8.2 Freeman's categorisation of stakeholders in Active Travel

Primary	Secondary	Influencers
Cycling commuters in Galway	Bike accessory retailers	Galway City Council
Bike-selling retailers	Galway Chamber of Commerce	Radio stations: Galway Bay FM, RTE
	Local cycling clubs	Newspapers: Connacht Tribune, Galway Advertiser
		Magazine: This is Galway
		Galway Bike Festival, Galway Bike Week

secondary, and influencers. Primary stakeholders are those individuals and organisations whose economic (or social) welfare depends on the system, for example, retailers selling bikes or everyday cycling commuters. Secondary stakeholders are individuals or organisations whose system–related welfare is dependent on the primary stakeholders, for example, retailers selling repair kits or bike locks or school pupils, whose cycling activity depends on that of primary stakeholders. Influencers are those persons or entities who shape the system such as the local city council with their provision of bike lanes, or not (Table 8.2).

The SMWG also classified the system stakeholders using a macromarketing classification mechanism (Layton, 2015). The result was three different groupings – incumbents, challengers, and regulating agencies (Table 8.3). Incumbents are the dominant organisations within your focal system context; they are relatively happy with the way things are and, in general, bar minor changes; wish to preserve the status quo. Challengers are less privileged than the incumbents are. Challengers often conform to the prevailing order while waiting for opportunities to emerge to transform the structure and/or processes and/or context of the existing focal system. Regulating agencies are in the system to defend the general status quo and governance of the system to facilitate the smooth running of it.

Stakeholders with clearly defined roles and status quo, for example, dominant or incumbent stakes will fit well into the framework, but other classifications of stakeholders, for example, emerging or dormant stakeholders' present difficulties. Stakeholders emerge in response to political, technological, cultural, and social issues. The difficulty lies in identifying and predicting these stakeholders and which adjacent or complementary system they will come from; what values inform their interests; and how the stakeholders strategically frame markets. Thinking about stakeholders as incumbents, challengers, or regulators sensitises the SMWG as to the stakeholders' role and function in the focal system. It begins to give power insights as to who is doing what and why.

Stakeholder analysis in a systems setting 119

Table 8.3 Layton's stakeholder classification mechanism

Incumbent Stakeholders	Reasons Why This Stakeholder Is Considered an Incumbent
Galway City Council (GCC)	GCC is responsible for a range of services in the city. The GCC has authority to develop and improve the Galway transport system and oversee the compliance with system rules. It develops cycling network development strategy for the city and implements various measures directly related to cycling. Having stressed the key role of GCC in affecting the local cycling system, it is known that "local authorities, on the other hand, have neither a mandate to shape transport policy nor sufficient funding to undertake any significant change" (Rau et al., 2016, p. 50).
Department of Transport, Tourism and Sport (DTTS)/ Transport Infrastructure Ireland (TII)/Road Safety Authority/other state and semi-state bodies and quasi-autonomous non-governmental organisations	These are central government departments in the area of the national and regional transport policy and infrastructure development. DTTS is responsible for sustainable transport and smarter travel manifestation. Rau et al. (2016, p. 45) call their commitments to support sustainable transport as 'declaratory.'
Businesses related to car parking revenues (e.g. large shops)	These entities are interested in preserving car-oriented status quo, thus both advertently and inadvertently opposing cycling. They can dominate in the question of car-centred infrastructure spread in many areas of Galway city.
Large companies in the field of transport planning and infrastructure projects (e.g. Arup Group, Systra Group)	These companies dominate many decisions related to the allocation of funds for transportation-related projects. In Freeman's stakeholder categorisation scheme, they are strong influencers, with a capacity for the system lock-in and stabilisation.
An Garda Síochána (or Gardaí)	Gardaí is the police service of the Republic of Ireland. It is responsible for policing roads, including maintaining their safety for cyclists. Duties may involve punishing cyclists. Apart from being an Incumbent, it could be considered a Regulating Agency, but in influencing upon the Galway Cycling System, its role is more decisive and status quo-oriented.
Motorist community	Motorists, as an entity with a peculiar logic and behaviour (often aggressive in relation to cyclists in Galway), remain a dominant force behind further implementation of car-centred culture in Galway.
Media e.g. Galway Bay FM, Connacht Tribune, This is Galway magazine.	The media is a powerful tool and has a big influence on people in particular the target audience.

(continued)

120   *Christine Domegan et al.*

Table 8.3 (Cont.)

Incumbent Stakeholders	Reasons Why This Stakeholder Is Considered an Incumbent
Challenger Stakeholders	**Reasons Why This Stakeholder Is Considered a Challenger**
Regular cycling commuters	As an entity, it is a main force that maintain the cycling system running and operable. It acts as major source of change but is grossly underprivileged.
Cycling-related NGOs (e.g. Galway Cycling Campaign, AMR – a bike community workshop affiliated to the National University of Ireland Galway)	Highly motivated when promoting Active Travel/ physical exercise to the target groups, these entities try to challenge the car-centric state of things and transform the system. They are less privileged with respect to influence and financial resources.
City Council councillors	Some of them represent a force, which directly challenges the system and demands its transformation. Weakness at the local level of elected politicians puts them into the underprivileged position.
Public Participation Network (e.g. Galway City Community Network or GCCN) and other entities from community and voluntary sector (CVS)	This entity acts as a mediator between social initiatives and local authorities, as well co-ordinates and supports the representation of the community, voluntary, and environmental sectors in Galway city. GCCN is highly supportive of cycling and Active Travel but has to conform to the prevailing order. The diverse CVS sector and its activities are a clear manifestation of the self-organisation social mechanism within the local cycling system.
Galway walking club/tours (e.g. private company Hillwalk Tours)	Communities gather walking amateurs by organising walks, hikes, and rambles. The walking amateurs can influence other people to join the community. These clubs form an adjacent system to the cycling system.
Galway Bike Festival, Galway Bike Week, Get Ireland Walking, Ireland Active, Parkrun Ireland and other initiatives and events	These events, which involve stakeholders across various domains, have a capacity to influence the system, though large-scale transformation is hardly possible due to the limited impact and short duration of such events.
Galway Tourism	The Galway Tourism is an entity which provides extensive online information to visitors to Galway and the entire of the west of Ireland. It promotes cycling/walking tourism and greenways, though has to conform to the existing underdevelopment of the cycling system.
Regulating Stakeholders	**Reasons This Stakeholder Is Considered a Regulating Agency**
Local, national, and supranational regulating agencies and civil servants (e.g. Galway City Council)	The system regulation is executed at different levels, including local, national and supranational. "Responsibility for transport policy is now spread across different levels of decision-making ranging from the local to the supranational," involving the EU institutions (Rau et al., 2016, p. 49).

Stakeholder analysis in a systems setting 121

Table 8.3 (Cont.)

Incumbent Stakeholders	Reasons Why This Stakeholder Is Considered an Incumbent
Civil society	Diverse civil society groups help monitor and regulate the system, preventing it from becoming fully car-centric.
Galway Chamber of Commerce	Galway Chamber of Commerce service includes influencing decisions and lobbying on behalf of businesses, providing opportunities for business networking, export documentation, trade information, business promotion & support, and encouraging mutual business support between members. By merging different interests, it provides a regulatory effect on the system.

Step 3 – Identify stakeholders' interests and benefits/barriers to participation

The aim of this third analysis step is to gain a deeper insight to understand the nature of the system stakeholders (Bunn et al., 2002). This involves a description of the stakeholders who will either help or block Active Travel in Galway city, in terms of their goals, motivations, and interests, the benefits they perceive from participating in the Active Travel system, as well as barriers to participation. Opportunities to overcome the barriers to participation are also identifiable by the working group. Table 8.4 highlights the power and interests of Active Travel (cycling) stakeholders on a continuum of high/low power and high/low interest.

Compliment the power/interest analysis with a power/interest map or visualisation as shown in Figure 8.3. Literature reviews, key informant interviews, surveys, and observation research are useful tools for this step. Remember, as the system changes and new aspects emerge in relation to the issue under consideration, the power/interest map maybe revisited to capture developments as stakeholder jockey for position in relation to the changes in the environment, context, structure, or processes in the system.

The segmentation of stakeholders by their interest-power relation to the focal issue, as shown in Table 8.4, prevents from seeing the finer gradation along the interest-power dimensions. However, Figure 8.3 helps to mitigate this problem by placing stakeholders in such a way so as to show subtler character of positioning with respect to interest and power. Table 8.4 and Figure 8.3 demonstrate actual (or at least close to actual) positions of stakeholders within the interest-power continuum. This combats aspirational visioning of the system when locations of stakeholders on the interest-power grid are guided by where the SMWG *wants* them to be. Figure 8.3 also shows what can be characterised as the 'value action gap line,' an abstract threshold below which stakeholders' pro-environmental values, if any, do not entail system-changing actions.

122 *Christine Domegan et al.*

Table 8.4 Stakeholders power and interest

Low-Interest/Low-Power Stakeholder	*Reasons This Stakeholder Belongs in This Quadrant*
General commuters	General commuters in the city have already chosen the transport mode(s) they use on a daily basis. Such habits are hard to change. The interest in cycling may be subdued. The chaotic level of organisation, lack of funds, and prevailing car-centric culture result in low power.
Local families	This category of stakeholders has a low capacity to change the cycling system and shows little interest in a transport mode which is not backed by proper and safe infrastructure. The predominant car-centrism characterises this category of stakeholders.
Local inhabitants	Like families, local inhabitants *en masse* are extremely rigid for change. They may influence high-power stakeholders via direct action or via electoral procedures, but this influence lacks regular impact and maintenance needed for the system improvement. Again, car-centrism shapes the attitude to mobility.
Low-Interest/High-Power Stakeholders	**Reasons This Stakeholder Belongs in This Quadrant**
Galway Chamber of Commerce	This rather influential entity is interested in the transportation issue and its solution for Galway (especially as a way of facilitation of business activities) but is unlikely to be able to generate a fair amount of steady interest towards cycling.
Large local businesses	Likewise, large local businesses, especially operating from centralised business parks and hubs, are interested to address the transportation issue, but hardly consider cycling as a viable approach, which can stimulate their interest.
Large companies in the field of transport planning and infrastructure projects (e.g. Arup Group, Systra Group)	These companies, which may have a large stake in the city's infrastructural projects, dedicate lots of time and efforts to addressing mobility issues, but cycling may constitute only marginal concern of such companies.
An Garda Síochána (or Gardaí)	Garda, with a strong capacity for keeping the roads safe, has a low concern about cycling.
Bus companies, taxi	While interested in mobility, they may view cycling as a competitor and are mostly preoccupied with motorised transport facilitation.
Businesses related to car parking revenues (e.g. large shops)	They are in direct opposition to cycling infrastructure development. Their support lies with motorised transport and car infrastructure.
Motorists	This category of stakeholders may be cyclists themselves, but they are interested in automobility and do not view cycling as an effective transport mode. Their behaviour to cycling is often aggressive and denigrative.

Stakeholder analysis in a systems setting   123

Table 8.4 (Cont.)

Low-Interest/Low-Power Stakeholder	Reasons This Stakeholder Belongs in This Quadrant
High-Interest/Low-Power Stakeholders	**Reasons This Stakeholder Belongs in This Quadrant**
Cycling commuters, sports cyclists	This category of stakeholders forms a group, which is probably the most interested in the development of cycling. Without proper infrastructure, funds, and influence, they have low capacity to change the system.
Cycling clubs, NGOs	This category supports cycling and is highly interested in its development, but it lacks power.
Tourists	Tourists may be mildly interested in cycling as a travelling option but has small power or intention to change the situation.
Students	This category of stakeholders has one of the highest cycling rates in the city and is interested in physically active safe and cheap way of transportation. Their power remains low.
Cycling events	They offer large opportunities to stir interest towards cycling but as short-term events are unable to change the situation.
Galway 2020 (related to the activities in Galway as a European Capital of Culture of 2020) and other festivals	The Galway 2020 event might arouse certain interest towards various elements of culture, including cycling culture, which has long traditions in Galway. However, the event has not capacity to affect the system.
High-Interest/High-Power Stakeholders	**Reasons This Stakeholder Belongs in This Quadrant**
Healthy Ireland, Galway Healthy Cities Forum	The organisations of such kind are extremely interested in the development of cycling as a healthy way of living and a social cohesion instrument. However, their power level is insufficient for providing a distinct impact on the issue.
Local government (e.g. Galway City Council)	This entity is rather influential and has a high degree of interest towards addressing the transportation issue in Galway. However, its role in the development of cycling is limited due to lack of funds and poor level of consultation with cycling experts. Overall power is limited too.
National government	It has power but lacks interest and understanding in the development of cycling as a mobility option both nationally and regionally.
Mass media, social media	Mass media, being rather an influential stakeholder, plays a very limited role in the cycling promotion in Galway, often demonstrating car-centric agendas and thinking.
Coca Cola Bikes (a bike rental scheme in Galway and a few other Irish cities; funded by the national government)	Being a single operator of the bike rental scheme in Galway, the entity has a limited power in the cycling system development and often shows limited overall interest in the general state of things with cycling.

124 *Christine Domegan et al.*

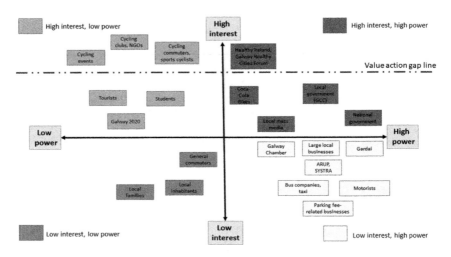

Figure 8.3 Stakeholder power/influence grid of Active Travel in Galway city.

Step 4 – Map the stakeholder dynamics of the focal system

Understanding not just the detail but the dynamics at work in a focal system of stakeholders is the fourth and final step in any multi-stakeholder assessment. The analysis now focuses on the relationships, perceptions, exchanges, actions, and reactions between the active and passive stakeholders in the system, however large or small. The stakeholder dynamics within a focal system are not linear in nature – stakeholders can engage and shift in any order at any point in time. Stakeholder dynamics are not an event; they are adaptable, flexible, and ongoing social mechanisms in a social system (Giesler et al., 2017). Dynamics are fluid, constantly changing and as a result, mapping the stakeholder dynamics is a process, an iterative process.

Importantly, the dynamics may never grow beyond micro exchanges into collective or societal outcomes. Failures and/or value destruction happens, as tensions remain unresolved and conflicts escalate, especially when there are substantial inconsistencies between stakeholders, their interests, power, and their actions (Laarmanen and Skálen, 2015).

One highly useful dynamic mapping tool from marketing science for the SMWG is an exchange systems map capturing all the direct and indirect exchanges currently happening among the various stakeholders in the focal system such as those shown in Figures 8.4 and 8.5 (Bagozzi, 1975). Another dynamic mapping tool from systems science highlights the structural, relational, and process dynamics at work between the various stakeholders in the system as shown in Figure 8.6.

As to be expected, both Figures 8.4 and 8.5 show complex exchanges at work for different segments within the focal system with some stakeholders,

Stakeholder analysis in a systems setting 125

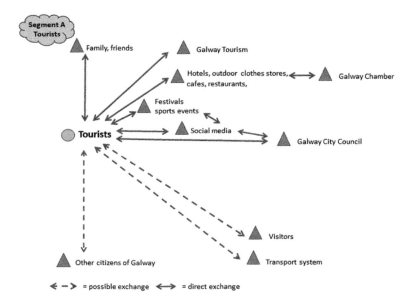

Figure 8.4 Tourists stakeholder value-based exchange map of the focal system.

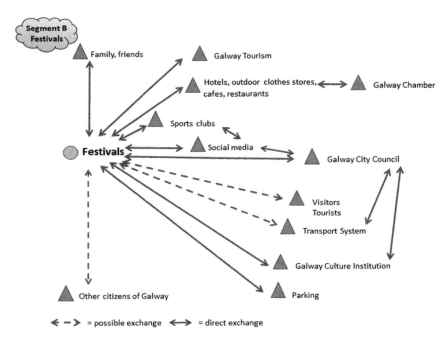

Figure 8.5 Festival stakeholder value-based exchange map of the complementary system.

126 Christine Domegan et al.

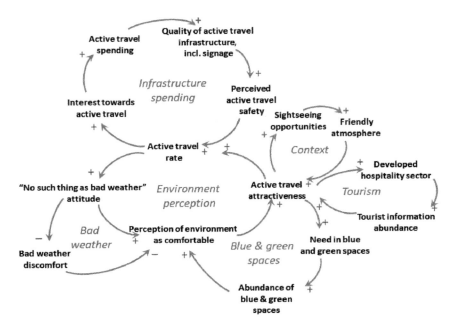

Figure 8.6 Stakeholders dynamic focal system mapping.

such as hotels and Galway City Council, dominating many segments. The exchange analysis together with the previous steps can be used to generate a list of all the system barriers and enablers currently at work in the focal system. Using the SMWG and extended stakeholder participation, the dynamic complexity of the system can be examined and mapped (Figure 8.6).

The stakeholder dynamics map (Figure 8.6) shows a complex array of interrelated barriers and enablers at work within the focal Active Travel system (predominantly the walking system) for Galway city stakeholders. The barrier and enabler dynamics affect different stakeholders and segments in different ways. The examples below illustrate some factors that participate in the barrier and enabler dynamics in the walking system in Galway.

1. Signage
    - *Sign colour scheme*: Current signage is coloured in black with golden font which makes them hard to read.
    - *Sign position*: Walking signs are placed too high, which makes them difficult to read.
    - *Abbreviation on signs & sign clarity*: Abbreviated content on signs results in difficulties in orientation for non-residents.
    - *Vandalised signs*: Some signs are vandalised, which makes them difficult to read.

Stakeholder analysis in a systems setting   127

- *Lack of signs*: There is a general lack of signage across Galway city.
- *Sign size*: Smaller signs are more likely to be affected by vandalism. Besides, the smaller the sign the harder it is to read the information.
- *Confusing signs*: Signs across Galway city are confusing, as they are lacking at some places and point in the wrong directions at others.

2. Bad weather conditions
   - *Bad weather:* Rain, cold, wind, storms, and hail can influence the decision not to walk/cycle and also increase the danger of floods, which is a serious issue in Galway.

3. Infrastructure
   - *Lighting*: Bad lighting could result in lesser safety and security.
   - *Footpath quality*: Too narrow footpaths make walking uncomfortable and more stressful, particularly at Salmon Weir Bridge where the walking space is just enough for one person. Some cobbled footpaths are low which results in puddles when it is rainy. Also, walkers need to pay more attention on where they step, particularly during night.
   - *Lack of pedestrian zones*: Lack of footpaths and construction sites results in a lower walking experience as walking in pedestrian zones is more relaxed, stress-free, and less noisy.
   - *Feeling unsafe*: Due to the lack of crossing facilities, heavy motorised traffic/busy roads impede walking. High traffic speed leads to walking restrictions in Galway.
   - *Not accessible for wheelchairs*: Some curb stones are too high, or footpaths lack quality so that access for wheelchairs is difficult or even impossible.
   - *Lack of left-luggage facilities*: It is a barrier for walking when luggage is too heavy to walk. Visitor might be dependent on buses or taxis.

Enabler dynamics include the following factors:

1. Abundant blue and green spaces
   - *Picturesque scenery*: The accessibility of green and blue spaces increases the level of enjoyment. Nice scenic walkways, for instance, increase the likability of people to walk.
   - *Animals and nature*: Bird and wildlife watching increase the level of adventure and excitement, and walking enables people to get closer to them.

2. Tourist information
   - *Tourist offices*: Tourist offices offer free maps that show walking routes and tourist sights. Staff can help with choosing the nicest walking routes which leads to a higher walking likeability.

3. Context
   - *History of Galway & sightseeing*: Galway is a cultural city and its history offers great sightseeing opportunities that can be reached within walking distance.

128   *Christine Domegan et al.*

- *Friendly people & atmosphere*: Galway is renowned for its friendly people who are the reason of a nice and friendly atmosphere when strolling through the city centre.
- *Google maps*: Journey planner apps improve orientation and time management and facilitate the walking experience.

Central to the success of understanding the stakeholder dynamics is the inclusion of stakeholders in the mapping phase. Co-opt stakeholders (macro, meso, and micro levels; primary, secondary, and influencers as well as incumbents, challengers, and regulating agents) into the working group to undertake the dynamics mapping. Such a stakeholder dynamics mapping exercise has the benefit of ensuring all potential groups and individuals affected by a focal system can be included to "work with, not against, the energy and motion of the system" they are living in and experiencing everyday life (Ricigliano, 2016, p. 61). Including a diversity of stakeholders (based on the above categorisation schemes) helps highlight the different perspectives at work. It can also uncover hidden tensions and conflicts and allow for their management. It proves a safe facilitated space for stakeholders to examine their assumptions and decisions from a holistic, multiple causality stance.

There are many software packages available on the market to assist with systems dynamic mapping. Many are free, for example, Draw.io, Scapple, Coggle, Lucidechart, Mental Modeller, and STELLA. Using all the barriers and enablers generated from the previous three steps, use modelling software to systematically map individual causal loops that are then combined to give a collective causal loop diagram capturing the complexity and dynamics of the system, stakeholders, and problems within it.

Be under no illusion, such systems' dynamic modelling is time consuming for stakeholders, and they may decline to participate in the mapping exercises. Furthermore, the more vocal stakeholders will have a bias towards self-inclusion. A viable alternate is for the working group members to conduct in-depth interviews with all individual stakeholders to validate the dynamics at work. Recognise not every stakeholder group will come to the table. On average, about 5% of stakeholders will not participate at a point in time.

Conclusion

Like the little fish and water fable from David Foster Wallace in 2008, we all live our lives surrounded by stakeholders in systems that influence and shape our daily actions, reactions, and behaviours. For social marketing to contribute to societies in the face of wicked problems such as obesity, health inequalities, and climate change, classic management stakeholder analysis, while necessary, is no longer sufficient. Multi-stakeholder assessment that is systemic and holistic is the way forward. This incorporates multi-societal stakeholder research strategies to provide a rich and informative understanding of the causal dynamics at work between the diverse stakeholders. In turn, understanding the dynamics

Stakeholder analysis in a systems setting 129

together with the details of stakeholders in a system acts as the strong basis for co-designing and co-creating change strategies for complex and wicked problems. Taking the time to analyse stakeholders get to grips with their dynamics and understand the system you are in ultimately gets you more change.

Every individual and organisation in a focal system is a stakeholder with a stake in that system, whether that stake is high on their agenda or not. Ensuring all stakes and stakeholders are heard and system stakeholders are not restricted to only those who are aware, have power, or have a vested self-interest in an issue, problem, challenge, or opportunity offers the potential for better outcomes for societies. Our ability to assess and engage multiple stakeholders in a system will, in part, determine whether we achieve the UN's 17 Sustainable Development Goals, the WHO's Health for all and OECD's improved quality of everyday life for humanity.

Acknowledgements

The authors would like to thank the MSc Marketing Management class and Fiona Donovan, Healthy Cities and Counties Ireland for their Social Marketing Service-Learning work with Healthy Cities Galway which informed this case study.

References

Australian Transport Council (2006). National Guidelines for Transport System Management in Australia. Available at www.transportinfrastructurecouncil.gov.au/publications/files/National_Guidelines_Volume_1.pdf.

Bagozzi, R. (1975). Marketing as exchange. *Journal of Marketing*, 39(4), 32–39.

Bossel, H. (1999). *Indicators for Sustainable Development: Theory, Method, Applications. A Report to the Balaton Group.* Winnipeg, Canada: International Institute for Sustainable Development (IISD).

Brennan, L., Previte, J., & Fry, M.L. (2016). Social marketing's consumer myopia. *Journal of Social Marketing*, 6(3), 219–239.

Bryson, J.M. (2004). What to do when stakeholders matter? *Public Management Review*, 6(1), 21–53.

Bunn et al. (2002). Stakeholder analysis for multi-section innovation. *Journal of Business and Industrial Marketing*, 17(2/3), 181–203.

Buyucek, N., Kubacki, K., Rundle-Thiele, S., & Pang, B. (2016). A systemic review of stakeholder involvement in social marketing interventions. *Australasian Marketing Journal*, 24, 8–19.

Domegan, Ch., McHugh, P., Flaherty, T., & Duane, S. (2019). A dynamic stakeholder engagement framework for challenging marketing system times. *Journal of Macromarketing*, 39(2), 136–150.

Freeman, R.E. (1984). *Strategic Management: A Stakeholder Approach.* Boston, MA: Pitman.

Freeman, R.E. (2017). Five challenges to stakeholder theory: A report on research in progress. In: Wasieleski, D.M., & Weber, J. (Eds.) *Stakeholder Management (Business and Society 360, Volume 1).* Bingley, UK: Emerald, 1–20.

130   *Christine Domegan et al.*

Geels, F. (2004). From sectoral systems of innovation to socio-technical systems insights about dynamics and change from sociology and institutional theory. *Research Policy,* 33, 897–920.

Geels, F. (2005). Processes and patterns in transitions and system innovations: Refining the co-evolutionary multi-level perspective. *Technological Forecasting & Social Change,* 72, 681–696.

Gharajedaghi, J. (2011). *Systems Thinking: Managing Chaos and Complexity. A Platform for Designing Business Architecture.* 3rd edn. Burlington, MA: Morgan Kaufmann.

Giesler, M., & Fischer, E. (2017). Market system dynamics. *Marketing Theory,* 17(1), 3–8.

Hastings, G., & Domegan, Ch. (2017). *Social Marketing: Rebels with a Cause.* 3rd edn. London, UK: Routledge.

Healthy Ireland (2013). *Healthy Ireland – A Framework for Improved Health and Wellbeing 2013–2025.* Retrieved from https://health.gov.ie/wp-content/uploads/2014/03/HealthyIrelandBrochureWA2.pdf.

Healthy Ireland (2016). *Get Ireland Active! National Physical Activity Plan for Ireland.* Retrieved from www.getirelandactive.ie/Professionals/National-PA-Plan.pdf

Hillebrand, B., Driessen, P.H., & Koll, O. (2015). Stakeholder marketing: Theoretical foundations and required capabilities. *Journal of the Academy of Marketing Science,* 43, 411–428.

The Institute of Public Health in Ireland (2011). *Active Travel – Healthy Lives.* Retrieved from www.publichealth.ie/files/file/Active%20travel/Active%20travel%20-%20 healthy %20lives.pdf.

Kennedy, A.M., & Parsons, A. (2012). Macro-social marketing and social engineering: A systems approach. *Journal of Social Marketing,* 2(1), 37–51.

Kennedy, A.M., Kapitan, S., Bajaj, N., Bakonyi, A., & Sands, S. (2017). Uncovering wicked problem's system structure: Seeing the forest for the trees. *Journal of Social Marketing,* 7(1), 51–73.

Kleidon, A. (2016). *Thermodynamic Foundations of the Earth System.* Cambridge: Cambridge University Press.

Laarmanen, M., & Skálén, P. (2015). Collective-conflictual value co-creation: A strategic action field approach. *Marketing Theory,* 15(3), 381–400.

Laczniak, G.R., & Murphy, P.E. (2012). Stakeholder theory and marketing: Moving from a firm-centric to a societal perspective. *Journal of Public Policy & Marketing,* 31(2), 284–292.

Layton, R.A. (2015). Formation, growth and adaptive change in marketing systems. *Journal of Macromarketing,* 35(3), 302–319.

Lindgreen, A., Kotler, P., Vanhamme, J., & Maon, F. (Eds.) (2012). *A Stakeholder Approach to Corporate Social Responsibility: Pressures, Conflicts, Reconciliation.* Farnham, Surrey: Gower Publishing.

McHugh, P., Domegan, Ch., & Duane, S. (2018). Protocols for stakeholder participation in social marketing systems. *Social Marketing Quarterly,* 24(3), 164–193.

Mitchell, R.K., Agle, B.R., & Wood, D.J. (1997). Toward a theory of stakeholder identification and salience: Defining the principle of who and what really counts. *The Academy of Management Review,* 22(4), 853–886.

Peterson, M. (2013). *Sustainable Enterprise a Macromarketing Approach.* London: Sage.

Rau, H., Hynes, M., & Heisserer, B. (2016). Transport policy and governance in turbulent times: Evidence from Ireland. *Case Studies on Transport Policy,* 4(2), 45–56.

Ricigliano, R. (2016). *Making Peace Last: A Toolbox for Sustainable Peacebuilding.* London: Routledge.

Senge, P. (1990). *The Fifth Discipline*. New York: Doubleday.

Skyttner, L. (2005). *General Systems Theory: Problems, Perspectives, Practice*. 2nd edn. Singapore: World Scientific Publishing.

Vargo, S.L., & Lusch, R.F. (Eds). *The SAGE Handbook of Service-Dominant Logic*. London: SAGE.

Wallace, D. (2008). David Foster Wallace on life and work. *Wall Street Journal,* September 23, 2019.

Weaver, W. (1948). Science and complexity. *American Scientist*, 36, 536.

Werhane, P.H. (2011). Globalisation, mental models and decentering stakeholder approaches, Chapter 5, 111–129. In: Philips, R.A. (Ed.) *Stakeholder Theory, Impact and Prospects*. Cheltenham: Elgar.

Werhane, P.H. (2008). Mental models, moral imagination and system thinking in the age of globalization. *Journal of Business Ethics*, 78, 463–474.

9 Co-production of social experiments to promote health and well-being among disadvantaged groups together with key stakeholders

Tomi Mäki-Opas, Janet Carter Anand, Csilla Veszteg, and Marja Vaarama

Social inequalities in health and well-being are a well-acknowledged societal challenge – Why do we still fail to tackle it?

The evidence of social inequalities in health and well-being is overwhelmingly convincing (Atkinson, 2015; Marmot, 2014; WHO, 2014), but effective solutions as how to address social inequalities remain elusive. Recent Finnish population surveys (Kestilä & Karvonen, 2019; Koponen, Borodulin, Lundqvist, Sääksjärvi, & Koskinen, 2018) emphasise that health and social policies in Finland are failing to reach the most disadvantaged groups in the society: *youth not in education, employment or training (NEETS), long-term unemployed, refugees in early stage of resettlement, and older people with multiple care needs and living alone at home* (Marmot, 2014; WHO, 2014).

Critical analysis of current health and welfare promotion strategies in Finland forces us to question why past and current efforts have failed to reduce the health and well-being inequalities (Rotko, Kauppinen, Mustonen, & Linnanmäki, 2012; Sihto & Karvonen, 2016; STM, 2008). It is clear that current top-down, expert-led policies, and programmes are failing (Abel & Frohlich, 2012; Green et al., 2015; Robinson, 2009; Rotko et al., 2012; Sihto & Karvonen, 2016). Several evaluations on Finnish social and health policies (Abel & Frohlich, 2012; Rotko et al., 2012; Sihto & Karvonen, 2016) have concluded that a broader commitment and participation of various stakeholders and focus on the 'root causes' (such as poverty, living conditions, work environment, and access to services) are needed to diminish inequalities in health and well-being. Regarding disadvantaged groups, the importance of empowering disadvantaged individuals to improve and maintain their health and well-being should not be forgotten (Abel & Frohlich, 2012; Green et al., 2015; Sihto & Karvonen, 2016). Empowerment refers to the promotion of an individual's capabilities (e.g. agency, personal abilities, and skills) so as to live a life they

Co-production of social experiments   133

value and enjoy being able, and look positively at their future regardless of possible structural barriers, such as poverty, unemployment, and poor access to services (Nussbaum, 2011). For empowerment of the disadvantaged groups, there is a need to fully encompass and understand the various needs of disadvantaged groups and engage them as active key stakeholders. However, disadvantaged population groups are often regarded as hard-to-reach for population study purposes (Kestilä & Karvonen, 2019; Koponen et al., 2018). More inclusive methods of outreach to engage disadvantaged groups in social research are required so that comprehensive theoretical frameworks, and mixed and participatory methods, may effectively address their needs (Green et al., 2015; Hastings & Domegan, 2014; Sihto & Karvonen, 2016).

Inclusive, multidisciplinary, and mixed research methods are offered by social marketing in the context of health and well-being promotion (French & Gordon, 2015; Hastings & Domegan, 2014; Lefebvre, 2013). By mixed methods, we refer to the evaluation, development, and piloting of new inclusive methods to promote health and well-being, which should be evaluated simultaneously, using both quantitative and qualitative participatory methods (Rubin & Babbie 2017). Trust building and collaboration with disadvantaged and difficult-to-access populations are essential to engage socially excluded groups in social research. There is a need for effective participatory methods to promote collaboration between disadvantaged groups and their key stakeholders (Hastings & Domegan, 2014; Lucca, Hibbert, & McDonald, 2016; Vargo & Lusch, 2006).

In this chapter, we describe the comprehensive PROMEQ framework and the inclusive social marketing processes employed within these (see Table 9.1). At the end, we conclude the key results from the social marketing experiments and key experiences and challenges of working with these stakeholders.

Central for *inclusive promotion of health and well-being,* an approach used in PROMEQ, was the employment of social marketing as a meaning of promoting both individual and structural change. To the best of our knowledge, this approach has rarely been applied to inform the design and delivery of services among disadvantaged groups. The involvement of the individual participants into the research process was performed by using participatory methods by a common study protocol. The partnership between public services, private enterprises, and third sector organisations, herein referred to as 'PPP' (public–private–people partnerships), was supported by establishing regional and local stakeholder forums and workshops. The term 'third sector organisations' is used in the Finnish context to refer to non-governmental and non-profit organisations, civic societies, and associations (typically based on voluntary personnel). For example, in Finland, many community organisations, sports associations, neighbourhood associations and several well-being associations are third sector organisations.

While there are different methods and strategies for social marketing applied in health and well-being promotion (Andreasen, 2002; French & Gordon, 2015; Hastings & Domegan, 2014; Hopwood & Merritt, 2011), we

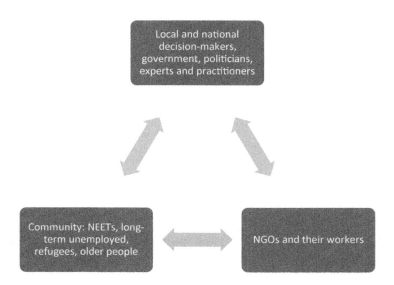

Figure 9.1 Social marketing as a triangle of social relations in PROMEQ.

utilised co-design, co-creation, co-production, and common value creation (Hastings & Domegan, 2014; Lucca et al., 2016; Vargo & Lusch, 2006) to develop tailored quasi-experiments within the PPP partnership as follows (see Figure 9.1).

1) *Co-creation*: Researchers together with representatives of the disadvantaged groups in question identified the key challenges and resources for their health and well-being using the common theoretical framework of quality of life, capability, and social quality.
2) *Co-design*: Based on these challenges and resources, researchers defined need and resource profiles for each group, and together with the representatives of disadvantaged groups defined meaningful, motivating, and effective solutions to the situation.
3) *Co-production of tailored and segmented social marketing experiments*: Together with regional public, private service provides, third sector non-government organisations (NGOs) (PPP), researchers, and the representatives of the disadvantaged groups, tailored segmented quasi-experiments were developed and tested over at least six months using social marketing methods and strategies to support the experiments.
4) *Common value creation*: The effectiveness, cost-effectiveness, and implementation of the social marketing experiments were evaluated applying a mix of relevant quantitative and qualitative methods, after which the results and policy recommendations were subjected for evaluation with the

study populations and their key stakeholders as well as in the regional and national congresses.

The stakeholder analysis is one of the key processes in planning the social marketing experiments and promotion of health and well-being programs (Hastings & Domegan, 2014; Green et al., 2015; Buyucek et al., 2016). Stakeholder theory suggests that inclusion of PPP stakeholders is the key to enhance the outcome (Buyucek et al., 2016), and this applies especially for complex social problems such as promotion of health and well-being among disadvantaged groups. It is, therefore, important to systematically map the potential PPP stakeholders that are offering services but also those stakeholders that are making the decisions of the services offered to the disadvantaged groups (Hastings & Domegan, 2014). Moreover, it is essential to consider how power is distributed among the key stakeholders, given that different stakeholders hold different levels and types of interests and motivations for finding solutions and for the promotion of health and well-being among disadvantaged groups (Hastings & Domegan, 2014; Green et al., 2015; Buyucek et al., 2016). The general definition of stakeholders is all those groups and individuals that can affect or are affected by the social marketer's behaviour change proposal (Freeman, 1984). In PROMEQ, the stakeholders were defined as representatives of the state, regions, local authorities, and NGOs working the geographical areas where the PROMEQ study was implemented.

The aim of the PROMEQ was to collect new scientific information on disadvantaged groups, and to test and develop inclusive and effective health and well-being promotion methods for disadvantaged groups. The PROMEQ study applied a comprehensive theoretical framework combining *Social Quality* (Beck, Van Der Maesen, & Walker, 1997; Pieper, Vaarama, & Karvonen, 2019; van der Maesen & Walker, 2012), *Capability* (Sen, 1993; Nussbaum, 2011, Abel, 2012), and *Quality of Life* (Vaarama, Pieper, & Sixsmith, 2008; Veenhoven, 2000; WHOQOL Group, 1998). PROMEQ considered the promotion of quality of life as the central aim for social marketing experiments, and growing capability (agency) as the central resource for promoting health and well-being among disadvantaged groups while considering social quality, that is the structural barriers for individual's agency and structural conditions that create and maintain inequalities in health and well-being. Experimental designs and mixed methods approach were applied to evaluate the effectiveness of the tailored social marketing experiments.

Four social experiments with disadvantaged groups

The study applied quasi-experimental research designs and utilised mixed methods to evaluate the effectiveness of four case studies. The four experiments included (1) digital online group intervention with NEETs, (2) multi-professional case management with long-term unemployed people, (3) participatory group-based case management with older people, and (4) employment,

Table 9.1 PROMEQ approach to social marketing of tailored experiments: Co-design and co-creation together with PPP partnership

	NEETs	Long-Term Unemployed	Older People Living Alone with Multiple Needs	Refugees
(1) Co-design of needs and resource profiles for intervention designs	Focus groups interviews and workshops, $N = 10$–15 participants per group	Focus groups interviews and workshops, $N = 10$–15 participants per group	Focus groups interviews and workshops, $N = 10$–15 participants per group	Focus groups interviews and workshops, $N = 10$–15 participants per group
(2) Co-creation of the interventions and social marketing means with the target groups	Focus groups & workshops Tailored intervention $N = 10$–15	Focus groups/ workshops for details of two pre-defined interventions $N = 10$–15 in both target groups	Focus groups/ workshops for details of two pre-defined interventions $N = 10$–15 in both target groups	Focus groups & workshops for details of four pre-defined interventions $N = 10$–15
(3) Co-creation of tailored interventions in PPP partnership	Participation in one-off workshops to share their thoughts of priorities in life, ingredients of health and well-being, needs concerning support, sources of inspiration as well as ideas on the potential of social media as a platform for receiving and giving support. The data collected in workshops was used to (re-)define the content of intervention.	Discussion on quality of life, preferences, problems, wishes, and living habits. Discussions were taped and post-it pads classified and all data was analysed, resulting to the needs, resource, and motivation profiles of the target group.	Discussion on quality of life, preferences, problems, wishes, and living habits. Discussions were taped and post-it pads classified and all data was analysed, resulting to the needs, resource, and motivation profiles of the target group.	Community Forums and planning sessions for each intervention: (1) Employability together with North Karelian Society for Social Security (2) Access to education together with University of Eastern Finland (3) Language acquisition together with Immigration Unit of the City of Kuopio, Setlementti Puijola, Multicultural Center Kompassi (4) Social participation together with ANTI – Contemporary Art Festival

Co-production of social experiments   137

education, language, and social participation experiments with people with refugee background.

Mixed quantitative and qualitative methods were used to assess the effectiveness of the four social marketing experiments (see Table 9.2). We collected self-administered survey information from the participants at the baseline and six months follow-up. The survey included self-reported information such as background information, living conditions and work, health, quality of life (WHOQOL GROUP, 1998), social participation, loneliness (Junttila et al., 2013), capabilities (Anand et al., 2005), use of health and social services, use of cultural services and participation in health promotion activities, healthy lifestyle (nutrition, physical activity, smoking, drinking), weight, and height (Murto et al., 2018). All measures are validated and reliable and allow comparability to local and national level surveys. Additionally, group-specific measures (questionnaire) and other methods (e.g. focus group methods, workshops and community forums) were employed. Multivariate analyses and statistical modelling (e.g. regression and structural equation modelling) were used for the analysis of the survey data gathered in RCT and quasi-experimental design, and qualitative content analysis for focus groups interviews and reflective diaries (Rubin & Babbie, 2017).

Experiment 1: A digital online community experiment to promote social connectedness among NEETs

Defining key stakeholders: The recruitment for NEETS was based on voluntariness and went through youth and social workers. The inclusions criteria were young adults 15–29 years of age not in education, employment, or training in the cities of Kouvola and Vantaa and in the Kuopio region. The experiment was conducted together with youth and social workers in the three cities.

Outcomes of stakeholder engagement: Based on the focus groups interviews with NEETs and professionals working with them, it was revealed that many NEETs had difficulties in participation into face-to-face meetings due to, for example, school bullying experiences or poor other social relationship skills. Moreover, the professionals working with these stakeholders did not have resources and skills for using web-based solutions to answer this kind of need for anonymised group-based online services.

Social marketing strategies: Based on the stakeholders' needs and NEETs resource profiles (Table 9.2), we developed a tailored digital online community to promote social connectedness and diminish loneliness among NEETs. The tailored experiment tried to answer to the need of more segmented online-based and anonymised services compared to traditional ones, such as face-to-face services. Researchers suggested the idea for the digital online community intervention, but the online-forum and the discussion topics were co-designed together with all stakeholders, that is NEETs, youth, and social workers. The experiment lasted for nine weeks. The experiment included pre-planned weekly online discussions on various themes such as friends, loneliness, hobbies,

Table 9.2 The needs and resource profiles of the disadvantaged groups

	NEETs	Long-Term Unemployed	Older People, Living Alone and with Multiple Needs	Refugees
Focus group interview & Workshops:	• Lack of social connections • Stigmatisation • Experiencing no opportunities for improving their quality of life	• Lack of confidence • Insecurity related to health, livelihood, and future planning • Concerns related to own or others health issues • Economic problems • The need of services is not fully satisfied. • Bad attitudes and ageism against the unemployed • Cannot get job nor pension	• Mobility problems • Lack of social connections • Poor service experiences, not answering the needs of older people • Lack of opportunities • Lack of knowledge	• Practical language opportunities • Employability actions • Information on educational opportunities • Participation and social interaction with local people
Baseline data:	• Have problems in the physical and psychological dimensions of quality of life • Almost half had some kind of financial problems • Most felt lonely often or constantly, although were weekly in contact with friends and family • Most of interested to start doing new sports • More often to be daily smokers	• Have problems in psychological and social dimensions of quality of life • Had a higher sense of their capability for intellectual stimulation in their life, have good options in life and to act with personal integrity • Over half of them experienced a lot or to some extent age-, economical, or unemployed-related discrimination • Felt more often lonely than the Finns on average	• Lower quality of life than same aged Finns • Living alone • Have deficits in health and well-being • Use multiple social and healthcare services • Receive social assistance more often than same aged Finns living alone • Felt more often lonely and felt more often that loneliness was a problem	• Have lower scores in all dimensions of quality of life compared to Finns, especially in psychological and environmental dimension • One in three reported they are to some extent or fully unable to work. • Over third of the respondents reported having difficulties to concentrate. • About third of the respondents reported feeling loneliness all the time or often. • Over third reported it is very difficult or somewhat difficult to get acquainted with Finnish people. • Three of five respondents reported it difficult to cover their costs, and over half have been in situation in the last 12 months where there is no money for food. • Every fifth respondent reported avoiding some places because of their foreign background

Co-production of social experiments 139

well-being, and economical situation. The youth workers and researchers acted as moderators of the digital online community. The community was a closed one, and all the discussions were anonymous.

According to the Andreasen's (2002) social marketing benchmark criteria, we applied criteria 1–5 and criteria 7–8. Competition analyses were conducted, as this would support the current existing services and diminished the time, attention, and financial costs of participating to a face-to-face meeting.

Reflection on results: The digital online community experiment proved to be successful in promotion of social connectedness and diminishing loneliness among young NEETs. NEETs who reported loneliness and problems with participation in group activities benefitted most from this kind of digital online communities. In the targeted youth work, digital online engagement offers a mean to work with NEETs who are seeking youth work, or a means to employ in rehabilitation workshops. However, due to the selectiveness bias among participants, we are not able to demonstrate changes in quality of life. One reason may also be the difficult baseline situation among NEETs, which had been causing them to search for youth services, such as difficult life situations, mental health problems, or losses in their families.

Experiment 2: Multi-professional case management to promote health and well-being among long-term unemployed

Defining stakeholders: The inclusion criteria for participation in this multi-professional case management intervention were: persons aged 35 to 54 years, having been at least 12 months in continuous unemployment and having not taken part in the active employment promotion programmes. Recruitment was performed in collaboration with the local social and health care professionals and employment services in the cities of Kuopio, Jyväskylä, and Joensuu. These unemployed persons are in most vulnerable situation; they are usually not part of this kind of multi-professional case management services but are directed as clients to the adult social work services.

Outcomes of stakeholder engagement: The effect of the stakeholder engagement revealed that there were multiple needs related to physical health, and social, psychological, and environmental problems, such as poor access to services and poor financial situations. These needs call for a tight collaboration between various kinds of services, including health, social, and employment professionals of social and rehabilitation services.

Social marketing strategies: Based on the needs and resource profiles (Table 9.2), a multi-professional case management intervention was designed that would fulfil the selected social marketing methodology. First, as unemployment is found to impact largely on people's health, self-images, and social well-being, the experiment aimed to promote the health and well-being among long-term unemployed people by multi-professional services given by the health, social,

140 *Tomi Mäki-Opas et al.*

and employment professionals. Second, customer-oriented working methods were applied, starting with comprehensive examination of the individual's life's situation. Third, the multi-professional case management services were strongly based on segmentation. Fourth, the services utilised multiple tailored methods and means. Finally, to further develop the services, the PROMEQ research team provided to the services a new comprehensive theoretical framework (*social quality, quality of life, and capability*) and evidence of their effectiveness.

Reflection on results: The multi-professional case management experiment was both effective and cost-effective in promoting physical and psychological quality of life, as well as strengthening capabilities among long-term unemployed people. The major reason for the established effectiveness of the experiment was the fact that there were plenty of unmet needs among the study population, but usually the collaboration and coordination across the different service sectors was poor, leading to unmet needs. Effectiveness was achieved because the importance of the collaboration between employment, social, and health services was emphasised during the experiment, and the applied theoretical framework guided adoption of a comprehensive approach to health and well-being among long-term unemployed people.

Experiment 3: Participatory group-based case management to promote health and well-being among older people living alone at home and having multiple needs

Defining stakeholders: Inclusion criteria were people aged 65 years or older, retired full-time, living alone, who had expressed (at least one) well-being deficit such as insecurity or loneliness. In addition, older people who had used or been in contact with social and healthcare services (e.g. doctor, nurse, care manager, social worker) during the past six months were also included. Exclusion criteria were any diagnosed memory disorders, substance abuse, or serious mental health problems. All participants needed to be able to participate in Finnish-speaking group activities. The regions included cities of Kuopio and Jyväskylä, the South Carelia Social and Health Care (Siun Sote) region, and the Central Finland Social and Health Care (Eksote) region. The study participants were recruited in collaboration with the local social and healthcare professionals.

Outcomes of stakeholder engagement: The intensive stakeholder engagement showed that the public and private service providers had not been able to meet the needs of the older people while the third sector organisations had mostly been taking care of them. A lot of the services for older people were targeted to home, but the intensive stakeholder engagement revealed that the older people do not want new services to home but services to get out of home. Moreover, these services should be based on PPP partnerships, especially more public and private services, to answer multiple needs of the older people living alone, are needed. In the co-design phase, case management was shown to be the most promising method in developing new models for promoting health and well-being among older people together with key PPP stakeholders.

Co-production of social experiments 141

Social marketing strategies: Based on the needs and resource profiles of the older people living alone (Table 9.2), a participatory group-based case management experiment to promote health and well-being together with primary stakeholders and service providers was developed. The experiment combined social support, guidance, and information delivery as well as support for agency. The groups had five meetings during the experiment, and one meeting lasting about 2 to 3 hours. Each group included six to eight older persons, a service worker, and a researcher. The themes of the meetings varied based on the needs and wishes of the older people belonging to the group. The meeting schedules and topics were planned together with the older people so that they could influence what were done, what kind of information and guidance (e.g. housing, use of local services, information on physical activity and nutrition) was provided. During the meetings, groups visited the local environments relevant for the older people, such as swimming pool, service centres, and museums as well as culture services. In the meetings, peer-support was essential but also included space for free discussion as well as time to spend together.

Reflection on results: The participatory group-based case management experiment was an effective and cost-effective way to promote social well-being and diminish loneliness. Moreover, the intervention improved trust in other people and to the public institutions. In addition, participation in the experiment empowered primary stakeholders and promoted their social connectedness and social inclusion. Peer-support and experiences shared helped many participants to learn relevant information on services and leisure-time opportunities. Finally, service providers reported that they had gained new information of the health and well-being as well as barriers of the services not reaching the older people. According to our analyses, the effectiveness of the experiment on social well-being was mainly due to increased social support, social connectedness, and new leisure-time opportunities. Improvement of trust was due to closed meetings, where group members had equal opportunities to discuss together and ask questions from experts and service providers, as well as gather information they needed that supported their own trust to the future and their own capabilities.

Experiment 4: Educational, employment skills, language, and social participation experiments to promote well-being and integration of refugees in the early-stage resettlement

Defining stakeholders: The inclusion criteria were refugees between the age 18–65 years, who spoke either Arabic, Farsi-Dari, English, or Finnish, arrived as quota refugee or had been granted with asylum status, and were living in Eastern Finland since 1 January 2014. The second category of stakeholders were the local service providers and social workers, community and NGO service workers, who participated in the intervention, while the local municipalities were the third category of stakeholder identified.

Outcomes of stakeholder engagement: Extensive stakeholder engagement revealed that the municipality-provided refugee integration services were not always

142   *Tomi Mäki-Opas et al.*

fulfilling the exact needs of more recent refugees. NGO-based service providers were bridging the gap between clients and local service providers and helping to facilitate the discussion between the parties. NGOs had the resources and the knowledge to reach out to clients, engage and motivate to build the sense of agency among the refugee communities.

Social marketing strategies: Several focus groups in two selected cities involving recent refugees in Eastern Finland reported that they needed more language opportunities, support for employment actions, information on the services and education, and participation and social interaction with local people to improve their new start in Finland. A series of focus groups and planning sessions with existing NGO and integration experts from the field identified the challenges in engaging recent refugees in existing integration programs. Four small-scale experiments were planned to target different refugee groups:

1) *Higher Education Group*, run by a local university, focused on increasing refugees' access to higher education through digital pathways, to raise awareness and realistic expectations of university educational opportunities in Finland.
2) *Employability Skills Groups* run by a community development organisation, focused on promoting new refugees' sense of agency in working with local employment services to more effectively negotiate the local labour market.
3) *Women's Language Acquisition Group*, delivered through a community settlement house, focused on the integration of refugee women who, because of domestic and cultural reasons, lacked opportunities for participating in activities outside their home. In the context of a language course women were encouraged to develop their strengths, talents, and expertise and change in the perceptions of women about living in Finland via a language course and knowledge-based activities, social and cultural integration through peer-support and social networking.
4) *Social Participation Group* focused on increasing social participation of younger male refugees through a series of social media workshops and a community event, including opportunities for exchange with Finnish youth. This experiment was not able to engage regular participants because of flaws in following the social marketing approach, we will come to this more in discussion, although it provided invaluable lessons on the importance of co-creation and a ground-up approach to service design.

Reflection on results: While there were no statically significant changes to quality of life resulting from the interventions, there were promising descriptive results and qualitative data obtained from focus groups with participants and stakeholders, indicating that some participants received new knowledge on negotiating community services, self-confidence, and additional capabilities. This case study reflects some of the challenges in evaluation in results small-scale real-life social marketing studies.

Co-production of social experiments   143

1) *Employability Skills Groups* participants reported that they have got to know new peers from their community, made new friends, got to know more Finns and professionals and accessed new sources of information. They also learnt more about Finnish culture and environment. Some participants, however, expressed that they still feel lost in the system, not knowing where to turn for help and support.

2) *Higher Education Group* participants significantly increase in learning Finnish by self-study and planning to apply for higher education, and confidence in work finding was observed. Participants felt that their aspirations and needs have been heard, if not always fulfilled. Involving 'experts by experience' talks with people from refugee and immigrant background to talk about their personal pathways to Finnish higher education gave a great motivation and provided new networks to participants. The project received an equality award from a local university, indicating awareness that structural changes are required to achieve equity for students with a refugee background. A small group of participants went on to be accepted in Open University courses and all participants left the programme with a personal plan and a source of ongoing support. Some participants expressed continued frustration and challenges regarding entrance into Finnish universities.

3) *Women's Language Acquisition group* participants reported positive changes in their everyday life in connection with the intervention. Participants adopted new language learning methods, learnt about Finnish system and culture as well as gender equality, how to use the bus and know the schedule, and how to use computer. All participants were motivated to continue to participate in language programmes. The segmentation of participations by gender and cultural background was also found to be important for promoting inclusive group processes. The impact of more participatory and action approaches to language acquisition was acknowledged by the service provider.

The details of research design, methods, aims, and outcomes of each case study are summarised in Table 9.3.

Discussion

To summarise, the PROMEQ approach, which utilised a comprehensive theoretical framework and inclusive social marketing strategies in developing and implementing tailored intervention for promotion of health and well-being among disadvantaged population groups, proved to be effective. The findings of the needs and resource profiles of the disadvantaged groups supported the comprehensive theoretical framework, and many of the social marketing experiments (Table 9.3) proved to be effective and even cost-effective in promotion of health and well-being, especially among long-term unemployed and older people.

Table 9.3 Experimental designs and mixed methods approach applied to evaluate the effectiveness of the tailored social marketing experiments

	NEETs	*Long-Term Unemployed*	*Older People Living Alone and with Multiple Needs*	*Refugees*
Study design and randomisation:	Quasi-experimental design, experimental group $N = 42$ and control group $N = 105$	Quasi-experimental design, experimental group $N = 85$ and control group $N = 78$	RCT-design, Experimental group $N = 180$, and control group $N = 180$	Quasi-experimental design, experimental group $N = 46$ and comparative group $N = 96$
Type(s) of intervention:	Digital online group intervention	Multi-professional case management	Participatory group-based case management	(a) Employment (b) Education (c) Language (d) Social participation
Aim:	To foster social connectedness, reducing stigma, displaying opportunities, acknowledging young adults' status as 'experts by experience'	To promote long-term unemployed client's well-being and quality of life	To improve health and quality of life of 65+ aged older people living alone and with multiple need of services	(a) To promote new behaviours and attitudes toward employment seeking (b) To change academic attitudes and practices, increase opportunities in higher education (c) To motivate stay-at-home mothers, to acquire the Finnish language (d) To increase social participation of younger male refugees through digital media including opportunities for exchange with Finnish youth
Methods:	• Structured discussion threads • Invitations to share thoughts and • Photos of everyday life	• Assessment of service needs • Regular meetings with multi-professional team	• Organised group meetings • Care managers and researcher as group tutors	(a) Series of community panels, interactive workshops, group work process involving refugees, agencies, and employers (b) organised group events, social media promotion, share information by educational experts, and expert by experience talks

				(c) Intensive community-based activities program, six weeks, 30 hours total. Volunteers (Finnish) provide child care while participants are in the pilot activities
		• Writing and updating personal employment plan • Works on one-stop-shop principle	• Participants are encouraged to plan and arrange shared social activities and participation between the provided group meetings	(c) Intensive community-based activities program, six weeks, 30 hours total. Volunteers (Finnish) provide child care while participants are in the pilot activities (d) 12 inclusive art-based workshops and final public event led by a professional artist
Evaluation:	Two measurement waves (baseline-end) with common and target group –specific questionnaires, focus groups for intervention evaluation, documentation and analysis of project communications and interactions of all partners over the course of the project	Two measurement waves (baseline-end) with common and target group –specific questionnaires, focus groups for intervention evaluation, documentation and analysis of project communications and interactions of all partners over the course of the project	Three measurement waves (baseline, middle, end) with common and target group –specific questionnaires, focus groups for intervention evaluation, documentation and analysis of project communications and interactions of all partners over the course of the project	Two measurement waves (baseline-end) with common and target group – specific questionnaires, focus groups for intervention evaluation, documentation and analysis of project communications and interactions of all partners over the course of the project

146 *Tomi Mäki-Opas et al.*

The experiments for NEETs and refugees require further development and research. The adequacy and applicability of the PROMEQ approach and social marketing strategies need more discussion but we suggest that there are real opportunities to engage disadvantaged population groups to inclusive promotion of their own health and well-being. It has been argued that the assumption of a 'rational individual' making choices among options does not apply well to members of vulnerable or disadvantaged groups. The violation of this assumption might impact on the effectiveness of social marketing experiments (Langford & Panter-Brick, 2013; Weinreich, 2011). In the perspective of health and well-being promotion (Green et al., 2015), the lack of information and education is assumed to apply among disadvantaged groups, and methods of developing knowledge and capabilities are seen as necessary elements of effective communication. Combining health and well-being strategies (Green et al., 2015; Sihto & Karvonen, 2016) with social marketing strategies (French & Gordon, 2015; Hastings & Domegan, 2014) and methods of social work to promote capabilities (Abel & Frohlich, 2012; Sen, 1993) among disadvantaged individuals provided a comprehensive approach to tackle social inequalities in effective and multidisciplinary way.

From the perspective of stakeholder analysis and theory (Buyucek et al., 2016; Hastings & Domegan, 2014; Green et al,. 2015), our experiences of stakeholder engagement point out not only some difficulties and barriers but also some success stories. In the case of NEETs, one of the main challenges with PPP partnerships was that professionals working in targeted youth services thought themselves as 'gate keepers' of the disadvantaged groups and did not respond well to our stakeholder engagement and our aim to study NEETs into come their field. One of the main reasons for this might be their work overload. It may also be due to miscommunication that we were not able to motivate them and communicate the benefits they may gain from this kind of comprehensive and alternative approach compared to the traditional ones. However, in the end most of the stakeholders saw that online services might be beneficial as additional services, but they would need more financial resources and education to utilise this kind of online service in their daily practices among NEETs.

In the case of refugees, the social participation experiment for refugees was not able to include regular participants in the end. Based on the qualitative results, the stakeholders had no prior contact with refugees on the local level, and they had difficulties to engage and recruit both refugees and Finns. Moreover, the social participation experiment may have been too complex and difficult to articulate the benefit of the participation for refugees, whose needs were more about everyday life. We also learnt effective recruitment strategies for refugees such as through word of mouth within the diverse communities, using printed information in relevant languages, and a direct approach via the social workers with home visits, as well as provision for childcare and the involvement of male family members. In addition, a paid peer researchers' group from the local refugee community was helpful in providing cultural interpretation and advice.

Co-production of social experiments   147

In the case of long-term unemployed people, the operating model of multi-professional service coordination together with key PPP stakeholders was able to correct the unfilled service needs of the target group as well as boost more efficient cooperation between PPP stakeholders. The engagement of several key PPP stakeholders was both effective and cost-effective way to promote health and well-being as well as strengthen capabilities among long-term unemployed persons. This was mainly due to the utilisation of more comprehensive theoretical framework as well as the success of inclusive methods of social marketing. Among older people, the utilisation of comprehensive theoretical framework provided essential new understanding of the service needs of disadvantaged groups to the stakeholders. The inclusion of key PPP stakeholders also improved older people's trust in other people and, especially, their trust of public institutions. The inclusive approach and methods of experiment design empowered older people and promoted their social connectedness and social inclusion as well as helped many to gather relevant information on services and opportunities.

To conclude, the PROMEQ approach offers an alternative approach to improve health and well-being, and to strengthen the commitment with individual and structural social change, as well as to the further development of social, health, and employment services. Strategically, PROMEQ follows the recommendation of embedding strategic social marketing in social policies, programmes, and projects to improve collaboration with policymakers and key stakeholders. Practically, PROMEQ used the rich mix of social marketing methods and strategies in the collaboration with disadvantaged groups and PPP stakeholders. Finally, PROMEQ introduced a new approach not only for tailored and segmented programs, services, and policies to the individuals but also for improving the responsiveness of services and collaborating with various stakeholders.

Acknowledgements

PROMEQ was funded by the Strategic Research Council of the Academy of Finland (#303615). PROMEQ consortium was lead by professor Marja Vaarama from the University of Eastern Finland. Consortium included Research Institute of the Finnish Economy (ETLA), University of Helsinki (UH), Finnish Youth Research Society (FYRS), University of Jyväskylä (JyU), University of Tampere (TAU) and University of Lapland (ULapland).

References

Abel, T., & Frohlich, K. (2012). Capitals and capabilities: Linking structure and agency to reduce health inequalities. *Social Science & Medicine, 74*, 236–244.

Anand, P., Hunter, G., & Smith, R. (2005). Capabilities and well-being: Evidence based on the Sen-Nussbaum Approach to welfare. *Social Indicator Research, 74*(1), 9–55.

Andreasen, A. (2002). Marketing social marketing in the social change marketplace. *Journal of Public Policy & Marketing, 21*(1), 3–13.

148　*Tomi Mäki-Opas et al.*

Atkinson, A.B. (2015). *Inequality. What Can Be Done?* London: Harvard University Press.

Beck, W., Van Der Maesen, L., & Walker, A. (Eds.). (1997). *The Social Quality of Europe.* The Hague, The Netherlands: Kluwer Law International.

Buyucek, N., Kubacki, K., Rundle-Thiele, S., & Pang, B. (2016). A systematic review of stakeholder involvement in social marketing interventions. *Australasian Marketing Journal, 24,* 8–19.

Freeman, R. (1984). *Strategic Management: A Stakeholder Approach.* Boston: Pitman Series in Business and Public Policy.

French, J., & Gordon, R. (2015). *Strategic Social Marketing.* London: Sage.

Green, J., Tones, K., Cross, R., & Woodwall, J. (2015). *Health Promotion – Planning & Strategies.* London: Sage.

Hastings, G., & Domegan, C. (2014). *Social Marketing: From Tunes to Symphonies.* Abingdon: Routledge.

Hopwood, T., & Merritt, R. (Eds.). (2011). *Big Pocket Guide to Social Marketing.* National Social Marketing Center.

Junttila, N., Ahlqvist-Björkroth, S., Aromaa, M., Rautava, P., Piha, J., Vauras, M., Lagström, H., & Räihä, H. (2013). Mothers' and fathers' loneliness during pregnancy, infancy, and toddlerhood. *Psychology and Education, 50,* 98–104.

Kestilä, L., & Karvonen, S. (2019). *Suomalaisten hyvinvointi 2018: Terveyden ja hyvinvoinnin laitos.* PunaMusta Oy. Helsinki.

Koponen, P., Borodulin, K., Lundqvist, A., Sääksjärvi, K., & Koskinen, S. (2018). *Terveys, toimintakyky ja hyvinvointi Suomessa – FinTerveys 2017-tutkimus.* Helsinki: Terveyden ja hyvinvoinnin laitos (THL).

Langford, R., & Panter-Brick, C. (2013). A health equality critique of social marketing where interventions have impact but insufficient research. *Social Science & Medicine, 83,* 133–141.

Lefebvre, R.C. (2013). *Social Marketing and Social Change.* San Francisco: Wiley.

Lucca, N.R., Hibbert, S., & McDonald, R. (2016). Towards a service-dominant approach to social marketing. *Marketing Theory, 16,* 194–218.

Marmot, M. (2010). Fair Society Healthy Lives (The Marmot Review). Retrieved from www.instituteofhealthequity.org/projects/fair-society-healthy-lives-the-marmot-review.

Marmot, M. (2014). *The Health Gap. The Challenge of an Unequal World.* New York: Bloomsbury.

Murto, J., Kaikkonen, R., Pentala-Nikulainen, O., Koskela, T., Virtala, E., Härkänen, T., Koskenniemi, T., Jussmäki, T., Vartiainen, E., & Koskinen, S. (2018). Alueellisen terveys-, hyvinvointi-ja palvelututkimus ATH:n perustulokset 2010–2016 (Available in Finnish). Accessed February 8, 2018, Retrieved from www.thl.fi/ath.

Nussbam, M. (2011). *Creating Capabilities. The Human Development Approach.* London Belknap Press of Harvard University Press.

Pieper, R., Vaarama, M., & Karvonen, S. (2019). The SOLA Model – A theory-based approach to social quality and social sustainability. *Social Indicators Research, 146,* 553–580.

Robinson, L. (2009). The problem with Social Marketing. Why you can't sell change like soap. Retrieved from www.enablingchange.com.au/The_problem_with_Social_Marketing.pdf.

Rotko, T., Kauppinen, T., Mustonen, N., & Linnanmäki, E. (2012). National action plan to reduce health inequalities 2008–2011, final report. (English abstract). Retrieved from Helsinki: www.julkari.fi/bitstream/handle/10024/90863/URN_ISBN_978-952-245-671-7.pdf?sequence=1.

Rubin, A., & Babbie, E. (2017). *Essential Research Methods for Social Work*. Boston: CENGAGE Learning.

Sen, A. (1993). Capability and well-being. In M. Nussbaum & A. Sen (Eds.), *The Quality of Life* (pp. 30–53). Oxford: Clarendon Press.

Sihto, M., & Karvonen, S. (2016). *Terveyden edistäminen ja eriarvoisuus – lähestymistapoja ja ratkaisuja*. Helsinki: Terveyden ja hyvinvoinnin laitos.

STM. (2008). National action plan to reduce Health Inequalities 2008–2011 (English Abstract). *Publications of the Ministry of Social Affairs and Health*. Retrieved from http://urn.fi/URN:NBN:fi-fe201504225427.

Vaarama, M., Pieper, R., & Sixsmith, A. (2008). *Care-Related Quality of Life in Old Age*. New York: Springer.

van der Maesen, L.J.G., & Walker, A. (2012). *Social Quality. From Theory to Indicators*. New York: Palgrave Macmillan.

Vargo, S. L., & Lusch, R. F. (2006). Service-dominant logic: What it is, what it is not, what it might be. In R. F. Lusch & S. L. Vargo (Eds.), *The Service-Dominant Logic of Marketing: Dialog Debate and Direction* (pp. 43–56). Armok: ME Sharpe.

Veenhoven, R. (2000). The four qualities of life. Ordering concepts and measures of the good life. *Journal of Happiness Studies*.

Weinreich, N.K. (2011). *Hands-On Social Marketing. A Step-by-Step Guide to Designing Change for Good*. London: Sage.

WHO. (2014). The equity action spectrum: Taking a comprehensive approach. Guidance for addressing inequities in health. Retrieved from www.euro.who.int/en/data-and-evidence/equity-in-health-project/policy-briefs.

WHOQOL Group. (1998). Development of the World Health Organization WHOQOL-Bref QoL assessment. The WHOQOL Group. *Psychological Medicine*, *28*(3), 551–558.

10 Plural rationality approach to stakeholder engagement

Kathy Knox and Joy Parkinson

Introduction

Stakeholders in environmental phenomena have deeply rooted disciplinary or cultural origins, values, epistemologies, and ideologies. Representing and translating the heterogeneity of stakeholders' perspectives and dealing constructively with value-based issues in decision-making is therefore inherently difficult. Social marketing application in environmental issues is on the increase (Kim, Rundle-Thiele, & Knox, 2019), where tools like co-design have been adopted. Current literature on co-design recognises the importance of understanding diversity of objectives (Trischler, Kristensson, & Scott, 2018) and so is well suited in environmental issues. On the other hand, in some places, the law mandates the importance of including stakeholder perspectives in environmental decision-making. For example, the participation of stakeholders in the decision-making process surrounding landslide risk management is mandated by the European Union (Scolobig, Thompson, & Linnerooth-Bayer, 2016). In the context of environmental decision-making, stakeholder engagement increases decision legitimacy, likelihood of implementation, and quality of outcome (Scolobig & Lilliestam, 2016).

This chapter describes the process and outcomes of integrating stakeholder consultation in a social marketing programme within an environmental context, using a plural rationality approach. The goal was to inform the design, implementation, and evaluation of a behaviour change programme to manage domestic dog and koala interactions in one local government area in Australia. The interplay between stakeholders and numerous influences on the environmental context indicates the complexity of wildlife conservation, with the result being a situation where each of the stakeholders in this complex system has multiple goals, and each is subject to multiple pressures and influences. For example, property developers have an economic interest in planning legislation, pet-owners call for autonomy in caring for their pets, and wildlife conservationists are concerned with the welfare and conservation of local wildlife. As such, their actions can appear to conflict with each other, and the ramifications of each action on other parties are often unclear. Thus, to guide the development of a programme aiming to reduce dog and koala

Plural rationality approach 151

interactions it was important to take the relevant stakeholder perspectives into consideration. In the following case study, we describe the methodology based on plural rationality approach which we employed to co-produce knowledge with stakeholders in developing a social marketing campaign to address this environmental issue. We describe the implementation and results of the process of integrating stakeholder perspectives based on theory of plural rationality and reflect on the process as it translated into options for addressing the environmental issue.

Stakeholder engagement in environmental issues

Stakeholder theory is one of the major approaches in social, environmental, and sustainability management research (Montiel & Delgado-Ceballos, 2014). There is increasing recognition of the importance of integrating stakeholder perspectives in developing policy or models in the context of environmental decision-making (Scolobig & Lilliestam, 2016). Explicit and comprehensive analysis of diversity of objectives for stakeholder engagement leads to practical ways to strengthen stakeholder engagement, identify new solutions, and improve the legitimacy of decisions. Stakeholder engagement is therefore a critical component of social marketing benchmark criteria (NSMC, 2008) and is shown to improve buy-in (Hodgkins, Rundle-Thiele, Knox, & Kim, 2019). Stakeholder engagement is important because behaviour change attempts operate within broader systems each with a range of actors and contributors. That said, there are considerable challenges pertaining to stakeholder engagement in environmental issues. We provide a brief overview of considerations here: determining the objectives of stakeholder engagement in environmental issues, identifying who qualifies as a stakeholder in environmental issues, establishing how to engage stakeholders when it comes to environmental issues, and ways to integrate perspectives translating to practical decisions. The issues are discussed, and then we describe the plural rationality approach to stakeholder engagement, before presenting the case study where we applied this approach to a local environmental issue.

What are the objectives of stakeholder engagement in environmental issues?

The objectives of stakeholder engagement in relation to environmental issues include gaining an understanding of the diversity of values, increasing the transparency of decision-making processes, and gaining support from stakeholders for solutions to problems. Stakeholder engagement seeks to influence a variety of outcomes through consultation, communication, negotiation, compromise, and relationship building. Stakeholders have diverse rationales for engagement, which can be implicit, understood from different perspectives and suit different purposes or motivations. Characterising the diversity can serve to challenge the predominant tendency to focus only on a few objectives (Garard & Kowarsch, 2017). In the current example, stakeholder engagement in addressing the local

152 *Kathy Knox and Joy Parkinson*

issue of declining koala populations was driven by the objective to explicitly address multiple conflicting interests, knowledge and value systems, and geographic contexts. In South East Queensland (SE QLD), Australia, there are wide variations in community behaviours and attitudes towards conservation of biodiversity in urban and peri-urban areas, including actions to conserve koalas: traffic calming, conservation schemes, development, and council-led initiatives (Shumway, Seabrook, McAlpine, & Ward, 2014) such as fencing, confinement of domestic pets, regulations governing the presence of dogs in public spaces, parks and beaches, and so on. The topic is highly emotive and regularly debated in public media. Debate often becomes heated, with protests, rallies, and energetic lobbying (Figure 10.1). Sensitivity to local community attitudes and perceptions is needed to minimise conflict and promote collaborative solutions (Shumway et al., 2014).

Who are the stakeholders in environmental issues?

A general definition is provided by Freeman (1984, p. 25), who describes stakeholders as "those groups and individuals who can affect or be affected" by the actions connected to value creation and trade. Stakeholders may be individuals, groups, or organisations affected by the outcome of the initiative proposed or in a situation to affect that outcome. However, there is a challenge to identify which stakeholders are involved in an environmental issue since the success of a behaviour change programme depends on the appropriate stakeholders' input, and therefore the lead organisation management has a commitment to their involvement and representation. A stakeholder is any individual involved but could encompass non-involved audience members (Garard & Kowarsch, 2017). In environmental decision-making, stakeholders can be any individual involved in some capacity, including representatives of international organisations, national, state, or local government representatives, expert scientists from diverse disciplinary and geographic backgrounds, non-government organisations, business, industry, target audience members, and non-involved target audience members (Garard & Kowarsch, 2017).

Specifically, in the context of human–wildlife conflict, the community of stakeholders frequently involves conflict between stakeholders with different goals, attitudes, values, feelings, and levels of empowerment (Madden, 2004). In the context of koalas in developed suburban locations in SE QLD, the community of stakeholders is diverse and can be characterised by heated emotion and opposing goals (see Figure 10.1). Stakeholders at different levels within the system seek to establish and maintain rights and responsibilities with respect to the issue that may either contribute to the problem or attempt to solve it (Brennan, Previte, & Fry, 2016). There are a range of stakeholders which influence koala conservation including policymakers and government officials from local, state, and national levels (Governance); ecologists, biologists, zoologists, veterinarians, business operators (Professionals); community action groups, lobbyists, campaigners, wildlife rescue volunteers, advocates (Volunteers); and pet-owners, land owners, residents, and the broader community (Locals).

Plural rationality approach 153

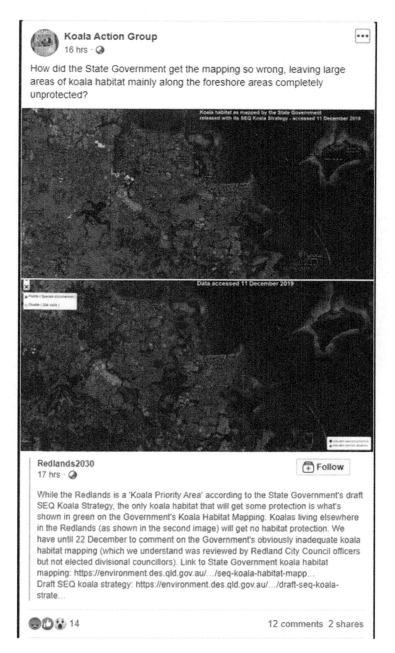

Figure 10.1 (a and b) Koala conservation in the Redland City Council is a heated topic.
Source: www.facebook.com/KoalaActionGroup/, retrieved 13 December 2019.

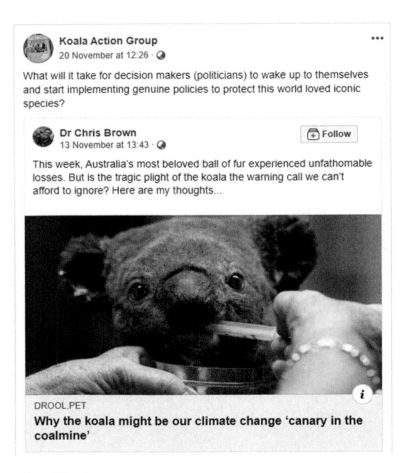

Figure 10.1 (Cont.)

What are the methods of stakeholder engagement in environmental issues?

Qualitatively different methods for stakeholder engagement in environmental issues exist: for example, multi-criteria analysis (Esteves, 2008) and scenario construction (Tompkins, Few, & Brown, 2008) to name but two. Each approach sits within a paradigm, and there are differences between approaches in their assumptions about stakeholder rationality, who oversees the framing of problems (i.e. stakeholders or experts), type of input from stakeholders, how input from stakeholders is used. Evidence indicates that intensive stakeholder engagement processes result in high-quality decisions in the sphere of environmental decision-making (for a review, see Beierle, 2002). Stakeholder engagement improves environmental decisions by adding new information, ideas, and analysis (Beierle, 2002). In the current example, a plural rationality approach was applied, which featured four steps: (1) identification of stakeholder perspectives, (2) co-production of options, (3) discussion of options in working groups, and (4) devise a clumsy (imperfect) compromise solution. The approach is described in more detail later.

How to integrate stakeholders' perspectives regarding environmental issues?

Effective stakeholder engagement and integration has important benefits for environmental decision-making and can lead to identification of novel solutions (Rundle-Thiele et al., 2019) and improve the legitimacy of decisions made (Beierle, 2002). Effective stakeholder consultation and integration of resulting 'insight' is thought to increase the likelihood that campaign or policy implementation will be effective, reduce psychological reactance, and contribute to the overall sustainability of action. In environmental applications, social marketing is a relative newcomer. In our case we sought to integrate perspectives from parties who shared a stake in the issue (dog-owners, residents, conservation volunteers, wildlife carers, scientists, community members) but in other ways were at conflicting standpoints. We applied the four steps of plural rationality approach to facilitate integration of stakeholder perspectives.

How to translate stakeholder perspectives into environmental decision-making?

There are various ways to engage stakeholders and integrate their perspectives in environmental decision-making (see Scolobig & Lilliestam, 2016 for comparison). Best practice suggests that social marketing campaigns incorporate some element of stakeholder consultation (NSMC, 2008). A core element of stakeholder theory is generating mutual interests between different stakeholders rather than focusing on trade-offs. Based on these mutual interests, stakeholder theory aims at creating value for all stakeholders involved (Freeman, Harrison, Wicks, Parmar, & De Colle, 2010). In this sense, the social marketing understanding of stakeholder theory substantially differs from purely instrumental interpretations that test the existence of an empirical link between differing stakeholder interests (e.g. stakeholder involvement and corporate financial performance), as we aim to explore opportunities for installing positive links between stakeholder interests. Thus, the social marketing stakeholder approach integrates stakeholder perspectives into decision-making to develop a mutually agreeable and beneficial solution. In the current case study, we applied a plural rationality approach to integrating stakeholder perspectives. The plural rationality approach is explained next.

Plural rationality approach

A rationality is a conceptual framework for perceiving what constitutes rational (i.e. logically valid, reasoned) action. The concept of plural rationality recognises the diversity of worldviews. Different rationalities exist which

156 Kathy Knox and Joy Parkinson

involve differences in tastes or preferences, interests and values, but more fundamentally, different frameworks for perceiving what type of behaviour can be regarded as 'rational.' The plural rationality approach originated in social anthropology (Douglas, 2002, 2013), then extended to economics as 'cultural theory of risk,' and later became integrated with sociology (Thompson, 2008b). Recently the notion of plural rationalities has been applied to understanding human responses to risk, for example, the global financial crisis (see Thompson, 2008a) and environmental planning (Scolobig et al., 2016).

According to the plural rationality approach, any social domain consists of a dynamic mix of a limited number of socially constructed stakeholder perspectives: hierarchy, individualism, egalitarianism, and fatalism (Douglas, 1992; Thompson, 2008b). These four archetypal perspectives are representative of fundamentally different and often conflicting worldviews and form the basis of understanding the sources of potential conflict in environmental planning (Verweij, Senior, Domínguez, Juan, & Turner, 2015). The hierarchical perspective is pro-control; problems demand expertly planned solution. This translates into a focus on top-down planning, featuring a reliance on government authority, and trust in a network of *experts*. The individualist perspective is pro-market: favours de-regulation and recognises individual freedom to innovate and take risks. The individualist rationality is characterised by explicit recognition of trade-offs among competing uses of resources. In contrast the egalitarian perspective is strident and critical, holding a sceptical view of both the individualist notion of trade-off and the hierarchical view that an expert-driven approach is best. The egalitarian perspective argues for a holistic, moralistic, or natural approach to problems. The fourth typology is the fatalist perspective: fatalism sees no possibility of affecting change for the better. These four opposing rationalities represent patterns of organising social relations, for example: attitudes to status, expertise, and power; and each has their associated cultural biases, perceptions, beliefs, and emotions (Perri, 2002). Plural rationality theory suggests that the actions of groups that are driven by these four belief systems functions to move the world from one type or level of risk to another.

The four archetypes can be adapted to environmental issues and, in this case study, provide a useful point of reference for constructing and understanding stakeholders' discourse (as a shared structured way of speaking, thinking, interpreting, representing ideas or sets of ideas). Applying the plural rationality approach in this study, the aim was to find a compromise solution. Rather than seek a consensus on one single best option, plural rationality theory proposes that social researchers may reach a compromise "through explicit elicitation of stakeholders' perspective on the nature and cause of the problem and its solution" (Scolobig & Lilliestam, 2016). Importantly plural rationality approach does not seek a single best option with consensus. Using the plural rationality framework, we looked for a 'fuzzy' or 'clumsy' imperfect compromise solution. Key steps in achieving this goal were to (1) identify stakeholder perspectives, (2) co-produce options, (3) discuss options in working groups, and (4) arrive at

Plural rationality approach   157

a compromise proposal. According to commentators, to achieve agreement or fuzzy compromise can be possible if we recognise diversity, learn and exchange information, and agree on principles (Wierzbicki, 1985). In the current case study, we adapted the principles of plural rationality to development of a community behaviour change program targeting wildlife preservation in South East Queensland.

Case study – Reducing domestic dog and koala interactions

The setting for this case study was Redland City Council, a local government area in South East Queensland with a significant koala population. The koala is an Australian iconic animal. Population levels are steadily decreasing (Redland City Council, 2016), and there was an estimated 80% decline in population density between 1996 and 2014 in South East Queensland (Rhodes, Hawthorne Beyer, Harriet Preece, & McAlpine, 2015). After habitat loss and traffic accidents, dog attacks, and predation are the third most common cause of death in koalas, and three out of four dog attacks are fatal (Queensland Government Department of Environment and Science, 2017). Statistics from the Koala Action Group QLD Inc. indicate that more than 600 koalas have been attacked by dogs over the past 15 years in the Redland City area. Redland City Council approached Social Marketing @ Griffith to help tackle this issue.

Redland City Council recognised that a city-wide behaviour change program to reduce koala injury, and mortality from domestic dog attacks would support councils regulatory provisions. To reduce koala and dog interactions, a behaviour change program was sought to identify and investigate community behaviours requiring change to reduce koala and dog interactions and develop and pilot a behaviour change program responding specifically to Redland's issues and needs regarding koala and dog interactions (targeting dog-owners). To address domestic dog interactions with native wildlife in the Redlands area, a research-based social marketing intervention was developed by Social Marketing @ Griffith (David et al., 2019; Hussenoeder et al., 2017; Rundle-Thiele et al., 2019). The focal goal was implementation of a community behaviour change initiative to reduce dogs interacting (*barking, chasing, injuring*) with koalas.

Initially we conducted a literature review (see Pang et al., 2017) which identified a complete absence of peer-reviewed research reporting interventions that targeted dog and koala interactions, although surveys of community attitudes (Shumway et al., 2014) and of koala populations had been published (de Villiers, 2015; Ng et al., 2014). Most of the relevant wildlife protection interventions reviewed were developed from environmental or ecological perspectives and failed to address individual voluntary behaviours such as pet-owners' willingness to contain dogs indoors at night. The next stage of programme planning was stakeholder engagement. The methodology we employed was aligned with the four key stages in plural rationality process: (1) identify stakeholder perspectives, (2) co-produce options, (3) discuss options in working groups,

158 Kathy Knox and Joy Parkinson

and (4) arrive at a compromise proposal. Campaign activities are described here in terms of the plural rationality approach with emphasis on the first stage, identifying stakeholder perspectives. Outcomes and evaluation research from this project have been published elsewhere (David et al., 2019; Lee & Kotler, 2019; Rundle-Thiele et al., 2019).

Identify stakeholder perspectives

A series of semi-structured interviews were conducted between January and February 2017 with identified stakeholders to enable rich contextual data to be collected. Expert consultation interviews were used to provide relevant detailed insights from experienced agents representing different rationalities (step 1, identify stakeholder perspectives) and reveal information about previous unpublished campaigns that might not otherwise have been accessible, and that fed into co-production of options (step 2) with stakeholder input in a series of co-design focus group sessions.

Following institutional ethics clearance, the research team consulted with the local government area working group to scope a framework of relevant stakeholder groups. The working group comprised parties with specialist ecological training; deep local knowledge of the local community; hands-on experience on the ground with stakeholders; and knowledge of relevant local, state, and national policy. A stakeholder framework was generated in consultation with the working group, and this framework deliberately included stakeholder groups known to hold discrepant viewpoints: community and volunteer groups (*Volunteers*), wildlife carers, veterinarians, trainers (*Professionals*), local council officers, canine behaviourists, and scientists working in research and policy (*Governance*), and local landowners (*Locals*). The working group members recommend three to four individuals within each stakeholder group for inclusion in interviews. The working group assisted to supply the researchers with publicly available contact information for potential interviewees. The researchers contacted nominated stakeholders for interviews. The resulting purposive sample contained 14 experts who represented a range of stakeholder groups with relevant expertise.

A semi-structured interview schedule was developed to gather contextual information, facts about existing or previous campaigns, and to identify potential facilitating factors and barriers to program participation. Interviews were consultative conversations organised around a series of predetermined questions or prompts, conducted with one participant at a time, and executed at the interviewees' convenience. The schedule incorporated prompts but allowed flexibility to enable comprehensive coverage of the key issues raised by stakeholders. One experienced researcher conducted all interviews.

Interviews commenced with collecting some contextual background information. Then the interview continued to elicit information about previous campaigns or activities conducted by relevant organisations and groups in and around the Redland City Council area. Interviewees were asked to identify behaviours that dog-owners currently do, or could do, to decrease dog and koala interactions and were asked to give their opinion on which is the most important behaviour to change. Interviews were audio recorded and later transcribed by a professional service. Identifying information was obscured. Participants did not receive any incentives. There were no objections or refusals to give an interview although some identified stakeholders could not be reached during the consultation timeframe due to illness or unavailability.

Applying the plural rationality approach to the data, the transcripts were thematically analysed to identify rationality typologies, represented by stakeholder perspectives on expertise, autonomy, power, dominance, interests, and status. Following the key phases of the plural rationality approach, this thematic analysis represents the elicitation of stakeholder perspectives (step 1). The purpose of the analysis was to identify stakeholder perspectives and needs, generate discourse, and elicit views from the four perspectives based on plural rationality archetypes. Examples of previous or current campaigns were extracted and verified by the research team. Campaign materials, documentation of campaign effectiveness, relevant collateral and reports were sought including PhD theses, advertising and promotional materials, news articles, and public information brochures. Previous campaign examples were summarised and compiled for inclusion in co-production (step 2).

Fourteen stakeholders participated in interviews. Individual interviews ran for approximately 30 minutes. Analyses are presented here according to plural rationality typologies. Within each stakeholder group or field of experience, individual stakeholders represented different fundamental approaches to rationality, or world views. Their rationality typology shaped their semantics and presentation of information as well as their dialogue around barriers and drivers of behaviour and causal pathways, and thereby the potential solutions. When considered according to plural rationality *archetypes* as opposed to stakeholder *groups*, a complex picture of the problem, the actors, and the solutions began to emerge.

Profile of stakeholders by rationality

Individual stakeholders within each rationality typology represented diverse fields of expertise. Accordingly, within a rationality archetype, the demographic characteristics, years of experience, professional role, and even dog ownership status varied (Table 10.1).

Five main themes emerged from thematic coding of the transcribed interview data. Across the four rationalities, each theme was discussed from a unique worldview, leading to four differing approaches to understanding the problem and the potential solutions. The five themes which consistently arose across the archetypal rationalities were development, legislation, management, training, and communication. Stakeholders' interviews revealed unique and often opposing viewpoints on these themes under the context of community behaviour change regarding domestic dog and native wildlife interactions (i.e. koalas), as shown in Table 10.2.

Table 10.1 Characteristics of stakeholders classified by rationality typologies

Archetype	Alias	Stakeholder group	Professional role	Years of experience	Dog-owner
Hierarchical	Diana	Volunteers	Lobbyist/President of Volunteer Organisation	28	Yes
	Dave	Governance	Animal Control Officer	9	Yes
	Sharon	Volunteers	Executive Manager of Professional Organisation	unknown	unknown
Individualist	Imogen	Volunteers	President of Volunteer Organisation	20+	unknown
	Mary	Professionals	Unqualified Dog Trainer	30+	Yes
	Elizabeth	Professionals	Principal Scientist	10	unknown
	Maria	Locals	Property Owner	unknown	Yes
Egalitarian	Clarke	Professionals	Veterinarian and Qualified Behaviourist	unknown	Yes
	Beth	Professionals	Qualified Behavioural Trainer	unknown	Yes
	Nicola	Governance	Scientist	35	unknown
	Rachel	Professionals	Wildlife Veterinarian	22	unknown
Fatalist	Kylie	Locals	Property Owner	35+	Yes
	Melanie	Volunteers	Wildlife Ambulance Volunteer	11	unknown
	Shane	Volunteers	President of Volunteer Organisation	18	unknown

Table 10.2 Archetypal rationalities, thematic categories, and exemplar quotes

	Hierarchical	Individualist	Egalitarian	Fatalist
Development	Look, people aren't going to do it. They're just not going to do it. They're just not going to, that's a fact of life. And – so, that's what I think that, if I was you, I'd be segmenting existing developments and future developments. So, future developments from the [organisation's] perspective, if they're in primary habitats, they have to be dog-free. They have to be! – Diana, Volunteer.	The cost of having to fence appropriately and contain the dogs of an evening against the koala problem, it's understandable – I've just listened to this lady and I feel devastated, but our basic problem is we have very large blocks where we live. Most of them are fenced appropriately with the dogs fenced in, but the requirement is that the fences have to be a certain height. – Maria, Local.	You know, you've got big apartment blocks being built on housing blocks that were chopped down now with no trees in it, it's less likely that koalas will go through those yards because there's, you know, that whole area now will have no trees that he can use and they've normally been using the street trees and moving around along the street. So, it's – yeah, it can work but it sometimes won't work as well. – Nicola, Governance.	Basically, my concern is that I really think everything's been too late here in getting on board with conservation. It's 20 years ago it should have started, 25 years ago when we did have quite a number of koalas. – Kylie, Local. It's not about the environment, it's not about having oxygen for ourselves of space so we can breathe, it's just wall to wall housing. It's money, money, money and so, once the koalas are gone, well hey, you don't need the trees any more do you so what are you getting upset about? – Melanie, Volunteer.

(continued)

Table 10.2 (Cont.)

	Hierarchical	Individualist	Egalitarian	Fatalist
Legislation	If I do pick up a dog that is micro chipped or it is registered and I can take it back home, which I like to do, while I'm there I can have a look at their enclosure. And, if the enclosure isn't adequate hit them with a 14-day notice, and I just keep following out – following up on it. – Dave So, if they're off lead and they're running around, boom, they're going to get a fine. – Dave, Governance.	[Organisation X] does not support making suburbs dog-free or necessarily saying, "They should only own small dogs," because a small dog could also attack a koala. So, we don't support that, but we do support rules around – you know, if you were in a high-koala area, we do support rules around the fencing and keeping your dog away from koalas. That is your responsibility. – Elizabeth, Professional.	There wasn't – well, there wasn't any police enforcing the – of the speed anyway. If there were speed cameras and stuff, people probably would have slowed down. That would have been an incentive, but you need to – it needed to be policed and people just aren't willing to do the right thing. – Nicola, Governance.	Let's say we're closing the door after the horse has bolted. – Kylie, Local. Protect koalas or protect or – protect koalas. We need to – I don't know. It's too big and we'd have to; you'd have to change the planning laws which is too big. – Shane, Volunteer.

Management	We don't want to hand over an animal to a member of the public or put it into a council area whereby that animal is going to again harm another animal and either cause issues for council or cause issues with what we would hope to be good neighbour relations. – Sharon, Volunteer.	We talk to people about the dog senses as well, but they have this acute sense of smell and hearing, many times greater than ours, so if our dog is inside, they will still smell or hear someone if they're lurking around the yard. Security is obviously the biggest thing we get back from pet-owners, they reason they want their dogs running in the yard all night is security. Again, I think if you educate people on the amazing things dogs are capable of with their acute senses, it might make people feel a little bit more – not everyone, but it might just help with people thinking. "Okay, if he's inside – not even inside, but if he's on the deck, he will hear someone if they're up around the back fence." – Imogen, Volunteer.	Well, the obvious thing is to lock up your dog at night. So, you know, it – it would be really nice if people living in koala habitat were prepared to confine their dog between sundown and sunrise. That would be a lovely thing. Then if not that, have a koala proof perimeter fence to stop koalas coming into your yard, and there, you know, koala proof perimeter fences can be things that are desirable fences. – Rachel, Professional.	To get fencing that a koala can't climb is probably fairly expensive. – Kylie, Local.

(continued)

Table 10.2 (Cont.)

	Hierarchical	Individualist	Egalitarian	Fatalist
Training	So, responsible pet ownership is something that we want to advocate with all of our councils we work with, keeping our dogs and cats in at night, because that's when our wildlife – we're fantastic here in Australia. We've got our native – our nocturnal animals. If we can keep our animals in at night, so many more animals would live – Sharon, Volunteer.	You know, didn't we have the biggest koala colony in Australia at one time? So, you know, are we proud of this or we're not proud of this? Let's just help. We're not – and not criticise people about it, just say, "Look, if you could work a little bit better, you know, we can – you can do a free class or something like that to just learn a little bit" – just basics. I want them to just learn basic control. – Mary, Professional.	Simply because we are all technically mammals and interestingly, when you look at behaviour, you look at body language. We mimic exactly what other animals do with our behaviour. – Beth, Professional.	So, I don't know how you educate people that we may save a lot of wildlife if that dog's inside at night. – Kylie, Local. It can be very difficult. You can't force people. – Kylie, Local.

Plural rationality approach 165

| Communication | It's not a very big island so it's up for – for me to be around police and to be seen there all the time. I go over there. I talk to – I give people a chance. No second chance. I speak to the locals and – and everything like that. – Dave, Governance. We are advocating to any of our councils with your animal control laws, we know, we train the animals, fantastic to have your pets inside with you at night, it's not harming them in any way. – Sharon, Volunteer. | I think it's actually creating – it's also – what's the word? Building a bridge between dog-owners and the environmental people. I think there's often seen to be this perception with dog people that environmental people hate dogs. I almost feel it's a bit of an us and them. I'm a dog-owner myself. As soon as I mention that, people kind of go, "Okay." So, I think there's a bit of a ways to go with building that bridge between people that are trying to give advice on how you can keep wildlife safe and still be a dog-owner. – Imogen, Volunteer. | When you explain to people the virtue and the value and the features of benefits of a dog being in a den, they are much more likely to – to come across with that and say, "Yes, I understand what you're saying now." – Clarke, Professional.

You can't get through to people. And, people, they don't want to know about it. They get very defensive when, you know, trying to educate them about their dogs and it's just like you can only do what you can do but they're not listening and nothing's enforced. – Melanie, Volunteer. |

166 *Kathy Knox and Joy Parkinson*

The hierarchical viewpoint representatives relied on legislative power to deliver messages and their discussion of themes reflected a strong support for planning, policing, and expert-driven solutions: *"Some people just don't care. But you've got to police that" (Dave, Governance)*. This pro-control approach applied to the management of animals and their behaviours, inspection, and enforcement of local legislation, communication, and outreach, as well as development and infrastructure change as it pertains to the context of domestic animal and native fauna interactions: *"I want a koala protection act which is going to force people to do this" (Diana, Volunteer)*. The advocates represented the hierarchical rationality in their words and their actions, and descriptions of how their personal experience interacting with the issue at hand reflected the worldview featuring top-down planning and solutions driven by legislation and enforcement, driven by expert opinion: *"We don't want to hand over an animal to a member of the public or put it into a council area whereby that animal is going to again harm another animal" (Sharon, Volunteer)*.

The individualist viewpoint strongly supported individual freedoms, recognising that there are trade-offs among competing functions of public and private spaces, and that in a free market people have the right to choose behaviours that they value: *"Most people want to do the right thing but they need to have reason to do it" (Imogen, Volunteer)*. The perspectives put forward by proponents of the individualist rationality articulated rejection of legislated guidelines while appreciating the sentiments behind them. Instead, the individualist viewpoint advocates for reasoned, justifiable behaviours, and explanations of behaviours are based on personalised notions of benefit:

> *Getting people to change is very difficult and for different people, the trigger to make them change is different. I'm not a social scientist; I'm a scientist, so this is not my area of expertise, but just from my experience, getting people to change is very difficult. People will complain about cost. They will talk about individual freedom. They will say it's all too difficult. There'll be lots of reasons why they don't want to do it. Some people will care enough about wildlife to do it and other people just don't.*

> (Elizabeth, Professional)

The egalitarian viewpoint respects and understands the multiplicity of motivations, barriers, and hurdles to behaviour change. Their discourse demonstrates a moral approach that considers the various competing factors that influence individual behaviour. The ensuing reasoning is holistic in that it considers the logic and reasoning behind a person's, an animal's, or a group's choices. The egalitarian archetype considers various viewpoints, how these interact to influence behaviour, and weighs up the associated values and motives underlying behaviours. This results in a balanced perspective which is critical of heavy-handed top-down legislation but understands the importance of enforcement, which argues for a fair and informed stance, and treats actors as agents making choices in a complex environment:

Plural rationality approach 167

when you explain to people the virtue and the value and the features of benefits of a dog being in a den, they are much more likely to — to come across with that and say, "Yes, I understand what you're saying now."

(Clarke, Professional)

The fatalist viewpoint was stark and depressing. The fatalist perspective perceives little to no practical means of altering the course of events to achieve positive outcomes, across thematic domains of development, legislation, management, training, or communication (see Table 10.2). What is interesting in this stakeholder context is that those whose viewpoints reflect a fatalist rationality were still active in some regards, in volunteering and tree planting, or preservation of habitat. It is possible that through the experience of inertia and having met resistance, a fatalist attitude had developed despite involvement in voluntary actions. The diversity of perspectives in this context further highlights that a fatalistic rationality might not necessarily align with apathy or helplessness.

Having identified stakeholder perspectives, the next step in the plural rationality approach was to co-produce options. To achieve co-production with stakeholders, we elicited examples of previous or current campaigns and approaches to environmental management of domestic animals and native wildlife, to use as stimulus in co-design sessions.

Co-produce options

Across the stakeholder groups it is possible to draw distinctions according to areas of expertise and experience (Table 10.3). Accordingly, the different stakeholder groups presented examples of previous or current campaign concepts and engagement approaches that varied in specificity and scope.

Expert stakeholders identified various campaign activities (Table 10.4) such as letter box drops, static education displays (https://environment.des. qld.gov.au/__data/assets/pdf_file/0025/86524/koalas-and-dogs.pdf), social media (Facebook) groups, a speed zone trial, visitor programs, surveys and microchipping, and registration drive events. Most examples were multifaceted

Table 10.3 Stakeholder framework and number of interviews

Stakeholder group	Area of expertise	Interviews
Volunteers	Wildlife preservation and advocacy, animal care and rescue	5
Professionals	Veterinary practice, animal behaviour, training and psychology	5
Governance	Environmental heritage and protection, ecology, habitat preservation	2
Locals	Homeowners, residents	2

168 *Kathy Knox and Joy Parkinson*

Table 10.4 Campaign concepts to reduce dog and koala interactions

Awareness	Marketing	Legislation
Letter box drops	Obedience training	Enforced speed zones
Static education displays	program	Animal control regulation
Visitor programs	Online videos	Microchipping and pet
School-based education	Koala alert smart phone	registration
program	application	Consistent enforcement
	Financial incentives	
	Wildlife focus in program	
	materials	

Source: Adapted from Rundle-Thiele et al., 2019.

and comprise actions or targets concerning (a) habitat preservation or restoration, (b) community education and awareness, (c) traffic calming strategies, and (d) animal control legislation, all of which require long time frames to implement. No explicit examples of social marketing campaigns were identified, and few campaigns had been evaluated for reach, outcomes or impact.

Community groups and volunteers from wildlife care organisations (Volunteers) typically conducted activities to raise community awareness and implemented tree planting programs. Such activities included occasional community events, static displays at information centres, reactive letterbox drops in response to koala sightings or dog and koala interactions, and ad-hoc information to residents. The approach reflected reactionary responses and emergent care in response to need.

Policy and governance scientific research stakeholders (Governance) worked to collate data to map habitat and monitor injuries and fatalities as well as review develop and implement action plans for local government areas management recommendations. The Governance stakeholder group indicated their involvement in research, consulting, and making submissions to inquiries or planning panels. The approach reflected a distinctly top-down evidence or policy-based approach.

Veterinarians, behaviourists, and animal management experts (Professionals) achieved behaviour change at an individual level through training and education of dog-owners. Professionals and animal behaviour practitioners epitomised an individualised behaviour management approach which was based on scientific study of animal behaviour and psychology.

We took example campaign concepts and collateral into co-design focus group workshops to co-produce options that stakeholder groups would engage with and value. Campaign concepts were incorporated as stimulus materials in a series of co-design sessions with stakeholder representatives, where pros and cons were discussed, needs and wants were considered, and stakeholders came together to co-produce options. Over 40 individuals representing community members and stakeholder groups participated in co-design sessions. To develop options the researchers facilitated and guided discussion to translate stakeholders' perspectives into technical options consistent with stakeholders' perspectives. The co-design process generated multiple options including novel campaign concepts based on awareness and education, marketing and service design, and legal structures. The unique and innovative ideas stemming from co-production of options were for a smartphone-based alert systems tracking koala movement in urban areas and for specialist dog training and obedience behaviour management coaching.

Discuss options in working groups

The third step stemming from a plural rationality approach was to engage in an analytical deliberative discussion aimed at reaching a compromise solution (as opposed to consensus). There are no prescribed methods for achieving this step. However, in the previous examples of stakeholder engagement in environmental issues, participatory processes including meetings, working groups, and consultations have been conducted at this step (Linnerooth-Bayer, Scolobig, Ferlisi, Cascini, & Thompson, 2016). In our case, following co-design processes and synthesis of the concepts generated therein, the research team settled on viable options. These options were presented to and discussed with the working group (comprised of client and stakeholder representatives) to further build the design and decide on the implementation of a process that would combine both previous steps (1) expert input and (2) public participation, in order to seek out a clumsy compromise solution.

At this step, researchers presented a compromise 'pilot strategy' proposal that combines insights from the plural rationalities identified in stakeholder consultation and incorporates concepts and insights generated at the co-design sessions. We strove to maintain sensitivity to the themes emerging from identification of stakeholder perspectives, balancing the plural conceptions of autonomy, power, and dominance across practical thematic categories such as legislation, management training, and communication. From the individualist viewpoint, any options we discussed should give motivation and reduce costs to participation. The egalitarian rationality showed us the importance of emphasising value to the individual and treating consumers as intelligent agents exercising independent choice. Inspired by the fatalist perspective, our proposal encompassed the surrounding community of active volunteers to break down any perception of inertia, overwhelm or hopelessness. From the hierarchical rationality, our solution should proactively communicate and emphasise the positive role of local enforcement and legislation in working together with the target groups.

A working group comprising stakeholders representing the various groups in our stakeholder framework and researchers discussed the pilot strategy options, identifying areas of agreement, areas of disagreement, and highlighting priorities for action. Based on campaign elements and key constructs from the discourse analysis and options generated in the co-design focus groups, the priorities emerged: a programme focused on dogs and dog-owners was preferred to a programme focusing on wildlife preservation; a whole-of community campaign was needed so as not to single out individuals. We hashed out next steps, generated a schedule of work going forward, and workshopped branding and messaging components.

Arrive at a compromise proposal

The fourth step in the process was to reach a clumsy compromise or fuzzy solution. With representatives from stakeholder groups including Governance, Volunteers, and Professionals, we began to design a compromise solution negotiated with some benefits for all stakeholders. Researchers provided the background to reach the compromise, by engaging with stakeholders and providing inputs. Pre-requisites for a compromise solution were accessibility (i.e. each perspective was able to make itself heard) and responsiveness (each perspective was engaged with, rather than dismissive of others). The critical point in arriving at a compromise solution was respect for the heterogeneity of stakeholder views and rationalities, as opposed to convergence or persuasion towards a consensus. Each viewpoint was important and was considered in the decision-making process.

For this project, the compromise proposal drew from divergent rationalities considering their perspectives and needs and took inspiration from existing examples and co-produced concepts generated by the stakeholders. The campaign ultimately focused on provision of services in the form of a behavioural obedience training program for dogs in the local area (see Figure 10.2). Trainers were invited to integrate wildlife aversion techniques into their program delivery and were given specialist training to do so. A series of public engagement events were coordinated to promote and advertise the training program. Incentives for dog-owners were embedded in the program. The wider community of pet-related services and businesses were recruited to partner with the campaign (see www.i-socialmarketing.org/index.php?option=com_content& view=article&id=244:decreasing-dog-and-koala-interactions--an-australian-social-marketing-pilot&catid=23:isma-news-desk&Itemid=119#.XfBG0-gzaUk). Process and outcome evaluations were included.

Discussion

Engaging stakeholders in environmental issues is fraught with difficulties. There are inherent complexities when representing and translating the heterogeneity of stakeholders' perspectives. Complexities are further complicated when there are value-based issues in decision-making, as is often the case with environmental issues. The problems stem from the representativeness of participants, selection bias, resources, and power imbalance between actors (researchers, client, stakeholders, consumers). While including stakeholders is important, it can slow the decision-making process. Further, bias in decision-making towards preferred solutions can undermine the democratic process. In this example

Plural rationality approach 171

Figure 10.2 Examples for the fuzzy compromise solution program design.

case study, a plural rationality approach was applied to deal with conflicting perspectives and address the inherent difficulty of integrating multiple realities in a compromise solution for a local environmental issue in a community characterised by divergent rationalities and heated debate.

The plural rationalities approach helped us to understand sources of societal conflict. The four opposing rationalities represented patterns of organising social relations, including attitudes to autonomy, dominance, and power; and each held their own perceptions, beliefs, and interests. The fundamentally straightforward process of (1) identification of stakeholder perspectives, (2) co-producing options, and then (3) discussing and workshopping options enabled researchers to focus on (4) building a clumsy compromise solution that encompassed potentially conflicting worldviews. This case demonstrates how, by understanding the origins of stakeholder behaviour and viewpoints, there is potential to assess if there is a path to working together to maintain a productive relationship to achieve a solution negotiated and acceptable to most stakeholders.

In many multi-actor decision situations, parties do not share a perception of rationality. In our case example from South East Queensland, priorities and perceptions surrounding local wildlife vary broadly. Actors and decision-makers come from different cultural backgrounds, fields of experience, and professional roles, but might share attitudes, behaviours, interests, views on what is relevant and why. Based on our analysis of discourse regarding the environmental issue and its management context, we found stakeholder groupings or categories did not necessarily share a common rationality. Stakeholders within a field of expertise or experience held vastly different values, world views, and epistemologies. The plural rationality approach afforded an alternative way to examine qualitative data and generate valuable material for designing campaign concepts: rather than consider the ideas of categories or groups of stakeholders with similar identities, by considering the archetypal rationalities new insights were uncovered. Rationalities have differing viewpoints on status, expertise, autonomy, power, dominance, interests, conflict, and co-operation: by exploring and discussing these viewpoints, we gained an insight into potential trigger points and motivations that were embedded into program design. Stakeholders highlighted important campaign components and messages that could inform behaviour change efforts targeting dog-owners. Further the expert interviews assisted the research team to identify a broad array of previous campaign approaches which were tested in co-design workshops with dog-owners.

International frameworks and case studies emphasise the importance of a multi-stakeholder approach. Yet research practice remains highly normative in which problems and their solutions are given from above. Top-down approach has limited applicability – limits local people and other stakeholders a chance to voice their concerns or influence measures. A top-down approach potentially limits the buy-in of these stakeholders which can impact the effectiveness of interventions implemented. Therefore, following a theory of plural rationality, a sustainable solution could be reached by including diverse voices in the decision-making process and building a clumsy compromise solution.

An implication of plural rationality is the need for an interactive, dynamic learning approach to any decision situation in which diverse rationalities/ stakeholders/viewpoints might occur. Plural rationality theory is applicable to many disciplines, ranging from philosophy and cultural anthropology, decision theory, game theory and economics, and applied mathematics and engineering. Applying a plural rationality lens allows reflection on the information shared by the experts that would otherwise not have been located and the value of this information to the development of the program. These experts were a rich data source, providing insights not otherwise available. Stakeholder engagement and consultation also enabled access to relevant collateral which otherwise would not have been found through the formative research process because it was not published in peer-reviewed academic literature or available online. Expert knowledge was therefore instrumental in uncovering relevant material.

Key insights gained through this process were the insider knowledge of the dynamics and local politics of the landscape, the important players, and situational factors that weigh on the issue, and the local tacit knowledge. However, there were questions left unanswered including understanding of the actual behaviours of the target audience, the perceived barriers and attitudes, and awareness of the consumers targeted for change. Hence, there are limitations to this approach, including the findings are somewhat biased towards those recommended by the reference group and those who were motivated to respond, but our research design was careful to seek a wide cross section of viewpoints from different players in the issue. Lacking in generalisability a highly localised picture of the issue has emerged, but this is a strength for developing a targeted community behaviour change campaign, given the uniqueness of the problem this study was seeking to solve.

This case study developed a detailed and theoretically grounded account of stakeholder integration in environmental campaign design following the plural rationality approach, thereby building and broadening our understanding of stakeholder engagement. In environmental issues, stakeholders have multiple perspectives often at odds. By focusing a social marketing lens on environmental decision-making in a complex community setting, this study has practical implications for managing modifiable factors that contribute to the decline of a threatened species. Previous campaign examples and evaluation data should be considered with the target audience and tested for applicability and acceptability. Exemplary campaigns are varied and multifaceted. Specific activities were identified by diverse stakeholders that subsequently informed our campaign approach, which was specifically centred on local behavioural obedience training for dogs. Important themes and practical strategies to overcome perceived barriers to behaviour change were generated through the steps in the plural rationality process. A plural rationality approach helped make sense of and bring together competing perspectives from invested stakeholders.

References

Beierle, T.C. (2002). The quality of stakeholder-based decisions. *Risk Analysis: An International Journal, 22*(4), 739–749.

Brennan, L., Previte, J., & Fry, M.-L. (2016). Social marketing's consumer myopia: Applying a behavioural ecological model to address wicked problems. *Journal of Social Marketing, 6*(3), 219–239.

David, P., Rundle-Thiele, S., Pang, B., Knox, K., Parkinson, J., & Hussenoeder, F. (2019). Engaging the dog owner community in the design of an effective koala aversion program. *Social Marketing Quarterly* (forthcoming), doi.org/10.1177/15245 00418821583.

de Villiers, D. (2015). *The Role of Urban Koalas in Maintaining Regional Population Dynamics of Koalas in the Koala Coast*. Brisbane, Australia: University of Queensland.

Douglas, M. (1992). *Risk and Blame: Essays in Cultural Theory*. London: Routledge.

Douglas, M. (2002). *Natural Symbols*. London: Routledge.

Douglas, M. (2013). *Essays on the Sociology of Perception*. London: Routledge.

Esteves, A.M. (2008). Mining and social development: Refocusing community investment using multi-criteria decision analysis. *Resources Policy, 33*(1), 39–47.

Freeman, E. (1984). *Stakeholder Management: Framework and Philosophy*. Mansfield, MA: Pitman.

Freeman, R.E., Harrison, J.S., Wicks, A.C., Parmar, B.L., & De Colle, S. (2010). *Stakeholder Theory: The State of the Art*. Cambridge: Cambridge University Press.

Garard, J., & Kowarsch, M. (2017). Objectives for stakeholder engagement in global environmental assessments. *Sustainability, 9*(9), 1571.

Hodgkins, S., Rundle-Thiele, S., Knox, K., & Kim, J. (2019). Utilising stakeholder theory for social marketing process evaluation in a food waste context. *Journal of Social Marketing, 9*(3), 270–287. doi:10.1108/jsocm-12-2017-0088.

Hussenoeder, F., Rundle-Thiele, S., Pang, B., David, P., Knox, K., & Parkinson, J. (2017). *Case Study: Using Social Marketing to Reduce Dog and Koala Interactions in a Local Council Area.* Paper presented at the UK Social Marketing Conference.

Kim, J., Rundle-Thiele, S., Knox, K. (2019). Systematic literature review of best practice in food waste reduction programs. *Journal of Social Marketing, 9*(4), 447–466. doi:10.1108/JSOCM-05-2019-0074.

Lee, N.R., & Kotler, P. (2019). *Social Marketing: Behavior Change for Social Good* (6th ed.). California: Sage.

Linnerooth-Bayer, J., Scolobig, A., Ferlisi, S., Cascini, L., & Thompson, M. (2016). Expert engagement in participatory processes: Translating stakeholder discourses into policy options. *Natural Hazards, 81*(1), 69–88.

Madden, F. (2004). Creating coexistence between humans and wildlife: Global perspectives on local efforts to address human–wildlife conflict. *Human Dimensions of Wildlife, 9*(4), 247–257.

Montiel, I., & Delgado-Ceballos, J. (2014). Defining and measuring corporate sustainability: Are we there yet? *Organization & Environment, 27*(2), 113–139.

Ng, C.F., Possingham, H.P., McAlpine, C.A., De Villiers, D.L., Preece, H.J., & Rhodes, J.R. (2014). Impediments to the success of management actions for species recovery. *PLOS ONE, 9*(4), e92430.

NSMC. (2008). *Social marketing national benchmark criteria.* London: UK National Social Marketing Centre.

Pang, B., Rundle-Thiele, S., Knox, K., Parkinson, J., David, P., & Hussenöder, F. (2017). *Extending social marketing's boundary: A systematic review of interventions aiming to protect wildlife by confining pets.* Paper presented at the ANZMAC 2017.

Perri. (2002). What is there to feel? A neo–Durkheimian theory of the emotions. *European Journal of Psychotherapy & Counselling, 5*(3), 263–290. doi:10.1080/1364253031000091363.

Queensland Government Department of Environment and Science. (2017). Koala Threats. Retrieved from www.ehp.qld.gov.au/wildlife/koalas/koala-threats.html.

Redland City Council. (2016). Redland Koala Conservation Strategy 2016. Retrieved from www.redland.qld.gov.au/download/downloads/id/2289/redland_koala_conservation_strategy_2016.pdf.

Rhodes, J.R., Hawthorne Beyer, Harriet Preece, & McAlpine, C. (2015). *South East Queensland Koala Population Modelling Study* (UniQuest Ed.). Brisbane, Australia: UniQuest.

Rundle-Thiele, S., Pang, B., Knox, K., David, P., Parkinson, J., & Hussenoeder, F. (2019). Generating new directions for reducing dog and koala interactions: A social marketing formative research study. *Australasian Journal of Environmental Management, 26*(2), 173–187. doi:10.1080/14486563.2019.1599740.

Scolobig, A., & Lilliestam, J. (2016). Comparing approaches for the integration of stakeholder perspectives in environmental decision making. *Resources, 5*(4), 37.

Scolobig, A., Thompson, M., & Linnerooth-Bayer, J. (2016). Compromise not consensus: Designing a participatory process for landslide risk mitigation. *Natural Hazards, 81*(1), 45–68.

Shumway, N., Seabrook, L., McAlpine, C., & Ward, P. (2014). A mismatch of community attitudes and actions: A study of koalas. *Landscape and Urban Planning, 126*, 42–52. doi:10.1016/j.landurbplan.2014.03.004.

Thompson, M. (2008a). Beyond boom and bust. *RSA Journal, 154*(5536), 34–39.

Thompson, M. (2008b). *Organising and Disorganising: A Dynamic and Non-linear Theory of Institutional Emergence and Its Implications*. Devon: Triarchy.

Tompkins, E.L., Few, R., & Brown, K. (2008). Scenario-based stakeholder engagement: Incorporating stakeholders preferences into coastal planning for climate change. *Journal of Environmental Management, 88*(4), 1580–1592.

Trischler, J., Kristensson, P., & Scott, D. (2018). Team diversity and its management in a co-design team. *Journal of Service Management, 29*(1), 120–145.

Verweij, M., Senior, T.J., Domínguez, D., Juan, F., & Turner, R. (2015). Emotion, rationality, and decision-making: How to link affective and social neuroscience with social theory. *Frontiers in Neuroscience, 9*, 332.

Wierzbicki, A. (1985, 1985//). *Negotiation and Mediation in Conflicts: II. Plural Rationality and Interactive Decision Processes*. Paper presented at the Plural Rationality and Interactive Decision Processes, Berlin, Heidelberg.

11 From care to prevention in the NHS

Tony Conway and Margaret Hyde

Stakeholder analysis: The social marketing and healthcare context

The imperatives of an ageing population, advancing technology, as well as poor lifestyle choices and budget constraints are creating increasing pressures on healthcare organisations to review and radically rethink approaches to service design.

There are many possible stakeholders involved in the provision of Health and Social Care, and managing the dealings that each stakeholder has with others is likely to be a challenging prospect. There is a need to invest time in identifying and seeking to understand what significant stakeholders want or expect as a whole. However, there does not seem to be an accepted definition of stakeholder theory or indeed, what is considered to be a 'stakeholder' (Polonsky et al., 2003). Some stakeholders may fall into several categories at the same time, and there may be several subgroups within any stakeholder classification. It is difficult to generalise about what a specific stakeholder group will expect in terms of their relationship with an organisation as expectations can also change. Although a primary motive for many stakeholders is profit, this is not necessarily the case where social welfare is the primary objective.

In attempting to identify and understand stakeholders and how relationships can be managed, there are a number of classification systems that have been offered. Table 11.1 presents example stakeholder classification systems.

Different stakeholders are likely to receive different levels of consideration, and thus there is likely to be a hierarchy of stakeholder interests. Winstanley et al. (1995) distinguishe between criteria and operational power. There is a clear distinction between the two, where the former sees the stakeholder holding significant influence in the setting and evaluation of strategy while the influence of operational power is around the allocation of resources and use of knowledge and skills to deliver the strategy.

Stakeholder interests can conflict and need to be managed. One way of looking at such interests is in deciding on which to prioritise. Mitchell et al. (1997) suggest measuring stakeholder 'salience' (the degree to which a stakeholder can grab attention). Prioritisation requires a consideration of power

From care to prevention in the NHS 177

Table 11.1 Examples of classifications of stakeholders

Types of Stakeholders	Authors
Capital market stakeholders Product market stakeholders Organisational stakeholders	Hitt et al. (2003)
Those who carry out strategic actions Those who have a stake in the outcome	Lynch (2008)
Primary stakeholder groups: Customers, employees, suppliers, shareholders, policymakers, and community Secondary stakeholders: Competition and media	Hull et al. (2011)
Customer Referral Influencer Employee Supplier Internal markets	Christopher et al. (1991)
Supplier partnerships Lateral partnerships Buyer partnerships Internal partnerships	Morgan and Hunt (1994)
Not-for-profit stakeholders Resource generators, regulators, employees, users	Gwin (1990)
30 types of relationships between stakeholders	Gummesson (2008)

and legitimacy as well as the urgency of a stakeholder's claims (Mitchell et al., 1997). The more these constructs overlap, the more salience.

Within a social marketing context, literature refers to moving 'upstream' (Hastings & Domegan, 2014; Hoek & Jones, 2011). In other words, to consider organisations other than just the individuals or groups of individuals for whom behaviour change is hoped. For example, Figure 11.1 illustrates the potential network of stakeholders in public health-related social marketing.

For an upstream focus, Stakeholder theory can aid the management of social marketing programmes. Stakeholders need to be considered in the design, planning, implementation, and evaluation of a social marketing intervention. Both Lefebrve (2012) and Domegan et al. (2013) recommend the involvement of the target group in the intervention process as this would allow for the co-creation of value. As such, stakeholders can be influential in the design of future interventions. Active engagement and value creation with members of the community (Kelly, 2013) are another similar approach to stakeholder management.

Given resource constraints, stakeholders need to be prioritised according to degree of importance for an organisation's survival. Each stakeholder should be considered considering their availability, reach, and convenience (Hoek & Jones, 2011). Similarly, Mendelow (1991) offers an approach that can be used to guide

Figure 11.1 Example of a potential network of stakeholders in public health.

Note: Clinical commissioning groups are responsible for the planning and commissioning of local health service. General practitioners are local community doctors.

interventions by categorising types of stakeholder based on power and level of interest. Such classifications are context specific and can change. There needs to be efficient coordination to achieve synergy between different stakeholders.

A role for relationship marketing

Stakeholder conflicts may be overcome through identification of key relationships and establishing and managing long-term partnerships that include different groups of stakeholders. Relationship marketing can be used to analyse relationship paradigms in social marketing interventions (Hastings & Saren, 2003; Margues & Domegan, 2011) with stakeholder theory being used as an additional perspective to help manage those relationships (Margues & Domegan, 2011; Rundle-Thiele et al., 2013; Domegan et al., 2013). Relationship-based approaches using a stakeholder agenda involve creating exchanges of mutually beneficial value (Christopher et al., 2002) or mutual commitment and trust (Morgan & Hunt, 1994).

From care to prevention in the NHS 179

Table 11.2 Six-market stakeholder model

Market	Types of stakeholder
Customer markets	Buyers, intermediaries, and final consumers
Referral markets	Two main categories: – Customer referral marketings (including advocacy referrals) – Company-initiated referrals
Supplier and alliance markets	Suppliers that provide physical resources to the business and alliance partners who supply competencies and capabilities which are knowledge-based
Influencer markets	Diverse range of constituent groups including financial and investor groups, unions, industry bodies, regulating bosied, media, user groups, political and governmental agencies, and competitors
Recruitment markets	All potential employees and third parties that serve as access channels, e.g. recruitment agencies
Internal markets	Sub-units of organisations: Special emphasis needs to be placed on behavioural characteristics for customer facing employees.

Source: Adapted from Payne et al. (2005).

Understanding the role of long-term relationships with both customer and other stakeholder groups is acknowledged in the relationship marketing literature. The six-market model of customer, referral, influencer, employee, supplier, and internal markets (Christopher et al., 1991; Payne et al., 2005) offers the opportunity for management to undertake a review of the key markets and stakeholders that may be important to an organisation in a social marketing context. There is also the potential to offer approaches that could effectively satisfy strategically important stakeholder groups and identify opportunities for improved success. In a general context, Payne et al. (2005) distinguish between the following stakeholder groupings (Table 11.2).

Payne et al. (2005) bring together stakeholder analysis and relationship marketing, and we believe that their model can be used as the basis for identifying relevant stakeholders that need to be considered in managing 'public health.' It is this aspect of partnership working that has a social marketing focus in that there is a requirement for marketing initiatives and interventions that aim to change behaviours and has a non-commercial focus. The classification of Gwin (1990) for not-for-profit organisations: regulators, resource generators, users, managers, and employees, has similarities with the Payne et al. (2005) classification, the main difference being the lack of a consideration of referral markets. We believe that although 'referral' (i.e. 'recommendation') could be considered within a social marketing context, it is possible to classify such recommendation as part of the customer market as an 'intermediary customer' category and could be presented as part of 'user' within 'customer markets' in a conceptual framework (see Figure 11.2).

180 *Tony Conway and Margaret Hyde*

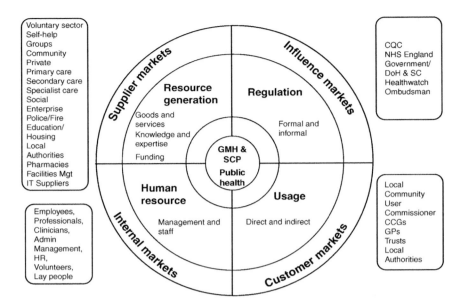

Figure 11.2 Relationship marketing and stakeholder approach to "local" UK Health Care.
Source: Adapted from Gwin (1990) and Payne et al. (2005).

Key to Figure 11.2:

> Self-help groups – Comprising members who all have similar conditions/experience.
> Private sector – This may include private sector health providers or social care providers such as residential/nursing homes.
> Secondary care – Hospital care.
> Primary care – Health and social care services available in the community.
> DoH&SC – Department of Health and Social Care (Government Department).
> CQC (Care Quality Commission) – Regulates and inspects health and social care services in England.
> NHS England – The organisation that leads the publicly funded National Health Service in England.
> CCGs (Clinical Commissioning Groups) – Clinically-led statutory NHS bodies responsible for the planning and commissioning of healthcare services for their local area.

We see resource generators as supplier markets, and we distinguish between the generation of: goods and services, knowledge and expertise, and funding.

Influence markets include Gwin's 'Regulators, and we classify these as both formal and informal regulation. Internal markets include Gwin's managers and employees. Finally, customer markets incorporate users (direct and indirect which in turn includes referrals).

The changing structure of health and social care in the United Kingdom

The UK National Health Service (NHS) employs approximately 1.7 million people making it the world's fifth largest employer (Nuffield Trust, 2017) and comprises employees across a wide spectrum and a myriad of disciplines. As one of the largest employers in the world, the UK's NHS operates within intensely complex systems and networks working at national, regional, and local levels. This chapter deals specifically with that part of the NHS that relates to a specific region within the English context and within this, a specific element which could be considered to involve social marketing.

Healthcare services in the United Kingdom are generally categorised as:

- Public health: which is responsible for improving the health and well-being of the general population and reducing health inequalities through the promotion of healthier lifestyles.
- Primary care: which includes general practice (family doctors), community pharmacists, dental, and optometry (eye health) services as well as providing community physiotherapy, district nurses, health visitors, walk-in centres and other local services.
- Secondary care: this usually refers to general hospitals, however some services can be provided in the community.
- Tertiary care: this refers to specialist centres such as cancer or cardiac care and tends to be centralised with expert staff and highly specialist equipment available.

(Gov.uk, 2018)

Because of its scale and complexity, the search for the optimum way to organise and control healthcare services in the United Kingdom efficiently and effectively has been a major issue over the years and has been subject to changes in structure and style of working. In the present structure, at the national level, links are primarily between the Department of Health and Social Care (DoHSC) with responsibility for the overall direction of strategy and policy, NHS England (NHSE) which implements those strategies, and Public Health England which is responsible for improving the health of the population and reduced inequalities in health across the country. At a local level, clinical commissioning groups (CCGs) work in the planning and purchasing of healthcare services, providing mental healthcare, ambulance services, hospital, and community services (NHS England, 2019). CCGs are led by clinicians and are responsible for approximately 60% of the NHS budget nationally. Such

182   Tony Conway and Margaret Hyde

services may be purchased from any one or more organisations. The CCGs receive funding directly from NHSE.

In recent years, there has been a shift towards the integration of health with social care services acknowledging the collaboration between the different services. The requirement of working across boundaries has long been recognised (Timmins, 2015) and offers opportunities for increased innovation in an environment where emphasis is being placed more on prevention rather than cure. It represents a new way of working which is essentially about introducing greater accountability and an inclusive, collaborative approach at local level so that different organisations from the health and care system work together to improve the health of their local population (Charles, 2018).

Of particular importance is the development of ongoing relationships between different interdependent parties/organisations, including other public services. Clearly, trust is of vital importance (Andresani and Ferlie, 2006; Osborne, 2006). Changes towards closer integration of health and social care are driving a new direction for service provision within the sector. Of particular relevance here is that funds are distributed to the local level through local authorities receiving budgets from Public Health England. The budgets are to be used for promoting health improvement and healthier lifestyles and towards reducing health inequalities within their own areas, working closely with the NHS (Gov.uk, 2019). Leaders argue that current strategy has been focused on care that has been 'over medicalised' (Patel, 2016) and should shift from simply treating sickness to promoting good health and well-being through innovative new thinking and by working with the other services. The over medicalisation is reflected in the traditional model of care which emphasises cure, while the wider issues such as environment, housing, and education have been emphasised much less. Now there are community strategies which engage with such aspects to a greater extent than in the past. New approaches that now place emphasis on prevention rather than cure have implications for the organisation of care.

In 2014 the UK Government produced a policy document: the 'Five Year Forward View' (NHS England, 2014), which has been superseded by the document: the 'NHS Long Term Plan' (2019). The initiatives have led to the piloting of different arrangements between commissioning and provider organisations and mark an acceptance that services need to be more tailored for local need (NHS England, 2014), and that devolution is a core part of this. There are many examples of integrated care partnerships that have been piloted representing a change in policy which will require integrated care organisations to find ways "to collaborate in harmony, focusing on a common purpose" (Worral & Leech, 2018, p. 2). Moving to new models of care based on integration creates challenges for providers and commissioners who also have longer term challenges such as those created by an ageing population, advancing technology, and budgetary constraints. Management appropriate for an integrated system of care is likely to be complex and not least because of the large number of diverse organisations that have an involvement with the local health

From care to prevention in the NHS 183

economy. In this context, it is noted that "new roles to support integrated care by working across organizational boundaries are only effective when they are part of a system-wide process of integration" (Gilburt, 2016, p. 4).

In an integrated system of health and social care there needs to be an understanding of a variety of models both within organisations and across the many organisations with which the NHS has to engage in order to deliver its goals (Kings Fund, 2011). Thus, there is a need to focus on social inter-action and multidirectional communication between organisations involved in the integrated system of planning and delivery which, in turn, may depend on developing mutual trust that is bound up with the effect on relationships. In health and social care, trust is particularly important given the strength of professional identity which can act as a barrier and basis for suspicion between different professional groups and managers (Gilburt, 2016).

Our case: The Greater Manchester Health and Social Care Partnership

Greater Manchester represents an example of the fully devolved organisation at the forefront of the previously mentioned developments. For the first time healthcare budgets and decision-making have shifted from central government to regional control which recognised the fact that decisions to meet the needs of the population are best made locally. The Greater Manchester Health and Social Care Partnership (GMHSCP) comprises not simply health and social care agencies such as NHS and local authorities but also the community, volun-tary, and social enterprise sector as well as a host of other agencies. Its health and social care plans focus on working in a pluralistic manner to reduce inequalities and improve life chances in the quest to improve health and well-being of the population.

With a population of 2.8 million residents, the ten authorities comprising Greater Manchester have long worked in collaboration through the Association of Greater Manchester Authorities (AGMA) (Kings Fund, 2017). A similar background of close working relationships exists between health and social care organisations (Healthier Together, 2015) and in 2016 the GMHSCP took over control of £6bn from central government (Kings Fund, 2015). Devolution has offered leaders an unprecedented opportunity to look at new ways of ser-vice design, taking on a far more holistic approach than has previously been the case in a region which has a record of poor health and social problems (GMHSCP, 2019).

The GMHSCP comprises the ten local authorities which make up Greater Manchester along with the ten CCGs from the Greater Manchester region. CCGs who are responsible for commissioning services and NHSE. However, it is not simply the health and social care agencies such as NHS and local authorities who are key to the partnership but also the community, voluntary, and social enterprise sector as well as Greater Manchester Police, the Greater Manchester Fire and Rescue Service, and universities among many others.

184 *Tony Conway and Margaret Hyde*

Setting its strategic aim also acknowledges the role that education, work, and housing contribute to the well-being of the population, and so the partnership is working to ensure an alignment between services. The rationale for our concentration on the public health context where social marketing rather than clinical interventions is the clear focus is two-fold:

- The Health and Social Care Act 2012 includes a clear agenda for public health and reducing health inequalities.
- In Greater Manchester, two thirds of early deaths are the result of poor lifestyle choices (GMHSC, 2019).

The aim is to offer opportunities for increased innovation in an environment where prevention rather than cure is emphasised representing a new way of working involving a wider network of partners than has previously been the case, allowing for a holistic approach to health and well-being.

The Greater Manchester Health and Social Care Partnership model

The focus on dyadic systems in healthcare has been replaced by complex service networks/ecosystems (McColl-Kenney et al., 2012). The World Health Organization (WHO) defines healthcare as including all actors, institutions, and resources used to improve health (Bengoa & Kawar, 2006; Evans et al., 2001). The extent of healthcare networks can be huge, and the GMHSCP is a working example of maximising the opportunities of working in close collaboration within an extensive and complex ecosystem of agencies. It is argued that the term ecosystem also acknowledges the diversity of the system of which networks are just one piece of the jigsaw (Henderson & Palmatier, 2010). The complex environment of health and social care, and particularly in the context of public health where both individuals and the wider community are fundamental to the process, contextualises an approach where reference to networks of stakeholders merely affected by an organisation's objectives is too simplistic a definition. It is a network of partners, interactions, activities and the integration of resources, knowledge, and expertise which all come together to create an effective ecosystem and to create value for society as a whole through a system of exchange (Edvardsson et al, 2011).

Nevertheless, there are challenges:

- Time taken in identifying stakeholders (Thomas, 2008)
- Conflicting interests (Hoeck & Jones, 2011)
- Perceived loss of control (Domegan et al, 2013; Lefebrve, 2006)
- Organisations having their own governance arrangements
- Objectives differing between agencies (Andreasen, 2006; Domegan et al., 2013; Lefebrve, 2006; Zainuddin et al., 2011)

From care to prevention in the NHS 185

- The complexities of communications including the maximisation of information sharing and digital integration
- The widely differing nature of staff between organisations (in healthcare they are likely to be highly qualified and used to working with a level of autonomy while in social care they are lower paid and have fewer qualifications)
- The access to resources and the allocation of resources
- The optimisation of capital and estate

The partnership has attempted to address these by the signing of a number of charters, known as memoranda of understanding (MoU), between partners which include shared objectives, governance arrangements, allocation of resources, capital/estates and research/innovation, and information/data sharing and workforce. Individual memoranda exist for ten different areas of focus, each with a number of partners (see Figure 11.3).

There is recognition that health, work, and the economy are inherently linked, and that health and social care alone cannot make the significant changes in the health of the population that are needed. Nor can public health groups change long-held poor lifestyles and social problems. Communities need help

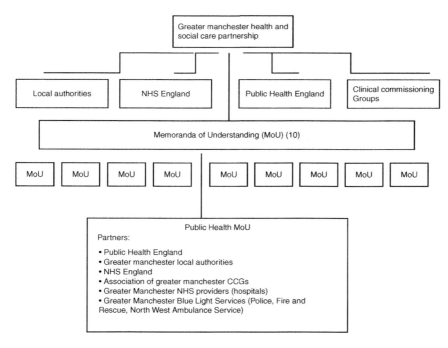

Figure 11.3 Greater Manchester structure.

and support to change their choices, and change depends on co-operation between a wide range of agencies to design and implement co-ordinated strategies. It is for these reasons that in Greater Manchester, more emphasis is being placed on community strategies including engagement, transport, environment, housing, and education to reduce inequalities and improve the quality of life and well-being.

Two of the objectives of the partnership are:

> To improve the health and wellbeing of all of the residents of Greater Manchester (GM) from an early age to the elderly, recognising that this will only be achieved with a focus on prevention of ill health and the promotion of wellbeing.
> To strengthen the focus on wellbeing, including greater focus on prevention and public health;

A third emphasises the importance of partnership working:

> To forge a partnership between the NHS, social care, universities and science and knowledge industries for the benefit of the population.
> (GMHSCP, 2014, p. 3)

"A rebalancing of investment towards prevention" (GMHSCP, 2015, p. 2) as one of the guiding principles of the MoU for public health highlights the shift of direction towards encouraging change in lifestyles, well-being, and prevention. A further charter exists with Sport England, the aim of which is to change behaviours towards sport and physical activity both for the individual and for communities.

Research by the Kings Fund provided evidence that, while actual structures of networks are important, the building of relationships between organisations is equally, if not, more important. Only through relationship development can there be effective integration at a sustainable level. Such development includes shared visions and objectives as well as regular and frequent communications between all parties (Kings Fund, 2017). The MoUs discussed play a leading role in helping to develop and maintain relationships through shared objectives and ways of working.

Thus, we suggest that stakeholder theory working with relationship marketing as a philosophy and as a strategic tool that can enhance the management of the GMHSCP, and this, in turn, should lead to positive patient and organisational outcomes. We therefore aim to assess the implications of our proposed conceptual model for stakeholder and relationship marketing theory, and implementation in this policy context (Figure 11.4).

Payne et al. (1995) map the gap between an organisation's present emphasis on each market and the desired emphasis at a future point in time. In the context of the GMHSCP, we offer a similar approach using six axes: three for Resource Generation and one each for Regulation, Usage, and Human

From care to prevention in the NHS 187

Figure 11.4 Stakeholders in the Greater Manchester Health and Social Care Partnership.

Resources. A scale of 1 through 10 reflects the degree of emphasis placed on each relationship market. Figure 11.5 is an example of its application.
For example, issues above would be an increased requirement in usage, for additional funding and for more staff.

Conclusion

Having highlighted the importance of stakeholders and stakeholder analysis in the context of the new integrated approach to public health in Greater Manchester, we have offered an approach that links stakeholders to a relationship marketing perspective. The below conceptual framework presents a way of identifying major stakeholders within key 'markets' for consideration and offers a way forward for analysing and assessing stakeholder relationships. The model suggests how future stakeholder strategies can be identified so that the effectiveness of social marketing interventions within a public health environment can be enhanced. Future research is necessary to test the models and to assess whether such an approach is relevant and appropriate.

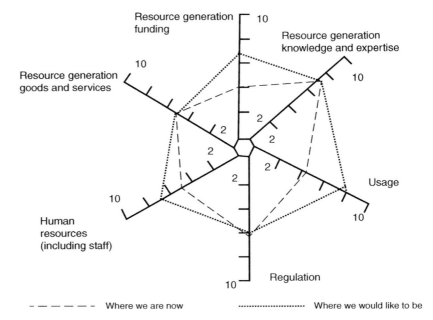

Figure 11.5 Map comparing GMHSP current priorities with future desired priorities.
Source: Adapted from Payne et al. (1995).

References

Andreasen A.R. (2006). *Social Marketing in the 21st Century*, Sage, California.
Andresani, G., & Ferlie, E. (2006). Studying governance within the British public sector and without. *Public Management Review*, 8(3), 415–431.
Bengoa, R., & Kawar, R. (2006), *Quality of Care – A Policy for Making Strategic Choices in Health Systems*, World Health Organization, Geneva.
Bryant, C.A., Forthofer, M.S., Brown, K.R.M., Landis, D.C., McDermott, R.J. (2000). Community-based prevention marketing: the next steps in disseminating behavior change. *American Journal of Health Behavior*, 24(1), 61–68.
Charles, A. (2018). Accountable care explained. 18 January, *Kings Fund*, London.
Christopher, M., Payne, A., & Ballantyne, D., (1991). *Relationship Marketing: Bringing Quality, Customer Service and Marketing Together*, Butterworth Heinemann, Oxford.
Christopher, M., Payne, A., & Ballantyne, D. (2002). *Relationship Marketing: Creating Stakeholder Value*, 2nd ed., Butterworth Heinemann, Oxford.
Domegan C., Collins, K., Stead, M., McHugh, P., & Hughes T. (2013). Value co-creation in social marketing: functional or fanciful? *Journal of Social Marketing*, 3(3), 239–256.
Edvardsson, B., Tronvoll, B., & Gruber, T. (2011). Expanding understanding of service exchange and value co-creation: a social construction approach. *Journal of the Academy of Marketing Science*, 39(2), 1–13.
Evans, D.B., Edejer, T.T.-T., Lauer, J., Frenk, J., & Murray, C.J.L. (2001). Measuring quality: from the system to the provider. *International Journal for Quality in Health Care*, 13, 439–446.

Gilburt, H. (2016). June, *Kings Fund*, London.

Gov.uk (2019). Retrieved from www.gov.uk/government/organisations/public-health-england/about.

Greater Manchester Health and Social Care Devolution (2014). Memorandum of Understanding.

Greater Manchester Health and Social Care Devolution, Memorandum of Understanding (2014). Retrieved from www.gmhsc.org.uk/wp-content/uploads/2018/05/1.-150227_HandSC_MoU-1.pdf.

Greater Manchester Health and Social Care Partnership (GMHSCP). (2015). Taking charge of our health and social care in Greater Manchester. Retrieved from https://www.gmhsc.org.uk/wp-content/uploads/2018/04/GM-Strategic-Plan-Summary.pdf.

Greater Manchester Health and Social Care Partnership (GMHSCP). (2019). Transforming the health of our population in Greater Manchester. Retrieved from https://www.gmhsc.org.uk/wp-content/uploads/2019/07/GMHSCP_-PopHealth_Progress-NextSteps.pdf.

Gummesson, E. (2008*). Total Relationship Marketing*, Butterworth-Heinemann, Oxford.

Gwin, J.M. (1990). Constituent analysis: a paradigm for marketing effectiveness in the not-for-profit organisation. *European Journal of Marketing*, 24(7), 43–48.

Hastings, G., & Saren, M. (2003). The critical contribution of social marketing theory and application. *Marketing Theory*, 3(3), 305–322.

Hastings, G., & Domegan, C. (2014). *Social Marketing: From Tunes to Symphonies* (2nd ed.), Routledge, Abingdon.

Healthier Together (2015). Consultation: your views [online]. Healthier Together website. Retrieved from https://healthiertogethergm.nhs.uk/decision-about-change/your-views/ (accessed on 7 January 2018).

Henderson, C.M., & Palmatier, R.W. (2010). Understanding the relational ecosystem in a connected world. In: Wuyts, S.H.K., Dekimpe, M.G., Gijsbrechts, E., & Pieters, F.G.M.R. (Eds.) (2010) *The Connected Customer: The Changing Nature of Consumer and Business Markets*, Routledge, New York, 37–36.

Hitt, M.A., Keats, B.W., & Yucel, E. (2003). Strategic leadership in global business organizations: Building trust and social capital. In: Mobley, W.H., & Dorfman, P. (Eds.) *Advances in Global Leadership: Vol. III*, JAI Press, Greenwich, CT, 9–35.

Hoek, J., & Jones, S.C. (2011). Regulation, public health and social marketing: a behaviour change trinity. *Journal of Social Marketing*, 1(1), 32–44.

Hult, G.T.M, Mena, J.A., Ferrell, O., & Ferrell L. (2011). Stakeholder marketing: a definition and conceptual framework. *Academy of Marketing Review*, 1(1), 44–65.

Kelly T.F. (2013). Fourteen more points: successful applications of Deming's system theory. *American Journal of Management*, 13(2), 36–40.

Kings Fund, (2011). The future of leadership and management in the NHS: no more heroes. Report from the Kings Fund Commission on Leadership and Management, *Kings Fund*, London.

Kings Fund (2017). Bottom up, top down, middle out: transforming health and care in Greater Manchester. Retrieved from: www.kingsfund.org.uk/blog/2017/11/transforming-health-care-greater-manchester.

Lefebvre, R.C. (2006). Partnerships for social marketing programs: an example from the National Bone Health Campaign. *Social Marketing Quarterly*, 12(1), 41–54.

Lefebvre, R.C (2012). Transformative social marketing: co-creating the social marketing discipline and brand. *Journal of Social Marketing*, 2(2), 118–129.

Lynch, R. (2006). Corporate Strategy. 4th Ed., *Financial Times*, Prentice Hall, London.

McColl-Kennedy, J.R., Vargo, S.L., Dagger, T.S., Sweeney, J.C., & Van Kasteren, Y. (2012). Health care customer value cocreation practice styles. *Journal of Service Research*, 15, 370–389.

McKenna and Dunn (2015). Devolution: what it means for health and social care in *Kings Fund*, London.

Margues, S., & Domegan C., (2011). Relationship marketing and social marketing. In: Hastings, G., Angus, K., & Bryant, C. (Eds.) *The Sage Handbook of Social Marketing*, Sage, London, 44–61.

Mendelow, (1991) cited in Johnson, Scholes, and Whittington, (2006) from Mitchell, R.K., Agle, B.R., & Wood, D.I. (1997). Toward a theory of stakeholder identification and salience: defining the principle of who and what really counts. *Academy of Management Review*, 22(4) 853–886.

Morgan, R.M., & Hunt, S.D. (1994). The commitment-trust theory of relationship marketing. *Journal of Marketing*, 58(July), 43–48.

NHS England (2014). *Five Year Forward View*, London.

NHS England (2019). *The NHS Long Term Plan*, 7 January, NHS England, London.

NHS England (2019). Retrieved from www.england.nhs.uk/ccgs/.

Osborne, S.P. (2006). The new public governance. *Public Management Review*, 8(3), 377–387.

Nuffield Trust (2017). The NHS workforce in numbers. Retrieved from www.nuffieldtrust.org.uk/resource/the-nhs-workforce-in-numbers.

Payne, A., Ballantyne D., & Christopher, M. (2005). A stakeholder approach to relationship marketing strategy: the development and use of the "six markets" model. *European Journal of Marketing*, 39(7/8), 855–871.

Payne, A., Christopher, M., Clark, M., & Peck, H. (1995). *Relationship Marketing for Competitive Advantage*, Butterworth Heinemann, Oxford.

Patel R. (2016). *The Future for Primary Care in Greater Manchester Westminster Health Forum*, Manchester.

Polonsky, M.J., Carlson, L., & Fry, M.-L. (2003). The harm chain: a public policy development and stakeholder perspective. *Marketing Theory*, 3(3), 345–64.

Rundle-Thiele, S., Russell-Bennett, R., Leo C., & Dietrich T. (2013). Moderating teen drinking: combining social marketing and education. *Health Education*, 113(5), 392–406.

Thomas, J. (2008). Happily ever after…? Partnerships in social marketing. *Social Marketing Quarterly*, 14(1), 72–75.

Timmins, N. (2015). The practice of system leadership-being comfortable with chaos. May, *Kings Fund*, London.

Winstanley, D.D., Sorabji, S., & Dawson S. (1995). When the pieces don't fit: a stakeholder power matrix to analyse public sector restructuring. *Public Money and Management*, 15(2), 19–26.

Worrall, R., & Leech, D. (2018). Will place-based leadership be the right remedy for health and social care? *British Journal of Healthcare Management*, 24(2), 90–94.

Zainuddin, N., Previte, J., & Russell-Bennett, R. (2011). A social marketing approach to value creation in a well-women's health service. *Journal of Marketing Management*, 27(3–4), 361–385.

12 Towards universal helmet use

Advocating for change in Vietnam

*Lukas Parker, Mirjam Sidik, and
Truong Thi Nguyet Trang*

Background

Globally, road traffic injuries are responsible for about 1.35 million deaths annually (World Health Organization, 2018). Deaths relative to the world's population have stabilised in recent years. However, the slow pace of reduction means that the United Nations' Sustainable Development Goals target 3.6 to halve the number of global deaths and injuries from road traffic accidents by 2020 (United Nations, 2019) is not likely to be met.

In Vietnam, road crashes result in approximately 24,970 deaths annually (World Health Organization, 2018). Vulnerable road users such as motorcyclists account for 67 per cent (National Traffic Safety Committee, 2017), and pedestrians account for 15 per cent (Ministry of Labour, Invalids and Social Affairs, Hanoi School of Public Health, World Health Organization, & United Nations Children's Fund, 2010) of these fatalities. Road traffic injuries are the third leading cause of premature death and disability in Vietnam and the seventh leading cause of child mortality (Institute for Health Metrics and Evaluation, 2017).

For most Vietnamese families the motorcycle is their primary vehicle. With motorcycles accounting for 93 per cent of registered vehicles (National Traffic Safety Committee, 2017), the vast majority of children are transported on motorcycles each day. Furthermore, higher speeds even in mixed traffic situations are increasingly possible due to improvements in infrastructure for efficient transport of goods, but not safety. Infrastructure such as traffic signals and sidewalk pavements as well as strict enforcement of traffic rules are ongoing issues (Hung & Huyen, 2011). This coalescence of interrelated issues results in roads being decidedly unsafe, particularly on major roads where there are greater numbers of heavy vehicles mixing with motorcycles.

Head injuries as a result of road crashes are the leading cause of death and disability in Vietnam: 78 per cent of motorcyclist fatalities are due to head injuries (Ngo et al., 2012). Helmets are the best way to reduce these deaths, and helmet non-usage is the most significant factor affecting the death rate of motorcyclists (Abbas, Hefny, & Abu-Zidan, 2012). In fact, wearing a quality helmet reduces a motorcyclist's risk of death by 42 per cent and head injury by 69 per cent in the event of a crash (Liu et al., 2008).

192   *Lukas Parker et al.*

Helmet use in adults was legislated as mandatory in Vietnam in 2007. Subsequently, helmets were also made mandatory for child passengers aged six and above in 2010. However, compliance with both laws have been markedly different, and while helmet use among adults is high (90%–99%), child passenger helmet use is typically low (15%–53%) (Nhan et al., 2019). This low compliance in child passenger use has posed a challenge for government and non-governmental organisation (NGOs) who are seeking to make Vietnam's roads safer.

Various explanations abound for the low child helmet use. Explanations include unfounded fears about the adverse effect of helmets on the development of children's skulls and potential neck injuries (Pervin et al., 2009; World Health Organization, 2009) – myths which have widely circulated in the country (AIP Foundation & FIA Foundation, 2017). Moreover, there is often a perceived low likelihood of having a crash (Duong, Brennan, Parker, & Florian, 2015; Duong & Parker, 2018) and belief that police enforcement of the child helmet laws is not rigorous (Center for Women's Studies – Vietnam National University & Asia Injury Prevention Foundation, 2011). Police enforcement has previously been described as sporadic and unreliable (Duong et al., 2015). Helmet costs have been cited as a factor previously (World Health Organization, 2009), but in more recent years the costs of helmets have dropped by comparison to median household incomes meaning that helmets are generally considered affordable. Lastly, common situational factors come into play: Multiple helmets are cumbersome to store on a motorcycle when dropping off and picking up children. This means that helmets may often be left at home, and extra helmets may simply not be with the parent motorcyclist at the time that it is needed for child passengers.

This case study is centred on Vietnam and the efforts of AIP Foundation, a road safety NGO, to act as a catalyst to increase road safety. The case is reviewed through the lens of stakeholder theory, whereby stakeholders are any groups or individuals who are affected by or who can affect the achievement of an organisation's purpose (Freeman, 1984). It therefore focuses on the ways AIP Foundation collaborates and partners with various stakeholders, individuals, communities, schools, other local NGOs, international NGOs, and various levels of government to develop and maintain strategies for sustainable behaviour change. In particular this chapter explores how AIP Foundation's approach can be effective in leading to lasting change through education, legislation, and enforcement. We review the dynamics between partners and stakeholders in order to draw conclusions about how AIP Foundation's stakeholder collaboration approach might be used in other similar behaviour change problems.

Engaging and mobilising stakeholders to promote sustainable change

An increasingly holistic view of behaviour change is being adopted by social marketing researchers and practitioners (Brennan, Previte, & Fry, 2016;

Hodgkins, Rundle-Thiele, Knox, & Kim, 2019). This holistic view recognises that the involvement of stakeholders during the planning, implementation, and evaluation stages of interventions may enhance social marketing outcomes (Buyucek, Kubacki, Rundle-Thiele, & Pang, 2016). This is the case with road safety interventions where a broad range of stakeholders must be mobilised to work together in order to sustainably promote road safety behaviour (Truong, 2016). Moreover, road safety problems are multifaceted, and therefore behavioural ecosystems need to be considered. In the case of helmets, the problem is not merely about the individual choice as to whether or not a child wears a helmet (Parker, Brennan, & Nguyen, 2015) but also their ecosystem of influences and influencers that each have a part to play (Brennan, Binney, Parker, Aleti, & Nguyen, 2014).

On an individual level, parents, friends, and peers' compliance or non-compliance behaviours and attitudes' impact on children's behaviour need to be considered, particularly when the burden of responsibility for encouraging this behaviour is placed upon parents. Moreover, parents are influenced by their own friends' and peers' behaviours and attitudes. At a local level there are the school and neighbourhood influences, such as whether/what teachers are teaching children about road safety in school. At a community level there are governance, policy, legal, and media influences. For instance, whether local district Peoples Committee (district government) is actively promoting helmet use, whether police are enforcing helmet use, and whether the media (in this case an extension of government) see the issue of helmet use as newsworthy all have a part to play in what people do. In addition, there are overarching social and cultural factors at play.

The challenge of getting children to wear helmets is manifold and complex requiring a coordinated response to build an ecosystem of prompting, support, and reinforcement. For this reason, a common scenario that can lead to children passengers not wearing helmets during school drop offs and pickups has been the focus of AIP Foundation and its stakeholders. Helmets are awkward to stow on a motorcycle once a child is dropped off, and schools are rarely equipped to store helmets during the day. So once the child is dropped off at school, there is often not an easy solution for helmets to be stored until they are needed again. These barriers mean that parents are often reluctant to make their child wear a helmet on the way to school at the start of the day, because there is no easy place to store the helmet until needed again. Moreover, these barriers are further compounded by the fact that trips between school and home are often short and not via major roads, which increases the temptation to "not worry" about a helmet for this type of everyday travel.

Given the complexity of this road safety challenge, responses cannot be limited to an individual focus. Coordination and mobilisation of parents, students, road users, schools, teachers, government, police, and other influences and influencers are required to build an ecosystem that promotes, supports, and reinforces safe behaviour. Moreover, given that the desired behaviour, helmet use, provides the user with no immediate sense of benefit (most road users do

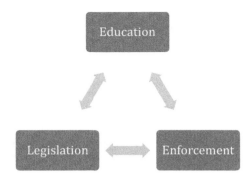

Figure 12.1 Tripartite model of behavioural compliance.
Source: Adapted from Snitow and Brennan (2011).

not experience a crash regularly), consideration to mechanisms to encourage and enforce safe behaviour is required.

Road safety social marketing campaigns and interventions, such as increasing seat belt use, maintaining safe driving speeds, adherence to traffic signals, and not driving while impaired by drugs, are focused on behavioural compliance, i.e. adhering to a road law. Legislation provides a legal framework with which citizens are expected to comply, and there can be penalties associated with non-compliance. Behavioural compliance campaigns typically have three elements: a legislative element, an enforcement element, and an education or advertising element (see Figure 12.1). Education and advertising may focus on the full range of benefits of maintaining the desired behaviour, but there is typically underlying alignment to both legislation and enforcement elements. For instance, wearing a helmet will make you less likely to suffer a head injury in the event of a crash (benefit). Also, you might be fined by the police if you are caught not wearing a helmet (consequence of non-compliance). The challenge for social marketers in this space is that in most instances people will not crash, if they do crash it is typically only minor, and law enforcement is limited to police resources.

AIP Foundation and its stakeholders

AIP Foundation was founded in Vietnam in 1999 to address the growing problem of injuries to motorcyclists and the low use of helmets. Since initiation, AIP Foundation has designed programs and interventions to (1) improve the public's understanding about the safety value of helmet wearing, (2) provide access to high-quality and low-cost helmets that are suited to the environment, and (3) evaluate the impact of policies that reinforce helmet use (Craft et al., 2017). Over time through successful advocacy, AIP Foundation has led to improvements in helmet laws in Vietnam and vastly improved numbers of motorcyclist and their passengers wearing helmets. The roads in Vietnam have changed over the intervening two decades, but AIP Foundation's focus on road safety has evolved to new developments.

AIP Foundation works in partnership with local governments and communities throughout Vietnam to address road safety employing its "five gears" approach which it has since employed in other neighbouring lower- and middle-income countries including Cambodia, Myanmar, and Thailand. AIP Foundation is a founding member of an international coalition to put a helmet on every motorcyclist's head, globally.

AIP Foundation's five gears approach includes:

1 *Targeted programs* to promote helmet use in vulnerable and high-risk populations such as children.
2 *Helmet accessibility and affordability* by designing and manufacturing high-quality, low-cost, climate-appropriate helmets that meet strict standards and by distributing them through retailers and other means.
3 *Public awareness and education* to improve knowledge about helmets' effectiveness, benefits of use, and consequences of non-use.
4 *Institutional policies and legislative advocacy* to effect sustainable behaviour change. Relationships are built with government entities to advocate for progressive helmet legislation combined with enforcement and also communications activities.
5 *Research, monitoring, and evaluation* to establish best practice, measure progress towards helmet usage behaviour and attitudes, and disseminate outcomes to the broader public and decision makers.

The five gears approach aligns well with the basic principles of social marketing in that they aim to increase helmet use (product), by reducing the various costs of acquisition (price), through programs that are targeted in the right locations (place) with communication and education components (promotion). Moreover, they address various elements of the behavioural ecosystem (Brennan et al., 2014) by different elements of their campaigns directed predominantly at the community and local levels (Hovell, Wahlgren, & Gehrman, 2002; Parker et al., 2015).

With a strong history of multisector collaboration, AIP Foundation implements programs and heads initiatives that engage and partner with public, private, and government road safety stakeholders. This ensures complex and inclusive interventions that target several aspects of road safety at the same time and that programs are appropriate and address the road safety needs of the population. AIP Foundation's projects are typically privately funded through philanthropic foundations and corporate donors. AIP Foundation plays a central role in bringing together various stakeholders to work in concert to promote change (see Figure 12.2).

AIP Foundation employs a research-driven approach that takes input from research bodies, such as the US Centers for Disease Control and Prevention

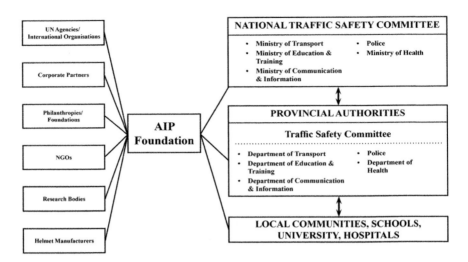

Figure 12.2 Relationships between the stakeholders.

(CDC), the Australian Road Research Board, the Hanoi University of Public Health (Vietnam), and United Nations agencies including the World Health Organisation and United Nations Children's Fund (UNICEF). It also engages with philanthropies, corporate sponsors, other NGOs, and helmet manufacturers to coordinate programs and funding. Given the complexity of the road safety problems, interventions often cross different levels of government (national, provincial, and local) and various community bodies. AIP Foundation engages and mobilises various stakeholders depending on the scale of individual interventions. This involves mobilising a network of dispersed government and community stakeholders with a broad range of remits, attempting to coordinate in order to build campaigns and systems to promote helmet use and road safety.

Over time, AIP Foundation's role in the development of road safety campaigns has evolved from being the facilitator of campaigns to that of catalyst and coordinator of the road safety campaigns of stakeholders. Into the future, this means an approach that builds the capacity of the various stakeholders to be more sustainable. This has resulted in more campaigns being led by the National Traffic Safety Committee (NTSC) with the support of AIP Foundation. The NTSC is an initiative that combines the resources of the national ministries of transport; education and training; communication and information; public security; labour, invalids, and social affairs; and health. The NTSC is responsible for assisting the Vietnamese prime minister to direct ministries, sectors, and localities to implement national strategies and projects on ensuring traffic safety and order as well as deploy interdisciplinary solutions in this field on a national scale. There are provincial level committees with similar mandates.

One of the effective ways that AIP Foundation has maintained both credibility and sustainable programs has been through engagement with philanthropic organisations and corporate sponsors and partners. Many of the foundation's activities are funded through effective sponsorship with corporate donors with aligned corporate social responsibility (CSR) objectives. Lee (2016) highlights that the most successful sponsored social marketing interventions are where there is alignment between the corporate donor and the issue, in this case, road safety. For instance, (1) the connection between the donor and the issue needs to pass the "smell test" (there needs to be an authentic and genuine commitment to the issue); (2) the target audiences are natural or aligned; (3) the desired behaviour is best for all; (4) the donor helps remove major barriers to behaviour change; and (5) the donor combines corporate social marketing with other corporate social initiatives (Lee, 2016).

The most successful partnerships between donors and AIP Foundation have been the ones that go beyond the mere transactional and are longer term. Successful sponsorships have included those from parcel delivery, petroleum, insurance, ride-share, and freight shipping companies: Each have a clear interest and commitment to road safety but also benefit from better road safety. For each of these sponsors there is strong potential to integrate the social messages associated with their projects into their own communications, amplifying the overall impact. Likewise, other long running sponsorships from companies that are associated with products related to the health and safety of children have similar synergies relating to health or protection of children.

In the case of fostering child helmet use, AIP Foundation works with schools, the Ministry and Departments of Education and Training, and the media to educate road users to encourage child helmet use (see Table 12.1). Schools are a central part of educating children and parents about the importance of helmets. This involves top-down collaboration with the Ministry of Education and Training to develop policy, curricula, and resources to promote within schools. The approach is concurrently bottom-up as AIP Foundation liaises with principals at individual schools, local governments, and local police to begin dialogues on how to foster change within a community. AIP Foundation assists the schools to tailor events, education, and training tailored to the requirements of each community. The foundation distributes helmets for free or heavily subsidised at the time of the education component to ensure the children have the capacity to enact the new behaviour concurrently with the campaign.

Aside from the in-school components of education, AIP Foundation concurrently implements its own communications directed to children and parents using mass media, direct communications, and social media (Nhan et al., 2019). To be successful, messaging needs to focus more broadly than merely compliance: It needs to present the facts and humanise the consequences of not wearing a helmet. To assist with this, AIP Foundation engages with and builds the capacity of the media via training to be able to report road safety issues in a way that is engaging to readers. Therefore, in road safety programs, communication

198 *Lukas Parker et al.*

Table 12.1 Fostering child helmet compliance

Element	Stakeholders	Activities
Education	AIP Foundation	Advertising and communications directed to children and parents. Public awareness campaigns using mass media, direct communication, and social networks. Providing free or subsidised helmets to children in schools.
	Schools	Facilitating school interventions and events. Developing education resources for schools and school teachers. Providing locations to store helmets at schools.
	Ministry or Departments of Education and Training (MOET/ DOET)	Development of teacher and student resource materials for inclusion in school curriculum. Advocacy and advice on curriculum.
	Media	Journalist training workshops to encourage reporting on road safety issues.
Legislation	Government (national, provincial, and local levels)	Advocacy for laws and policy. Building capacity to implement, sustain, and expand campaigns.
	School	Assisting policy development for helmet use in schools.
Enforcement	Traffic police	Police engagement and capacity building to enforce the child helmet law. Coordination of campaigns with Traffic Safety Committees and Traffic Police Departments. Conducting helmet enforcement blitzes.
	Parents	Communication to parents about the importance of ensuring child helmet compliance.
	Schools	Teacher or school monitoring of helmet usage.
	AIP Foundation	Monitoring helmet usage through observation by staff, trained volunteers, and sometimes third parties.

and education components are integrated to ensure that parents and children are receiving consistent messaging from multiple points during a campaign, reinforcing the same message.

In terms of legislation, AIP Foundation has had a long-term role in advocating for road safety policy and legislative change with various levels of government (see Figure 12.2). In fact, it was instrumental in advocating for the national child helmet laws enacted in 2010 (AIP Foundation & FIA Foundation, 2017). However, on a local level, AIP Foundation supports individual schools and school districts to develop school policies related to helmet use in the school environment. Furthermore, AIP Foundation coordinates with local police (where possible and practical) to focus on enforcement the helmet laws during the campaign to reinforce the compliance element of the campaign message.

Building better stakeholder engagement and coordination

Coordinating and mobilising such a diverse range of stakeholders present many challenges. All stakeholders have their own mandate, objectives, and focus (Lasker & Weiss, 2003), meaning that creating a united direction for the campaign can be a challenge. Moreover, many of the stakeholders are not familiar with collaborating with the other stakeholders meaning that communications and rules of engagement between partners and stakeholders need to be established for each campaign. Moreover, the timing of the various activities which are managed by different stakeholders can pose a challenge and lead to friction.

In an environment like Vietnam, a top-down approach to public health campaigns needs to work in concert with a bottom-up community-driven movement. Top-down only approaches are likely to lead to resentment from the general public and in the case of road safety lead to short-term changes in behaviour in order to merely comply with directives. Longer term, top-down approaches are often difficult to sustain because the parents, teachers, and children do things merely because they have to, not because they want to. A bottom-up "grass roots" only movement, without government support, is also difficult to maintain momentum and enthusiasm because there is little immediate incentive for lasting change.

As the Vietnamese Government has taken an increasing role in promoting road safety behaviour with the NTSC, AIP Foundation's role has evolved. Increasingly, AIP Foundation is moving away from being at the centre of the campaigns, to transferring ownership to government entities, and providing support. This leads to a sustainable response to road safety because the government takes ownership of the problems. AIP Foundation's role has adapted to become the capacity builder and the coordinator of road safety efforts. This means that AIP Foundation may appear less visible to the public as part of road safety efforts but more integral behind the scenes mobilising and advocating for the various stakeholders to act. These activities and their challenges are explored in the following.

As part of its coordination role, AIP Foundation is typically the bridge between individual schools and school districts and other stakeholders, in the formation and implementation of a campaign. School principals are central to the success or failure of a campaign. With the assistance and support of AIP Foundation, principals build school policy to mandate helmet use for students coming to and from the school. Principals are the ones who need to encourage teachers to be actively involved in teaching and compliance components. The principal may have the best intentions to make the program successful, but without the full support and resourcing of other stakeholders a sustainable outcome is not likely. It is hard to motivate people with merely words, so the coordination and support of AIP Foundation are key.

Another challenge to a successful campaign is that public health education had previously not been prioritised within the Vietnamese education curriculum and policy (Parker, 2013). A more recent encouraging innovation has seen the government mandate the Ministry of Education and Training to incorporate road safety education at all grade levels, increasing lesson times, encouraging more extra-curricular activities relating to road safety education, and the development of relevant materials for parents. However, implementation of road safety education is still challenged by limited budgets, capacity, and time constraints. Motivating and training teachers to deliver road safety education are therefore a difficult undertaking in a sustainable sense.

Aside from its advocacy role to bring about education policy and curriculum change, AIP Foundation has been assisting schools through the development of an e-curriculum. This new e-curriculum provides practical interactive road safety education materials/activities delivered online that are aimed at children but also involve parents. When it rolls out, the e-curriculum will be used in individual school interventions to maintain enthusiasm at the community level. The materials will be scalable and available for national dissemination and are designed for sustainable impact.

Police involvement and enforcement has been an innovative and successful component of AIP Foundation-led road safety campaigns. Police are involved in the full process of the campaigns from the initial meetings through to the end in order to garner support and to coordinate with campaign activities. From the outset, police are involved in initial stakeholder orientation meetings and workshops at the beginning of the program to engage with other key stakeholders, especially teachers and school principals, and other relevant stakeholders at a city level. Meetings connect stakeholders together, whereas normally each of the different groups work in their individual function without much thought to the other members in the intervention.

Each group of stakeholders come to the problem with different perspectives and resource constraints. The teachers and principals want what is best for the students but have little control outside the school grounds. The police share the concern for student helmet use but have many other road issues that compete for their attention and resources, and therefore sustainable ongoing enforcement can be a challenge. Moreover, there are legitimate concerns that zealous police enforcement of the law may only ultimately lead to fear of being fined by the police, rather than the other consequences of not wearing a helmet. Therefore, the approach requires balance as well as ongoing support and dialogue between all stakeholders.

Conclusion

Road safety behaviour change campaigns by their nature require a holistic approach given the broad range of influences and influencers. In the case of campaigns related to helmet use the use of communication or educational tools alone in social marketing communications campaigns is insufficient to encourage target audiences. Mobilising and engaging multiple stakeholders, community, schools, universities, hospitals, government, police, commercial sector, philanthropies, and research to unite on one common goal, is key. Sustainable behaviour change can only happen through an approach that involves a combination of education, legislation, and enforcement, which by nature involves coordination of various partners and sectors.

Campaigns merely focused on the individual level communications and education are unlikely to work on a sustainable basis when attempting to increase helmet use because there are no immediate benefits to helmet use, and therefore reinforcement is needed. Multilayered engagement activities involving multiple stakeholders and partners as well as a broader social- and ecosystems approach are required to facilitate and support sustainable behaviour change. Campaigns need to address human, situational, and cultural competitors in an integrated manner to support the change.

References

Abbas, A.K., Hefny, A.F., & Abu-Zidan, F.M. (2012). Does wearing helmets reduce motorcycle-related death? A global evaluation. *Accident Analysis and Prevention, 49,* 249–252. doi:10.1016/j.aap.2011.09.033.

AIP Foundation & FIA Foundation. (2017). Head First: A Case Study of Vietnam's Motorcycle Helmet Campaign. Retrieved from https://issuu.com/aipfoundation/docs/aipf-10-year-helmet-law-report-fina.

Brennan, L., Binney, W., Parker, L., Aleti, T., & Nguyen, D. (2014). *Social Marketing and Behaviour Change: Models, Theory and Applications.* Cheltenham: Edward Elgar.

Brennan, L., Previte, J., & Fry, M.-L. (2016). Social marketing's consumer myopia. *Journal of Social Marketing, 6*(3), 219–239. doi:10.1108/jsocm-12-2015-0079.

Buyucek, N., Kubacki, K., Rundle-Thiele, S., & Pang, B. (2016). A systematic review of stakeholder involvement in social marketing interventions. *Australasian Marketing Journal (AMJ), 24*(1), 8–19. doi:10.1016/j.ausmj.2015.11.001.

Center for Women's Studies – Vietnam National University & Asia Injury Prevention Foundation. (2011). Survey on Public Opinions on Child Helmet Use: "Head Safe. Helmet On" Project. Hanoi: Vietnam National University.

Craft, G., Van Bui, T., Sidik, M., Moore, D., Ederer, D.J., Parker, E.M., ... Sleet, D.A. (2017). A comprehensive approach to motorcycle-related head injury prevention: Experiences from the field in Vietnam, Cambodia, and Uganda. *International Journal of Environmental Research and Public Health, 14*(12). doi:10.3390/ijerph14121486.

Duong, H.T., Brennan, L., Parker, L., & Florian, M. (2015). But I AM normal: Safe? Driving in Vietnam. *Journal of Social Marketing, 5*(2), 105–124. doi:10.1108/jsocm-07-2013-0048.

202   *Lukas Parker et al.*

Duong, H.T., & Parker, L. (2018). Going with the flow: Young motorcyclists' misperceived norms and motorcycle speeding behaviour. *Journal of Social Marketing, 8*(3), 314–332. doi:10.1108/jsocm-10-2017-0064.

Freeman, R.E. (1984). *Strategic Management: A Stakeholder Approach.* Boston, MA: Pittman.

Hodgkins, S., Rundle-Thiele, S., Knox, K., & Kim, J. (2019). Utilising stakeholder theory for social marketing process evaluation in a food waste context. *Journal of Social Marketing, 9*(3), 270–287. doi:10.1108/jsocm-12-2017-0088.

Hovell, M.F., Wahlgren, D.R., & Gehrman, C.A. (2002). The behavioral ecological model. In R.J. DiClemente, R.A. Crosby, & M.C. Kegler (Eds.), *Emerging Theories in Health Promotion Practice and Research, Strategies for Improving Public Health* (1st ed., pp. 347–385). San Francisco, CA: Jossey-Bass.

Hung, K.V., & Huyen, L.T. (2011). Education influence in traffic safety: A case study in Vietnam. *IATSS Research, 34*(2), 87–93. doi:10.1016/j.iatssr.2011.01.004.

Institute for Health Metrics and Evaluation. (2017). Country Profile: Vietnam. Retrieved from www.healthdata.org/vietnam.

Lasker, R.D., & Weiss, E.S. (2003). Broadening participation in community problem solving: A multidisciplinary model to support collaborative practice and research. *Journal of Urban Health: Bulletin of the New York Academy of Medicine, 80*(1), 118–129.

Lee, N.R. (2016). Corporate social marketing. *Social Marketing Quarterly, 22*(4), 340–344. doi:10.1177/1524500416672550.

Liu, B.C., Ivers, R., Norton, R., Boufous, S., Blows, S., & Lo, S.K. (2008). Helmets for preventing injury in motorcycle riders. *Cochrane Database of Systematic Reviews,* (1), CD004333. doi:10.1002/14651858.CD004333.pub3.

Ministry of Labour, Invalids and Social Affairs, Hanoi School of Public Health, World Health Organization, & United Nations Children's Fund. (2010). *Vietnam National Injury Survey 2010.* Hanoi: Center for Injury Policy and Prevention Research, Hanoi School of Public Health.

National Traffic Safety Committee. (2017). *Report: Road Safety in 2016 and Key Missions for Road Safety in 2017 (Báo cáo: Kết quả Công tác Bảo đảm Trật tự, An toàn Giao Thông Năm 2016 và Nhiệm vụ Trọng tâm Năm An toàn Giao thông 2017).* Hanoi: National Traffic Safety Committee (Uỷ ban An toàn Giao thông Quốc gia).

Ngo, A.D., Rao, C., Hoa, N.P., Hoy, D.G., Trang, K.T.Q., & Hill, P.S. (2012). Road traffic related mortality in Vietnam: Evidence for policy from a national sample mortality surveillance system. *BMC Public Health, 12,* 561. doi:10.1186/1471-2458-12-561.

Nhan, L.D.T., Parker, L., Son, M.T.H., Parker, M., Moore, M.R., Sidik, M., & Draisin, N. (2019). Evaluation of an integrated multisector campaign to increase child helmet use in Vietnam. *Injury Prevention, 25*(3), 206–210. doi:10.1136/injuryprev-2017–042517.

Parker, L. (2013). Personal hygiene, environmental sanitation: A case of social marketing in the Mekong Delta. In L. Brennan, L. Parker, T. Aleti Watne, J. Fien, T.H. Duong, & M.A. Doan (Eds.), *Growing Sustainable Communities: A Development Guide for Southeast Asia* (pp. 241–253). Prahran, Australia: Tilde University Press.

Parker, L., Brennan, L., & Nguyen, D. (2015). Social marketing: Cambodia, Indonesia, the Philippines and Vietnam. In C. Rowley & B. Nguyen (Eds.), *Ethical and Social Marketing in Asia* (pp. 161–191). Amsterdam: Elsevier.

Pervin, A., Passmore, J., Sidik, M., McKinley, T., Tu, N.T.H., & Nam, N.P.N. (2009). Viet Nam's mandatory motorcycle helmet law and its impact on children. *Bulletin of the World Health Organization, 87*(5), 369–373. doi:10.2471/blt.08.057109.

Snitow, S., & Brennan, L. (2011). Reducing drink driving road deaths: Integrating communication and social policy enforcement in Australia. In H. Cheng, P. Kotler, & N. Lee (Eds.), *Social Marketing for Public Health: Global Trends and Success Stories* (pp. 383–403). Sudbury, MA: Jones & Bartlett.

Truong, V.D. (2016). Government-led macro-social marketing programs in Vietnam. *Journal of Macromarketing, 37*(4), 409–425. doi:10.1177/0276146716660833.

United Nations. (2019). Sustainable Development Goals Knowledge Platform. Retrieved from https://sustainabledevelopment.un.org/.

World Health Organization. (2009). *Summary of the Evidence. The Case for Motorcycle Helmet Wearing in Children: A submission to the Ministry of Transport*. Geneva: World Health Organization.

World Health Organization. (2018). *Global Status Report on Road Safety 2018*. Geneva: World Health Organization.

Index

Note: Locators in *italics* refer to figures and those in **bold** to tables.

accountability: DrinkWise case study 94; ethical tension in working with stakeholders 34–35; healthcare context 182; human rights framework 32

active travel case study, Ireland 112–128; focal system boundary analysis 113–115, **116–117**; focal system stakeholder dynamics 124–128, *125–126*; focal system stakeholders 115–118, **119–121**; setting 112–113, *113*; stakeholders' interests and benefits/ barriers to participation 121, **122–123**, *122*

ageing population 176

AIP Foundation 192, 194–199, *196*, 200

alcohol consumption and prevention interventions: challenging the alcohol social change space 93–103; collective intelligence 92–93; dissensus on 89–92; education programmes 4–5, 72–86; education programmes case studies 76–84; health dangers 26; moving forward 103–105; networks of stakeholder relationships 64–66; responsible drinking 90–91; Slovene culture 55–56; Slovenia interventions case study 4, 56–69; stakeholder analysis 5, 58, **59–60**, 62–64; stakeholder approach 57–58, 66–68; stakeholder ethical tensions 26–27; stakeholder identification 58, 60–64; stakeholder involvement 78–84; as wicked problem 89, 95

anti-smoking interventions 39, 42–51, **44–47**

Association of Greater Manchester Authorities (AGMA) 183

Australia: alcohol consumption in Australian culture 89, 97–98; *Blurred Minds* project 76–77, 78–84; DrinkWise 93–103; indigenous ways of knowing and being 8–9; reducing domestic dog and koala interactions case study 157–173

Australian Curriculum, Assessment and Reporting Authority (ACARA) 72

behaviour change: alcohol consumption case studies 95, 98–100, 102–105; campaign elements 194; holism 192–193; koala conservation 168, 172–173; plural rationality approach 150, 152, 156, 159–167; systems setting 108–109

Blurred Minds project (Australia) 76–77, 78–84

boundary analysis 113–115, **116–117**

brainstorming 115

capacity building, alcohol interventions case study 64, 67, 68

Centres for Disease Control and Prevention (the CDC) 14–15, *16*

challengers (stakeholder types) 28, **120**

Civil Rights Movement 17–18

climate change: dogmatism 18; indigenous peoples 21–22; inertia 16–17; new stories and new partners 19–20

clinical commissioning groups (CCGs) 181–182, 183

co-creation 134, **136**

co-design: alcohol interventions case study 76; plural rationality approach 150, 158, 167–169; public-private-people (PPP) partnerships 134, **136**; social experiments with disadvantaged groups 137, 140

co-production: koala conservation case study 167–169; public-private-people

Index 205

(PPP) partnerships 134; social experiments with disadvantaged groups 135–147; social inequalities in health and well-being 132–135
Coca-Cola 15–16
coercive power 30
collective intelligence 92–93, 104
common value creation 134–135
communications: alcohol consumption interventions 75, 83–84; new stories and new partners 21–22; participation and inclusion 33–34; plural rationality approach **165**
community: active travel case study 115, **116–117**; grass roots movements 199; helmet use case study, Vietnam 193; koala conservation case study 168; stakeholder values 10
consultation 33
consumer marketing 18
consumer society 19, 22–23
control 34
Corporate Social Responsibility (CSR): alcohol industry 90–91; avoiding regulation 16; helmet use case study, Vietnam 197

decision-making processes: alcohol consumption 97–99; human rights framework 32; participation and inclusion 33–34; stakeholder perspectives on environmental issues 155
delegation 34
Denmark: alcohol consumption interventions 72; *GOOD Life* project 77–84
Department of Health and Social Care (DoHSC) 181
Diageo Foundation 16
digital online community experiment 137–139
distraction in marketing 16
dogmatism 18–19
downstream social marketing *see* individual social marketing
drink driving 26
DrinkWise 93–103, 104–105
drug education 72–73
dynamism 111, 124–128, *126*
education: alcohol consumption interventions 4–5, 72–86, *73*; anti-smoking interventions 39; helmet use case study, Vietnam 195; schools-based 72–73; social experiments with refugees 141–143

Effective Public Health Practice Project (EPHPP) 74
egalitarian perspective, plural rationality approach 156, **160–165**, 166–167
employability skills, refugees 142, 143
employees, stakeholder values 10
empowerment: alcohol interventions case study 64; social inequalities 132–133
engagement *see* stakeholder engagement
environmental issues: climate change 16–17, 18, 19–20, 21–22; co-design 150; plural rationality approach 150–151, 156–157; reducing domestic dog and koala interactions case study 157–173; stakeholder engagement 151–155; stakeholder identification 152–153
equality: ethical tension in working with stakeholders 34; health and well-being 132–135; human rights framework 32; social experiments with disadvantaged groups 135–147
ethics: alcohol consumption interventions 79; ethical tension in working with stakeholders 25–27, 32–36; human rights framework 3; power asymmetry 29–32
ethnographic research 98
evaluation, researcher reflexivity 9–10
evidence mapping 95
expert power 31
experts: alcohol interventions 64; anti-smoking interventions 49; plural rationality approach 156, 148, 172; refugees, challenges faced 142

fatalist perspective, plural rationality approach 156, **160–165**, 167
Finland: social experiments with disadvantaged groups 135–147; social inequalities 132–135
focal system: boundary analysis 113–115, **116–117**; stakeholder dynamics 124–128, *125–126*; stakeholders 115–118, **119–121**
follow-up periods, intervention outcomes 81
food industry, stakeholder marketing 14–15
Framework of Engagement with Non-State Actors (FENSA) 91–92
Freeman, Edward 27, 41, 109
French, R. P. 30
frontline employees, stakeholder values 10
funding: healthcare context 182; power 30
future directions, stakeholder engagement 6

206 *Index*

Gaia Principle 22
Galway, active travel case study 112–128, *113*
Ghosh, Amitav 19–20
GOOD Life project (Denmark) 77–84
governance: alcohol interventions 92, 94, 95; healthcare context 184, 185; koala conservation case study 152, 158, **163**, 166, 168, 170
governmental organisations: alcohol interventions case study 61, 62; helmet use in Vietnam 199–200
grass roots movements 199
Great Derangement 19
Great Transition Initiative (GTI) 17
Greater Manchester Health and Social Care Partnership 183–187, *185*, *187*, *188*

health: promotion 5; social experiments with disadvantaged groups 135–147; social inequalities 132–135
healthcare context: Greater Manchester Health and Social Care Partnership 183–187, *185*, *187*, *188*; relationship marketing 178–181, *180*; stakeholder analysis 176–178; stakeholder identification and classification 176, **177**; UK National Health Service 181–183
helmet use case study, Vietnam: AIP Foundation 192, 194–199, 200; building better stakeholder engagement and coordination 199–201; child passengers 192, 193, 197–199, **198**; engaging and mobilising stakeholders to promote sustainable change 192–194; road traffic injuries 191; Vietnamese context 191–192
hierarchical rationality, plural rationality approach 156, **160–165**, 166
higher education, refugees 142, 143
holism 111, 192–193
how to drink properly (HTDP) initiative 93–103
human oppression 19
human rights framework 3, 32, 35–36

incentives, participation 82
inclusion: ethical tension in working with stakeholders 33–34; human rights framework 32; *see also* stakeholder engagement
incumbents (stakeholder types) 28, **119**
indigenous peoples: anti-smoking interventions **47**; climate change 21–22; partnerships 20–22; ways of knowing and being 8–9

individual social marketing: active travel case study 115, **116**; vs. organisational focus 40
individualist rationality, plural rationality approach 156, **160–165**, 166
inequalities *see* social inequalities
inertia 16–18, 22–23
information: active travel case study 127; indigenous ways of knowing and being 8–9; participation and inclusion 33; plural rationality approach 156
infrastructure, active travel case study 127
interest/power (stakeholder analysis) 121, **122–123**, *124*
Intergovernmental Panel on Climate Change (IPCC) 18
intermediaries 1
international frameworks, multi-stakeholder approach 172
International Olympic Committee (IOC) 16
intervention outcomes: alcohol consumption interventions 81–82; anti-smoking interventions 50; follow-up periods 81
Ireland, active travel case study 112–128; focal system boundary analysis 113–115, **116–117**; focal system stakeholder dynamics 124–128, *125–126*; focal system stakeholders 115–118, **119–121**; setting 112–113, *113*; stakeholders' interests and benefits/ barriers to participation 121, **122–123**, *124*

Kayapós 21–22
Kessel, Joseph 23
knowledge gaps 92–93
koala conservation: reducing domestic dog and koala interactions case study 157–173; stakeholder engagement *153–154*, 154–155; stakeholder identification 152
Kogis 21–22

language: alcohol interventions 101–103; new stories and new partners 19–20; refugees PROMEQ research 141–143
legal framework *see* human rights framework; regulation
legitimate power 31
long-term unemployed: multi-professional case management experiment 139–140; needs and resource profiles **138**; social experiments with disadvantaged groups 135–137, **136**, 143–147, **144–145**

macro decision-makers 115, **117;** *see also* organisational social marketing

management: human rights framework 36; plural rationality approach **163;** reputation 15–16; stakeholder theory 41, 85; stakeholder types 28; of stakeholders 1–2

marketing: dogmatism 18; and power 14; stakeholder theory 42; *see also* social marketing

markets, six-market stakeholder model **179,** 179–181, 186–187

meso decision-makers 115, **116–117;** *see also* organisational social marketing

micro decision-makers 115, **116;** *see also* individual social marketing

mixed methods research 133, **144–145**

MOSA (alcohol interventions case study) 56–69; networking and knowledge exchange 66–67; networks of stakeholder relationships 65–66; pillars of the MOSA network *65;* stakeholder analysis 58, **59–60;** stakeholder approach 57–58, 66–68; stakeholder identification 60–64

motorcycles 191; *see also* helmet use case study, Vietnam

multi-criteria analysis 154

multi-professional case management experiment 139–140

multi-stakeholder approach 2, 4, 172

multi-stakeholder partnerships 2

multi-stakeholder social marketing 4

multinational corporations (MNCs) 3, 13–14, 21

narratives: chances of success 22–23; changing the narrative 12–13; dogmatism 18–19; inertia 16–18, 22–23; new stories and new partners 19–22; power 13–16

National Health Service (NHS) 6

National Traffic Safety Committee (NTSC) 196, 199

networks of stakeholder relationships: alcohol interventions case study 64–66; healthcare context *178;* stakeholder theory 42

NHS England (NHSE) 181–182

non-discrimination: ethical tension in working with stakeholders 34; human rights framework 32

non-governmental organisations (NGOs): alcohol interventions case study 62, 63–64, 65–66, 67–68; helmet use case study, Vietnam 192, 194–199

not in education, employment, or training (NEETS): digital online community experiment 137–139; needs and resource profiles **138;** social experiments with disadvantaged groups 135–137, **136,** **144–145;** social inequalities 132

older people living alone with multiple needs: needs and resource profiles **138;** participatory group-based case management experiment 140–141; social experiments with disadvantaged groups 135–137, **136,** 143–147, **144–145**

Olympics 16

organisational social marketing: active travel case study 115, **116–117,** 118, **119–121;** alcohol industry 91; alcohol interventions case studies 60–61, 63–68, 100, 104–105; healthcare context 177–178; vs. individual focus 40; systems setting 110

Orwell, George 14, 19

Paris Agreement on Climate 19–20

participation: ethical tension in working with stakeholders 33–34; human rights framework 32; incentives 82; intervention outcomes 40

participatory group-based case management experiment 140–141

partnerships: approaches to 3; healthcare 183–187, *185;* indigenous peoples 8–9, 20–22; multi-stakeholder 2; new stories and new partners 19–20; participation and inclusion 33; public-private-people (PPP) 133–135, 146–147; purpose of 15–16; stakeholder cooperation 1

Piketty, Thomas 13, 18–19

plural rationality approach 5–6; rationality typology 156, 159–167, **160–165;** reducing domestic dog and koala interactions case study 157–173; stakeholder engagement 150–151, 155–157

policymakers 10

populist politics 16

power 13–16; asymmetry 29–32, 33, 34; definition 29; interest-power matrix 63, *63;* participation and inclusion 33–34; sources of 30–31; stakeholder ethical tensions 28; stakeholder interests 121, **122–123,** *124;* stakeholder salience 176–177

PROMEQ framework 5; social experiments with disadvantaged groups

208 Index

135–147; social marketing 133, *134*, **136**; stakeholder analysis 135, 146
public health *see* healthcare context
Public Health England 181, 182
public-private-people (PPP) partnerships 133–135, 146–147

randomised control trials (RCTs), alcohol consumption interventions 74–75, 76–84
rationality typology 156, 159–167, **160–165**
Raven, B. 30
recruitment: alcohol consumption interventions 80; incentives 82; long-term unemployed 139; not in education, employment, or training (NEETS) 137
Redland City Council, reducing domestic dog and koala interactions case study 157–173
referent power 31–32
reflexivity, researchers 9–10
refugees: educational, employment skills, language, and social participation experiments 141–143; needs and resource profiles **138**; social experiments with disadvantaged groups 135–137, **136**, 143–147, **144–145**
regulating agencies (stakeholder types) 28, **120–121**
regulation: alcohol interventions case study 61; anti-smoking interventions 39; helmet use in Vietnam 192, 195, **198**, 198–199; human rights framework 32, 35–36; plural rationality approach **162**, 166; social marketing to avoid 16
relationship marketing 178–181, **180**, 186
reputation management 15–16
researcher reflexivity 9–10
researchers as stakeholders 9–10
responsible drinking 90–91, 99; *see also* alcohol consumption and prevention interventions
reward power 30
risk, plural rationality approach 156
road traffic injuries 191; *see also* helmet use case study, Vietnam

scenario construction 154
schools: alcohol consumption interventions case studies 76–86; helmet use in Vietnam 197–200, **198**; interventions based in 72–75
scientists, stakeholder values 10
signage, active travel case study 126–127

Slovenia: alcohol consumption in Slovene culture 55–56; alcohol interventions case study 4, 56–69; networks of stakeholder relationships 64–66; stakeholder analysis 58, **59–60**; stakeholder approach 57–58, 66–68; stakeholder identification 60–64
smartphones 18–19
smoking: anti-smoking interventions 39, 42–53, **44–47**; health risks 39
social change: alcohol consumption interventions 93–103; consumer society 22–23; new stories and new partners 19–22
social inequalities: health and well-being 132–135; social experiments with disadvantaged groups 135–147
social justice 20, 35
social marketing: challenges and assumptions 7–8; choice to use 15; as concept 1; individual vs. organisational focus 40; purpose of 15–16; stakeholder involvement in 1–3
social marketing benchmark criteria 151
social marketing interventions 3–4
social marketing process 48–49
social marketing working group (SMWG) 114–118, 124
social media: active travel case study **117**, **123**; alcohol interventions 95, 100, 102–103; co-production 167; refugee social participation 142, **144**
stakeholder analysis 5; alcohol interventions case study 58, **59–60**, 62–64; focal system boundary analysis 113–115, **116–117**; focal system stakeholder dynamics 124–128, *125–126*; focal system stakeholders 115–118, **119–121**; healthcare context 176–178; public-private-people (PPP) 135; social experiments with disadvantaged groups 135, 146; stakeholders' interests and benefits/ barriers to participation 121, **122–123**, *124*; systems setting 110, 112
stakeholder approach, alcohol interventions case study 57–58, 66–68
stakeholder cooperation 1
stakeholder engagement: anti-smoking interventions 49–50; environmental issues 151–155; future directions 6; helmet use case study, Vietnam 192–194, 199–201; long-term unemployed 139; not in education, employment, or training 137; older people living alone with multiple needs 140; plural

rationality approach 150–151, 155–157; reducing domestic dog and koala interactions case study 158–163; refugees 141–142
stakeholder identification: alcohol consumption interventions 84–85; alcohol interventions case study 58, 60–64; classification of focal system stakeholders 115–118, **119–120**; environmental issues 152–153; guidance 42; healthcare context 176
stakeholder involvement: anti-smoking interventions 49–50; barriers to 121, **122–123**, *124*; in social marketing 1–3
stakeholder marketing 14–15, 16, 18, 42
stakeholder networks *see* networks of stakeholder relationships
stakeholder relationship marketing 178–181, 186
stakeholder salience 176–177
stakeholder theory: cations of stakeholders 41; environmental issues 151; limitations in managing ethical tension and conflict 28–29; marketing 42; origins 27; programme planning 85; relationship marketing 178, 186
stakeholder values: different perspectives 10; power asymmetry 29–32
stakeholders: challenges and assumptions 7; definition 27–29, 41, 109; identity and role 6–7; incumbents, challengers, and regulating agencies 28; systems setting 109–112, *110*
study design, alcohol interventions 80
sugar-sweetened beverages (SSBs) tax 15
systems setting 5, 128–129; active travel case study in Ireland 112–128; dynamism 111, 124–128, *126*; fish analogy 108–109; focal system boundary analysis 113–115, **116–117**; focal system stakeholder dynamics 124–128, *125–126*; focal system stakeholders 115–118, **119–121**; holism 111; stakeholders in 109–112, *110*; stakeholders' interests and benefits/ barriers to participation 121, **122–123**, *124*

target audience: alcohol consumption interventions 84–85, *96*; anti-smoking interventions 44; interventions 42–48
Theory of Planned Behaviour (TPB) 76
tobacco smoking *see* smoking
training, plural rationality approach **164**
transparency: environmental issues 151; ethical tension in working with stakeholders 34–35; human rights framework 32
travel *see* active travel case study, Ireland; helmet use case study, Vietnam

UK National Health Service 181–183; *see also* Greater Manchester Health and Social Care Partnership
upstream social marketing *see* organisational social marketing

values *see* stakeholder values
Vietnam, helmet use case study: AIP Foundation 192, 194–199, 200; building better stakeholder engagement and coordination 199–201; child passengers 192; engaging and mobilising stakeholders to promote sustainable change 192–194; road traffic injuries 191; Vietnamese context 191–192

Wallace, David Foster 108–109, 128
welfare promotion 5
well-being: social experiments with disadvantaged groups 135–147; social inequalities 132–135
wicked problems: alcohol consumption 89, 95; collective intelligence 92–93; human rights framework 35; social marketing approaches 2; systems setting 109
Williams, Rowan 23
Willis, C. D. 5, 90, 93–94
women's language acquisition 142, 143
World Health Organization (WHO): Framework of Engagement with Non-State Actors (FENSA) 91–92; healthcare 184; smoking 39
worldviews, plural rationality approach 156

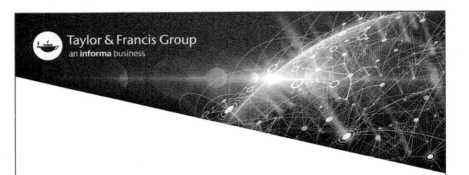